Up to now you may not have given the matter of your departure from this earth much thought. It has not been too pleasant or happy a subject to reflect upon—and there may have seemed little you could do about it anyway. Better just put off facing it as long as possible . . .

In this book which you hold in your hands, you will read the individual testimony of many sensible, sensitive men and women who profoundly believe—who not only believe but feel that they *know*—that there is personal survival after physical death.

Such people have one thing in common: They are free of fear, they say, as a result of psychic or spiritual experiences they have had. They are sure they can face the time for their departure from earth without apprehension, with—instead—a feeling of anticipation. They are not nearing an end of life but a new beginning. . . .

Also by Harold Sherman
Published by Fawcett Books:

HOW TO FORESEE AND CONTROL YOUR
 FUTURE
HOW TO MAKE ESP WORK FOR YOU
KNOW YOUR OWN MIND
YOU LIVE AFTER DEATH
YOUR KEY TO HAPPINESS

THE DEAD ARE ALIVE

They Can And Do Communicate
With You

Harold Sherman

FAWCETT GOLD MEDAL • NEW YORK

A Fawcett Crest Book
Published by Ballantine Books
Copyright © 1981 by Harold Sherman

ISBN 0-449-13158-0

Printed in Canada

First Ballantine Books Edition: January 1987
Tenth Printing: August 1993

To The
SEVEN
WHO
Will
LIVE
FOREVER

DEATH reached down and wrote upon the upturned faces around the world, leaving an image forever in their minds and hearts.

At that awful unexpected moment, the souls of five courageous men and two equally courageous women space travelers were released from earth bodies no longer existent.

Only a few there were in that vast assemblage of witnesses who actually realized what was happening. It had all been concealed by a spectacular, mammoth, explosive white cloud effect, followed by a fireworks of falling fragments of different shapes and sizes.

Then, after an awesome, stunned few seconds of unbelieving silence, there came a mighty heart-rending, anguished chorus of "Oh, God!.. Oh no!.. Oh God!" which rocketed and reverberated enough to shake the planet.

It couldn't happen, but it did! In some unaccountable manner, a flame seared its way into the fuel tank, and the Shuttle, with everything in it, was instantly incinerated.

But what of Ellison, Christa, Gregory, Judith Michael, Francis and Ronald? What happened to them?

We last saw their blue-clad figures marching happily, single-file, as they waved goodbye and disappeared, to be forever, inside the bird-like coffin.

Mortal eyes could not see simultaneous transformation from flesh to spirit ... mortal minds could not sense that Death had not touched REAL LIFE at all!

What is Death?

Death is nothing at all. I have only slipped away into the next room. I am I and you are you. Whatever we were to each other, that we are still. Call me by my old familiar name. Speak to me in the easy way which you always used. Put no difference in your tone. Wear no forced air of solemnity or sorrow. Laugh as we always laughed at the little jokes we enjoyed together. Play, smile, think of me, pray for me. Let my name be ever the household word that it always was. Let it be spoken without effect, without the trace of a shadow on it. Life means all that it ever meant. It is the same that it ever was. There is absolutely unbroken continuity. Why should I be out of mind because I am out of sight?

I am waiting for you, for an interval, somewhere very near, just around the corner. All is well.

Harry Scott Holland
1847–1918
Canon of St. Paul's Cathedral.

Contents

1. HOW IT BEGAN   1
2. VOICES FROM THE BEYOND   16
3. DEALING WITH THE EARTHBOUND   26
4. SPIRIT MESSAGES ON TAPE   35
5. THE HARRISON HAUNTINGS   50
6. A LIFE-TIME OF
   SPIRIT COMMUNICATION   61
7. EVIDENCES OF SPIRIT RETURN   87
8. AN AMAZING EXCEPTION   101
9. THE DAVE SAALFELD STORY   108
10. ASTOUNDING PROOF OF LIFE BEYOND   114
11. MIND-TO-MIND COMMUNICATION   141
12. WHAT THE AFTER LIFE IS LIKE   155
13. MY ASTRAL PROJECTION EXPERIENCE   174
14. SPIRIT COMMUNICATION
    BY TELEPHONE   187
15. AN AMAZING DEMONSTRATION OF
    PSYCHIC MEDIUMSHIP   203
16. THE REMARKABLE MECEVITCH CASE   238
17. THE RAYMOND CASS REPORT   259

18. DIMENSIONS OF LIFE BEYOND LIFE   279
19. THE CONTINUITY OF LIFE   284
20. YOUR PREPARATION FOR THE
    LIFE TO COME   303

Chapter 1

HOW IT BEGAN

On December 10, 1974, Wilma Plimpton left this life. She had been unconscious for 72 hours before passing. At least this is what doctors and nurses clinically thought. But Wilma told her husband, A.J., a year or so later after he had established two-way communication with her, that she had been out of her body, in her spirit form, trying to tell him she was still alive, and knew what was going on.

When death of the physical body occurred, said Wilma, she had blacked out, and when she returned to consciousness, she found herself in what appeared to be an almost endless hospital ward with rows of occupied beds and white-attired attendants. Her first thoughts were that A.J. had had her moved to another hospital, until she saw her formerly deceased father and mother standing beside the bed, smiling down at her.

Then, for the first time, the thought struck her: "I must have died! If I'm dead, where am I?" Her parents, sensing her thoughts, explained that she was in what might be called a Rest Home, one of many which exist around the earth, where most people are transported at death, to remain for longer or shorter periods, until they become adapted to the new conditions.

As Wilma became more and more aware of her surroundings, which seemed to be as real and substantial as her earth existence had been, she was almost overwhelmed by the emotional pull of A.J.'s grief upon her.

The effect on Wilma was such that, while she didn't know how it could be done, she felt she had to respond to A.J.'s mental call and return to earth and try to assure him that she was still alive—that there *was* a life after death, in which he had not believed—and that they, one day, could be re-united.

As Wilma had these thoughts, she suddenly found herself in the Plimpton home in Oklahoma, and in the physical presence of A.J. who was, at that moment, gazing fixedly at her photograph. She heard her own voice speaking to him but was frustrated to observe that he didn't hear it. She followed him about the rest of the day, in his car, wherever he went, trying to embrace him, to comfort him, to catch his attention in one way or another—and her fruitless efforts continued until night when A.J. finally retired, and went to sleep, calling her name.

It was then that Wilma intercepted his thought and sensed that he was contemplating suicide, since he felt he could not go on without her.

In January of 1975, a little more than a month after Wilma's demise, a despondent A.J. still intent on doing away with himself, passed a newsstand and was challenged by a paperback book title, YOU LIVE AFTER DEATH by Harold Sherman. He bought it on impulse, wondering skeptically if he could have been wrong, if there could be a form of continuing life after death. In any event, he decided that he would see what this writer had to say.

I, of course, was the author of this book. It had first been published in 1949, and after a number of editions in hard cover, had gone into paperback with Fawcett Publications, now known as CBS-Fawcett, New York City, where YOU LIVE AFTER DEATH has remained a best seller ever since.

A.J. took the book home and read it that night. When he came to the last page, he saw a letter from me wherein I invited all who had had psychic experiences to write me a report of them, in care of my ESP Research Associates Foundation in Little Rock, Arkansas.

A.J. was sufficiently impressed by what I had to say about the possibility of Survival to write me, asking if I knew any way he could learn how to communicate with his wife, Wilma, provided she still existed. He said he didn't know anything about the subject of Psychic Phenomena, but he was willing to approach it with an open mind if I could show him how he could undertake his own research and develop his own proof of life after death.

We exchanged correspondence until the day that A.J. motored from his home in Oklahoma to meet me in my home in north central Arkansas. We spent the first hour getting acquainted. He told me he had spent the major part of his adult life in the production end of the oil business; that he had also owned a Flying Service in Florida, engaged in the selling of new and old planes, as well as helicopters. "I owned a helicopter myself and Wilma and I used to cover the country on combined business and pleasure trips." Music was an avocation with A.J. who was a fine organist. He had a magnificent Theatre Organ installed in his home but all the music had gone out of his life when Wilma had

3

died and he sold the instrument and resolved he would never play again.

As I studied A.J., I found him to be a man of great intensity of purpose. He said that he wanted me to tell him all I could about different forms of research so he could decide how to go about it himself. If I thought there was a chance of his managing to communicate with Wilma, he was willing to devote day and night to it.

When I learned that A.J. knew a great deal about electronics, that one of his sons was an electronic engineer with NASA, I decided to suggest that he concentrate his efforts on experimentation with Electronic Voice Phenomena.

"What's that?" A.J. wanted to know.

"Let me take a few minutes to explain," said I. "It's known simply as the tape recording of spirit voices. There's a history connected with this development."

I went to my files and brought out a brief account, which I read to A.J.

" 'In 1959, Friedrich Jurgenson, of Molubo, Sweden, while recording 'bird sounds,' in a forest, was astounded when he played back the tape, to find human voices on it, one of which appeared to be his long deceased mother's voice. He heard his own name called and then the words, 'Friedrich, you are being watched.' The more he listened, the more he became convinced that these sounds were not radio signals; they were coming through on tape in different languages—Swedish, German or Latvian.

" 'Jurgenson concluded that these voices had to be emanating from another Dimension. Before making his discovery public, however, he devoted four years to a careful and systematic experimentation, during which time he recorded some several thousand voices. He encountered interference with what is called 'white sound,' through which the voices had to emerge, some

4

exceptionally faint or in whispers, and occasionally loud and easy to hear, often establishing their identity as entities who had formerly lived on earth.

" 'In 1965, Dr. Konstantin Raudive, psychologist and author of a number of philosophical books, visited Jurgenson and together they made a number of successful recordings. Later, returned to his home on the edge of the Black Forest, in Germany, Dr. Raudive undertook the enormous task of recording, analyzing and cataloguing some eighty thousand 'paranormal voices,' with the aid of fellow scientists and engineers. This job completed, he reported his findings in an epoch-making book titled, BREAKTHROUGH, which inspired electronically-minded researchers to undertake investigations of their own, with like significant results.

" 'One of them, G. Gilbert Bonner, well known English researcher, made many thousands of recordings, quite a number of which were in extended dialogue of nearly 30 minutes duration.

" 'On the evidence of such recordings,' said Bonner, 'and also on the content of the material, I am certain these voices have their origin in another Dimension. I challenge any parapsychologist to prove that these recordings are not paranormal. These cannot be explained away by radio intrusion or noises mistaken for voices. In some cases, the age, sex and even the personality of the speaker are clearly identified. It is hardly likely that all these are psychokinesis. The voices speak in logical sentences of five to ten words at a time—call to a person by name—and identify themselves as people who previously lived on earth. They also reveal that they can SEE us and, at times, even display a knowledge of the future.'

" 'Then Bonner added: 'Their manifestation through tape recording of their voices challenges the very foundation of scientific thinking.'

" 'Two of the pioneer investigators in the United States were the Lamoreaux brothers, Joseph and Mike, of Washington State. In their experimentation, they also recorded some thousands of voices, and received many messages in answer to questions which they carefully and systematically recorded for future checking and evaluation. When a friend, Jim Remich, was accidentally killed, they were able to contact him after a time, and in one communicative session, they asked him if there were any Rules for Living, like our 'Ten Commandments,' where he was.

" 'Yes, there are,' was Jim's recorded reply. 'If you will leave your tape running, I will try to give them to you.' The Lamoreaux brothers did as directed, and these are the exact words which appeared on the tape.

> *"There are Six Rules.*
> *"The First Rule is to live as though you are part of everyone.*
> *"The Second Rule is to help everyone.*
> *"The Third Rule is to not let anyone feel alone.*
> *"The Fourth Rule is to love everyone.*
> *"The Fifth Rule is to forgive everyone.*
> *"The Sixth Rule is to live like you are one with everyone and everyone is one with God."*

A.J. had listened intently to my reading of this information and seemed deeply impressed and moved by it.

"Our ESP Foundation is acting as a clearing house for many independent researchers who are experimenting with the tape recording of spirit voices," I told him. "There is much work yet to be done. Everyone is trying to reduce the volume of sound interference so the voices can come through with greater clarity. These investigators are checking with each other and exchanging helpful suggestions about methods they are using which have seemed to improve reception."

"Give me all the instructions you can. I'll buy the equipment needed, and get to work!"

For answer, I handed A.J. a pamphlet our ESP Foundation had prepared on information furnished us by William "Bill" Welch, author of TALKS WITH THE DEAD (Pinnacle Publishing). We had booked Bill to be on our Body, Mind and Spirit Healing Workshop program to be held in St. Louis, but Bill had died of cancer shortly before the scheduled date. A noted Hollywood screen writer, Bill had devoted many hours to "spirit voice" recording.

As a tribute to him, we established a William Welch Memorial Research Division of our ESP Foundation and have made his Instructive Message available to all "spirit voice" researchers.

It reads, as follows, opening with Bill Welch's statement: "This is how I have talked with the dead in receiving more than 20,000 of what I believe to be 'spirit voices.' If you wish to follow my simple methods, I feel you can, in time, achieve like results."

THE "LISTENING" EQUIPMENT NEEDED

Almost any type of reel-to-reel tape recorder will do. It should contain three speeds—1-7/8 i.p.s. . . . 3-3-4 i.p.s. . . . and 7-1/2 i.p.s. Depending on the tempo of the "spirit voices" recorded, you may wish to play it back at a slower or higher speed. I usually record at 3-3/4 i.p.s. so I can go either way.

I use the microphone to record my own voice on tape as I invite friends or loved ones, if present, to respond. You must be prepared to receive voices and fragmentary messages or words from strangers and "wandering spirits" as well as those you may know—or no voices at all.

When I have finished sending out the call for communicators, I let the tape continue running from five to ten minutes during this time but when I play back the tape, if voices appear on it, they have been magnetically projected. This is one of the still unsolved mysteries.

You will encounter what is called "white noise" and the "spirit voices" when they are present, must be detected through this static or interference. For this reason, it is often difficult to make them out or decipher words and meanings.

It will help if you start your listening period with a brief meditation or a simple prayer, to create a more receptive atmosphere, free of such emotions as grief or apprehension or doubt. Just relax and let what will happen, happen.

You will find after a little experimentation, that you will have to train your hearing in order to discern voices which exist in the background of the "white noise" and can only be brought out through repeated playbacks. Someday, electronic experts working on this problem, believe they will be able to filter out much of the "white noise" and communication between worlds will be greatly facilitated.

The best time and place to record must be determined by you. I have found, obviously, that the quietest room in the house or office is most ideal. The tape recorder will pick up every sound through the open mike. When you have made contact with the "spirit voices" the "spirit entities" can apparently follow you wherever you go.

I was able to give a demonstration for the National Enquirer staff, using their own equipment, to prove that these communications had no identification with my instrumentation. An evidential message came through for one of the Enquirer reporters during the test.

I should impress upon you, however, that it often requires a great amount of time and patience and determination to get such results as have come to me. I have devoted endless hours

8

not only to recording these spirit voices but to keeping a written record of the names and messages which came through, all carefully dated, and filed away with all tapes, for future study.

You should use the best grade of tape and turn the recording volume on full and the treble control on maximum. If you have a stereo tape recorder, use only one track at a time, recording monaurally.

When you have run the tape for five or ten minutes, play it back and listen intently. Whenever you feel there are sounds out of the ordinary, go back and listen to it again and again. If it is a voice, and of particularly low volume, it actually may increase as you attune your ear to it by replaying. You may have to identify the words syllable by syllable. The message may have come through at double speed so you will have to play it back at a slower rate. You need to remember that the speaker may be using an entirely different language.

I am convinced, through the many experiences I have had, that there are "spirit engineers" on the "other side," trying to help us solve the communication problems. They have apparently created devices designed to help us receive their transmission through our still imperfect electronic equipment. We have evidence that they sometimes shut off communication for reasons unknown. But it is encouraging to observe that they seem to be working with us.

This information, furnished by Bill Welch, was about all that A.J. required to start upon what proved to be the most exhaustive, almost around-the-clock tape recording effort, within my knowledge. It was three months before A.J. was able to bring through even *one* voice on tape and how his faith and determination held out that long seemed almost incredible to me. I was

9

actually concerned that his expenditure of effort might lead to a physical or mental breakdown. But A.J. kept on insisting that, if Welch and others could do it, he could do it if he kept on keeping at it.

Finally there came the great day for A.J. when he reported excitedly to me by phone that the first voices had appeared on tape.

"But I can't make out who they're from," he said. "I've begun to get a lot of them . . . they sound something like a crowd at Grand Central Station . . . everyone trying to talk at once . . . some voices are too faint to understand . . . others are in whispers . . . and some are loud enough to hear plainly against the static. I don't know why it took so long before I could get any voices at all—but I've sure got them now. No doubt about that!"

I knew what A.J. was getting. Every "spirit voice" researcher had reported the same encounter. I told him he was in touch with what is called "earthbound spirit entities"—those possessing such "low spirit gravities" that they had been held close to earth.

"But I don't want to talk to them," said A.J. "How do I get rid of them?"

"That's a problem no one has apparently solved yet," I replied.

Encouraged at the breakthrough he had achieved, A.J. put forth a renewed effort to make contact with the spirit of his wife, Wilma, but he only seemed to be opening the door wider and wider to the earthbound. They were all calling for help . . . they seemed to be in a confused state . . . some could not remember their identity . . . some did not know they had died . . . some could not tell where they were . . . they were surrounded by darkness and gloom . . . they were in a dream or nightmarish state . . . and they did not know how to get out of it. . . .

Others, A.J. discovered, when he called for his wife,

Wilma, would say *they* were Wilma, just to get his attention ... and would confess when he challenged them, that they were *not* "Wilma". . . .

A.J. said he no longer doubted that there was life after death, but the problem, as I had stated, was how to get through or past the "earthbound area," to the Higher Dimension where his wife, Wilma, might be.

A frustrating year followed, during which time A.J. had fantastic adventures with earthbound entities who filled his tapes with obscenities and often heart-touching pleas for help. He tried to tell them to leave him alone, that he wanted to reach and talk to his wife, Wilma. It was like a party line, the voices wouldn't get off.

Persistence finally won out. An elated A.J. reported to me one night: "I just got through to Wilma. I distinctly heard her say: '*Amour* (that's my first name) *this is Wilma!*' ... I have had a talk with her, a few words at a time. I'm convinced it's her, all right. Now I can hardly wait until I can get better communication."

By this time, A.J. was so impressed that he decided to sell his home in Oklahoma, and rent a house in an Arkansas town where his married daughter, Jeanette lived—so he could be within easy driving distance to me, and we could keep in closer touch. The move was made, and every few weeks, A.J. would bring his recent recordings and spend the day with Martha and me, discussing and analyzing the communications.

Some time later, A.J. phoned to report that he had caught the interest of scientifically-minded spirits who said they were responding to his expressed interest to improve the means of communication. They wanted

11

A.J. to know that they were trying to help him develop a *psychic ability* to communicate with the Other Side by *telepathy*—thus avoid all static that was interfering with good reception.

"If I could ever do that," said A.J., "I believe we'd really begin to get somewhere!"

One day, in January, 1977, it *happened!*

A.J. heard Wilma's voice, speaking to him over his left ear, as though through a telephone receiver. Her voice came through usually in loud whispers, not very plainly but there was no mistaking the words. No one else could hear Wilma's voice but he could instantly relay what she was saying to him . . . and she could answer any questions put to her. It wasn't long before A.J. was able to establish a two-way telepathic conversation.

A.J. drove over to see us and gave an impressive demonstration. He said he couldn't explain how this power suddenly began manifesting but there was no trouble in hearing not only Wilma's voice but other voices from known and unknown entities.

I, frankly, had not been prepared for such a development and I didn't accept the genuineness of this phenomenon at the very first. It seemed so unbelievable that I felt concerned that I might have encouraged A.J. to carry things too far, that he might, somehow, however logical the communications seemed to be, have become psychotic, possibly hallucinatory, subject to hearing voices of his own creation.

But something happened a few nights later, which convinced me that what was taking place might well be true. I'll let you, the reader, be the judge.

NOTE: In describing this incident, as in most cases, we are compelled to use fictitious names to protect the privacy of those involved. The publishers, however, have been acquainted with the real names and can vouch for the authenticity of every happening.

A.J. was awakened around three in the morning by a man's voice, which said to him: "A.J., I've been trying to get through to you for some time. This is your old friend, Ed Martin."

"Oh, no , it's not!" A.J. denied. "I know Ed Martin—and *he's* still alive!"

(The Martins had been long time friends of A.J. and Wilma. They lived in the state of Kansas . . . and the two couples had visited back and forth with each other, when Wilma was still on earth.)

"You're wrong, A.J." said the voice. "I died last September 28th!"

Thinking now that this voice was from a mischievous spirit, claiming to be Ed Martin, A.J. challenged—"If you died last September 28th, where were you buried?"

The Voice gave the name of the cemetery in another town in Kansas of which A.J. had never heard.

"Okay," said A.J. "How did you die?"

"I had a heart attack," answered the Voice. "They rushed me to the hospital and I died ten minutes after they got me there."

"Well," said A.J. "What color of suit and tie did they bury you in?"

The Voice gave immediate and specific answers to all questions asked.

"I still don't believe it," said A.J. "But I can soon prove it out. When morning comes, I'll phone Ed's wife, Cleo—and she'll set me straight."

"*Do* that," said the Voice. "*You'll* find out!"

When A.J. got Cleo on the wire, he said to her: "I know you'll think I'm off my rocker, but a Voice claim-

13

ing it was Ed woke me up last night . . . and told me he had died last September 28th."

Cleo cried out in shock. "He *did* die on the 28th!"

"Just a minute!" said A.J. "Don't tell me anything—let me tell *you* what else this Voice told me . . . !" A.J. then repeated his psychic conversation. An amazed Cleo confirmed everything that he had said.

"You've made a believer out of me," Cleo told A.J. "You couldn't have known all these things yourself!"

A few days later, Cleo phoned A.J. to tell him she had been taking inventory of Ed's tools in his tool shop . . . and she had found that his favorite hammer was missing.

"If you are in touch with Ed again," said Cleo, "please ask him if he remembers what happened to his hammer?"

A.J. promised to help if he could. When he was next talking to Wilma he asked her if she knew their friend, Ed Martin, had died.

"No," replied Wilma. "I hadn't heard. You know—it's a *big place* over here."

"If you can locate him," said A.J., "Cleo wants me to ask him a question."

"I'll see what I can do," said Wilma.

Several days later, Wilma contacted A.J. and announced that she had Ed Martin with her.

"What is it, A.J.?" asked Ed's voice. "What can I do for you?"

"It's Cleo," said A.J. "She wants to know if you recall what you did with your favorite hammer?"

"Why, I loaned it to So-and-So," said Ed, instantly, giving the friend's name.

A.J. passed the information on to Cleo. She contacted the friend—and *he had the hammer!*

If you, the reader, accept this little intimate account

14

as true—it should indicate that we not only survive with our *identity*, but with our memory of our earth life.

A year and more later, Ed Martin made contact with A.J. again, to tell him that Cleo had married George Knight, a man she had been going with for some time. George's wife had been hospitalized in a comatose condition for several years, and had finally died.

This was news to A.J. who phoned Cleo to check and learned she had, indeed, married George the past week.

"Can't I do anything Ed doesn't know about?" said Cleo.

"You'd better believe it!" said A.J. "But you should be glad to know that Ed approves of George. He thinks he's a fine fellow."

"Does that mean that Ed will still be hanging around?" Cleo wanted to know.

"I heard that!" Ed's spirit cut in. "Tell Cleo, NO. She's got a good man to care for her now and there is no need for me to remain. I'm free to go my way—sending her my love and wishing her well!"

Chapter 2

VOICES FROM THE BEYOND

When the Arctic Explorer Sir Hubert Wilkins and I conducted our pioneering experiments in Long Distance Telepathy from the North Pole region to New York City, where I acted as Receiver of Wilkins' thoughts, three nights a week for five and a half months, despite the fact that these experiments were witnessed by Dr. Gardner Murphy, then head of the Psychology Department at Columbia University, and other scientists, the world reaction was more of skepticism than wonder.

It was impossible, many scientists had contended, for the human mind to transmit and receive thoughts across a laboratory room, let alone a distance of three thousand miles, and on a regularly scheduled basis. This was in the years of 1937 and 1938. Our book, THOUGHTS THROUGH SPACE was published in 1942, in which Wilkins and I narrated the complete account of our telepathic adventure, together with the day-by-day record of what had happened to Wilkins in his search expedition for the lost Russian fliers, and my exactly worded impressions of these happenings received from Wilkins' mind.

Thirty-five years after our initial experiments Astronaut Edgar D. Mitchell, during the Apollo 14 Flight, January 31 to February 9th, 1971, with the aid of four selected sensitives, of whom I was not one, conducted a series of telepathic experiments, which were adjudged significant, from moon to earth, in the neighborhood of 150,000 miles, proving once again that time and space are no barrier to the mind.

In a foreword that Edgar D. Mitchell graciously wrote for the paperback edition of THOUGHTS THROUGH SPACE, under date of October 2, 1972, he said in part:

"It would be very nice for the scientists if telepathic abilities lent themselves to the types of investigations that are easily reduced to mathematical expressions and statistical scoring. Unfortunately, nature is seldom so kind. She does not adapt herself to the preconceived notions of man. It is for man to adapt the techniques of investigation to discover the truth about nature.

"Thus, it is that after many years of laboratory research, the scientist finds himself returning to a mode of investigation carried out by non-scientists, Sherman and Wilkins, thirty-five years ago. The success of that effort appears to be related to the empathy and understanding between two men in a 'survival' or emotionally charged situation. In such a climate of operation, the telepathic test was perceived with clarity. Certainly their success does not require statistical evaluation to be impressive to the thoughtful reader.

"Thirty-five years after their test, we see from the experiment on Apollo 14 that the mechanism which functioned in this earlier demonstration can also work at distances beyond planetary dimensions. The Apollo data, although they have satisfying statistical significance, for the scientist, do not capture the drama or the emotion of this early demonstration . . ."

From this, it is apparent that the pioneering long distance telepathic experiments between Wilkins and myself, confirmed some 35 years later by Astronaut Edgar D. Mitchell, from moon to earth, established the fact that communication has been conclusively proved from mind-to-mind regardless of distance.

More recently, the remarkable sensitive, Ingo Swann and I have conducted scientifically witnessed psychic probes of the planets Jupiter, Mercury and Mars, recording our impressions, independent of each other, before space modules either bypassed or landed (in the case of Mars)—impressions which proved amazingly accurate, some contrary to the expectations or concepts of astronomers.

As a result of these psychic accomplishments and other verified experiments of like nature by experienced sensitives, it is evident that the stage is being set for new adventures in the realm of mind—this time in dimensions which exist in the After Life.

In this connection, one of the emerging pioneers may well be A.J. Plimpton, whose real name must understandably be protected. He is just one of a developing group of modern researchers who are putting together the evidence and abilities that are evolving. They all know that they have a long way to go. They are about at the level of an Alexander Graham Bell when he tried to transmit the first voice over a wire—or Marconi, when he sought to send a voice through the air.

To the first ears that sensed these words, it must have seemed unbelievable. Anything, sound or apparition or whatever, that emerges from the Unknown Realms, is always mysterious if not actually frightening. We either doubt or fear what we do not understand.

One might be disposed to ask—can it really be a voice that is independent of any created sound on earth? Or can it be a fragmentary pick-up from some radio program, either past or present, that is still vibrating in the mysterious ether? If it is a voice from some other dimension or existence, for want of any other way to describe it—just *where* is this dimension and *what* is it?

Some parapsychologists have speculated that these voices could be psychokinetic creations of the mind, and that the investigator was actually conversing with himself in some sort of feedback manner. But this conjecture had been cancelled out by the fact that the voices were coming through in different languages, which the researcher did not speak, much less understand, and many of the messages made sense, with replies often in somewhat garbled form, to the questions which had been asked.

It is questionable, at this point, how much successful taping depends upon the psychic power of the investigator. It is possible, some think, that a certain energy is drawn from the researcher or the vibrations of his voice by the spirit communicators and when this energy is temporarily exhausted, the sound production grows faint or dies out.

In any event, assuming that survival after death is an accepted fact, we now know enough about human consciousness and its unlimited potentiality to be convinced that it is only a matter of time before mind-to-mind communication will be demonstrably possible between Beings from higher dimensions of existence or from intelligences on other planets.

It was early in 1975, as I have already stated, when A.J. Plimpton first got in touch with me as a result of reading my book, YOU LIVE AFTER DEATH. He had described his great loneliness in the loss of his wife,

Wilma, his desire to find a way to communicate with her if there really was a life after death, as I had contended, otherwise he had felt disposed to end it all.

I find a letter I had written him, in my correspondence file, dated April 4, 1975, in which I had suggested:

> "You might get a reel-to-reel recorder and sit quietly and speak into the microphone, stating your name, and expressing the wish that your wife would communicate with you on tape ... then let the tape continue for half a minute or so, and play it back and see if any voice appears on the tape. This requires patience but others have had comforting as well as evidential results. You must steel yourself against disappointment, as this method of communication is still in the experimental stage.
>
> "There are few really good professional mediums ... many of the better ones will not make their gifts available for money and the demand for their services would be so great that they would have no time for anything else.
>
> "To commit suicide would not assure you reunion with your wife. It would affect your 'spirit gravity' and you could upset your magnetic attraction, soul to soul. (Too detailed a matter to explain in a letter.) You MUST adjust yourself to her temporary separation from you ... and find something in life to live for, to increase the possibility of a contact with your wife."

A.J. had been visiting his wife's grave in a town in Kansas, when my letter arrived. On his return to his home in Oklahoma, he had written me as follows:

> "I have two tape recorders, one of them is a very expensive professional recorder, which I have used for recording my organ music. I have not played the organ since my wife's passing as

I have a very deep feeling of sadness when I even go near it. I presume this is because my wife loved to have me play for her. I have used the professional recorder for trying to get voices on the tape because it is much more sensitive than the small recorder. So far I have not been able to hear any voices but will keep trying . . ."

A.J. told me that, three months later, having gotten no results, he was about to quit when, responding to an inner urge he decided to try a couple of days longer. Apparently that did it. The first voice came through. Two words:

HELP ME!

"Who are you?" A.J. asked.

I DON'T KNOW!

"What's your name?"

DON'T KNOW!

"Where are you?"

RIGHT HERE!

"I can't see you!"

I SEE YOU!

As if a communicative circuit had been opened up, different voices began coming through, most of them in broken sentences—plaintive whispers for help against a "white sound" background.

Relieved, at long last, to be getting any type of re-cordings on tape, A.J. commenced talking back to these voices, trying to get more specific information from them—why they were all pleading for help—help *from* or *for* what?

Gradually, he was able to put together a picture in

his mind of a region or place or condition in which these voiced entities appeared to be existing. This was all a new experience to A.J. but he sensed that he was seemingly surrounded by an earthbound area, which might contain an inconceivable number of spirit forms, many of whom did not know they had died, and appeared to be, most of them, in a confused, bewildered state, not knowing where they were, or how to get out of their present predicament. They were actually much closer to the earth than they were to any so-called higher dimension or "heaven world."

In the few months that followed, A.J. recorded several hundred of these voices. During this period, however, he had managed to make contact with the voice of his wife, Wilma, on tape . . . and also his nephew, Jason, who had entered the next life through an accident when a boy of two and a half years. He would now have been about seven.

"Are you right here with me?" A.J. would ask Wilma and Jason. "Can you see me even if I can't see you?"

"Yes, we can see you," they would reassure him. "We've been trying to make you see us—but we don't know how."

"Can you see these earthbound people who are giving me such a time?" A.J. wanted to know.

"No, we can't see them—but we can hear their voices, just like you can," they would reply.

A.J. was led to presume that the earthbound spirits then existed in a different frequency, as the reason for their invisibility.

Many times, when A.J. would call for Wilma, hoping that her voice would come on tape, a voice would answer, "This is Wilma" and he had learned to tell when it was an earthbound spirit pretending or masquerading as Wilma, and say to it: "No, you're not Wilma. Why do you tell me you are?"

"We want to talk to you," a voice would answer.

It was frustrating, almost maddening, at times, and occasionally A.J. would lose his patience and tell the meddlesome spirits off, demanding that they stay off the tape so he could make contact with his wife, Wilma.

Every few weeks, A.J. would make the long motor trip to our home in Arkansas to confer with us, to play some of the tapes, and to discuss what might be done next. He had purchased much new equipment and was experimenting with more sensitive receiving instruments which other researchers had suggested, all for the purpose of reducing or eliminating the interfering static.

Finally, in December of 1975, A.J. sold his home in Oklahoma and rented a house in the town in Arkansas where his married daughter, Jeanette lived, so he could have easier access to us, and reduce his driving time to around two hours.

From about the first night of living in this old but nice-appearing Arkansas home, A.J.'s real troubles began. He had sought to resume taping and had just made contact with a voice he recognized as Wilma's, when it was cut short and an angry man's voice broke in, saying:

"That's *my* Wilma! You can't talk with my wife!"

"Who are you?" A.J. demanded.

"I'm Frank and you're in my house! Get out of my house!"

"Why is it *your* house?"

"I live here! I've always lived here!"

There followed a loud, rumbling, rattling sound which A.J. didn't hear physically but which was on the tape when it was played back. The whole atmosphere of the front room was electrically charged.

A.J., not easily frightened, talked into the microphone.

23

"You say your name is Frank. I just rented this house. What makes you think it's your home now?"

"I can't find my wife! What have you done to Wilma? Get out of here or I'll kill you!"

These words came through a few at a time. A.J. had to piece them together.

This was just the start! He not only had to contend against the earthbound people who had followed him from Oklahoma, but now a person by the name of Frank who insisted he had a wife named Wilma and who believed, somehow, that this was the Wilma to whom A.J. was trying to talk!

A.J. reported these strange happenings to me and I suggested that there may have been some violence—probably a tragedy that had taken place in this house some years ago. A.J. said he had come to the same conclusion and thought he would check with authorities on the house's history.

He came back a few days later with startling information. A lady who had lived in the house for ten years before he had, told him that a man had been murdered in it quite some time ago. This led him to the police records and the newspapers, with the disclosure that a man by the name of Frank Bradley had owned the house and had been brutally murdered in that very front room about 7:30 p.m., Monday evening, April 28th, 1947, by a man named Roy Hoyt. A.J. gave me a photostat of a newspaper copy of the front page story on the murder, part of which is reproduced here.

Hoyt, who was a friend of Bradley's daughter, Margaret, became infuriated at her, believing that she had had a date with someone else, and it was while in search for her that he is alleged to have committed the crime.

Sheriff Jeff Arnold said yesterday that five shots had been fired into Bradley's body, three in a close area in the back and two in the chest area, and that almost half of the skull had been clubbed away, apparently with a gunstock with a piece of metal attached to the end, and a 22 rifle which were found behind the body. The rifle had been broken.

The Sheriff said yesterday that Roy Hoyt had a very lengthy criminal record, and had been in trouble in various parts of the country.

A February 19, 1948 edition of the paper told of the execution of Roy Hoyt for the murder. The headlines stated that he showed courage as he went to his death. As part of the news item read:

Roy Hoyt, aged 26, convicted slayer of his prospective father-in-law, Frank Bradley, went to death bravely in the electric chair at the state prison farm.

Strapped in the chair before the curtain between him and witnesses was removed, Hoyt referred to the chair as "The Thunderbolt."

He asked undertaker, John Mason, to tell his Mom and Dad that he would wait for them in a better world, and told how he wanted his funeral conducted, even to the pall bearers.

So often tragedies like this one cause houses and business places to be "haunted" by the victims as well as the perpetrators of the crimes, and this well-established case is especially illustrative. More remarkable even than this was the unbelievable coincidence discovered by A.J. that Frank Bradley's wife's name was also Wilma, which accounted for Frank's feeling that A.J. was interested in her!

Chapter 3

DEALING WITH THE EARTHBOUND

Despite the fact that A.J. now knew the details of the crime that had been committed in the house, he continued to be plagued by the spirit presence of Frank Bradley who kept on trying with taped voiced threats and curses to make the place untenable.

It seems that Frank was so confused, he couldn't be sure whether he had been the victim or the killer. His wife, Wilma, had apparently preceded him in death and he, held in this earthbound condition, didn't know where to find her. A.J. told him his last name and what had really happened but while it stirred his memory, he still felt uncertain and disturbed.

Meanwhile there were five young women who had somehow become attached to A.J.'s wife, Wilma, and who often accompanied her wherever she went. They had forgotten their names and said they didn't really need them anyway. But A.J. told them he would have to give them names, so he could distinguish them from each other when they communicated. So he assigned these five names to them for identifying purposes and called them Cleo, Agatha, Lula, Mary and Helen, when he wanted to address them individually.

A.J.'s nephew, Jason had volunteered to be his messenger. He would try to locate different friends and relatives and other personalities for A.J. to find if possible where they were residing, what they were doing, and if they would care to communicate. Many of them expressed surprise that they could hear A.J.'s voice and that there was a way for them to tape their voices. Some tried to exchange messages without success. They said it required the exercise of energy and it was not easy to do. Anyway, it wouldn't be too long before everyone they had known on earth would be on their side of life.

A.J.'s father was reached by some of his relatives and told that A.J. wanted to speak to him. The father sent back word: "Tell A.J. I'm not interested in getting in touch with earth. I'm having too interesting a time where I am. Tell Amour I'll see him when he gets here!"

In the fall of 1977, A.J. came suddenly in possession of the telepathic ability to hear voices in his mind and to transmit his thoughts mentally. He found himself able, at times, to record messages from Wilma on tape at the same time he was receiving the same messages by telepathy. He had dreamed of having some such method of communication for months, and expressed his gratitude to whatever powers had helped him develop such a faculty, if this was how it had been brought about. As an experiment, A.J., who now had five different types of tape recorders, started them all going at once and all five recorders picked up the same voice messages, simultaneously. This reminded him of his being in a big television shop and seeing their sets tuned to the same station with the same program com-

27

ing in. Apparently thought vibrations are just as universal as radio and TV waves.

Able to communicate without the interference of the "white sound" effect on tape, A.J.'s sources of information were immeasureably increased. This did not mean that he was always correct in his reception of messages but when friends and relatives, skeptical of such a phenomenon actually taking place, asked him to see if he could locate and talk to deceased loved ones, A.J. would send Jason to "Information Centers" to find them, and if contact was made, their answers to questions were often so accurate as to convince many of their identity.

"I just tell what I hear," A.J. explained to me. "I don't try to embellish it or interpret it, or guess at it. I've stopped reading any books on ESP or Psychic Phenomena. I don't want my mind to be colored any more than I can help by what others think or report or speculate on. I'm not making any claims. Whoever is interested can take or leave what I am being told. I have just decided to let others decide whether to accept or reject what is coming through my tapings and my telepathic communications. This all just happened in response to my devoting full time and energy over the past few years, in a major effort to prove if there was a life after death, and if so, would it be possible to communicate with my wife Wilma? I am satisfied now that I have proved that everyone survives death, regardless of their religious beliefs or no belief at all, that it is a part of the scheme of creation, so if anyone prefers to doubt, it is all right with me. Let them go to work, if they will, and prove it out for themselves. I know it will seem fantastic to many. It seemed that way to me, at the start, and I don't know to what this present development is going to lead. But I am learning something new and wonderful every day and I am confident that many people could open up channels of communications as have come to me, if they would put aside their preconceived ideas and give these higher powers of mind a chance to function."

How to cope with the continuing threats and opposition of the "haunting spirit" of Frank Bradley was a problem along with the persistent appeals for help from increasing numbers of "earthbound people." Now that A.J. could "hear" their voices telepathically, he was using tape recording less and less.

One day, when A.J. was particularly hard pressed by the voiced pleas of the "earthbound" to help them, he asked prayerfully for an answer from someone on the Other Side, what could be done for these distressed people.

To his surprise, a deep toned, measured voice replied: "These people have to have a sense of direction to release them from the conditions they are in. Tell them to repeat after you: 'I want to leave this dark and dismal place and go to the 25th dimension which is warm and cheery and bright and beautiful, and where friends and loved ones are waiting to greet me.'"

"I've been told that what is called the First Plane has 25 dimensions," said A.J., "and that these earthbounds are on the 16th dimension at the present time. Can they reach the 25th without guidance?"

"I suggest you let your nephew Jason and the ladies take those who want to go," said the Voice.

"Can you tell me who you are?" asked A.J.

"That is not necessary," replied the Voice. "You have your answer."

Acting on these instructions, A.J. worked out a plan of action. He appealed to Jason and the ladies for help to which they readily assented. Then he spoke aloud to the earthbounds who, in some mysterious way, could hear his voice where they were—a dimension, like so many, situated in layers, superimposed over what might be called the earth plane. He explained to them a procedure he would like them to follow which would free them from their self-imposed bondage.

A babble of voices flowed through A.J.'s consciousness.

"What if we don't like it where you want to take us?"

"If you don't like it, I'll have Jason and the ladies bring you back to the 16th dimension where you now are," said A.J.

Jason reported: "Uncle Amour, there are hundreds of them gathering here. We can see them now. I wish people on earth wouldn't call them spirits . . . they have bodies just like they had before they died . . . only they are still mixed up in their minds . . . and they need to be taken some place where they can be helped. We can't take them beyond the 25th dimension because that's where the Second Plane begins and they're not ready to go there . . . they wouldn't be permitted. So just get them to say the word . . . and we'll be off!"

A.J. couldn't see the assemblage of earthbound people whom Jason had described, as he told them:

"I understand you can all hear my voice. Perhaps you can all see me . . . and Jason and these ladies. They are ready to be your guides and take you all to the 25th dimension—but you will first have to repeat after me these words:

"I WANT TO GO TO THE 25TH DIMENSION WHICH IS A PLACE THAT IS WARM AND CHEERY AND BRIGHT AND WHERE FRIENDS AND LOVED ONES ARE WAITING TO GREET ME."

The spirit of Wilma, who was with A.J. exclaimed: "Oh, Amour—I wish you could see! They are repeating these words in chorus. They have such a look of hope and expectation in their faces ... and now they are gone—they have disappeared ... and Jason and the ladies with them! They will be in the 25th dimension in no time! Oh, how wonderful!"

Incredible as it may seem—A.J. found that this simple method brought release to the earthbound spirits from their confused states of consciousness and enabled them to go to a higher vibrating level where they could be given help and loving care. He thenceforth set aside the times, twice a day, when he repeated this little demonstration, and by now, through his guidance, he estimates that thousands of spirit entities have been sent to "a place that is cheery and bright, where they have been met by friends and loved ones."

Fantastic if true, as well as comforting and reassuring!

It has been explained to A.J. that those who die, lacking a belief in an After Life, are still clinging to the "earth plane." They are able to see and hear those in this life, their body forms seem to be the same, and they cannot understand why they can no longer communicate. It is a frustrating experience and without direction from some source, they are inclined to remain in limbo for an indefinite period.

The practice of some religious peoples in praying for the souls of the departed would appear to have validity since we know now that thought can be transmitted and received, and their influence may well be of aid to those who have gone on in making adjustment to the Next Existence.

Perhaps, as we gain further knowledge of the interrelationship of one plane of existence to another, we will learn how to be of better help to the spirits of loved ones and speed them on their way with good and loving thoughts, rather than over-burdening them with

31

grief and mourning, in the mistaken notion that we are demonstrating our degree of affection and sense of loss in this manner.

I return again to the trouble A.J. had with the spirit of Frank Bradley who was murdered years ago, in the very room where A.J. had his recording equipment; trouble enough, at times, to drive him distracted.

Frank's spirit kept ordering A.J. to stop calling for his wife, Wilma, to which A.J. kept angrily replying: "I'm not talking to your Wilma. I'm talking to MY Wilma." But he couldn't make Frank understand this, and their denunciations and arguments were repeated again and again.

This turmoil, added to the many imposters who pretended that they were people with whom A.J. was trying to communicate, would often exasperate A.J. beyond words. He would shout: "You're not who you say you are, and you know it! Why don't you stop pestering me? Get your voices off the tape! Let me alone! I'm trying to reach my wife, Wilma!"

"*I'm* your wife, Wilma!" a voice would insist.

As stated, after A.J. had developed a telepathic ability to hear voices directly in his mind's ear, without need of taping, the bombardment still continued. This happened, as I have reported, until a mysterious Voice, in a commanding tone, told him how to help the Earthbound Spirits escape from their self-imposed imprisonment in the lower regions of the First Plane.

That done, A.J. still had the problem of getting rid of the spirit of Frank Bradley. Finally, armed with the information that Frank had been murdered, he asked him, at the first opportunity, if Frank remembered what had happened in this very room, quite some time ago.

"What do you mean? . . . I didn't kill anybody!" Frank protested.

"No—you're mixed up. You didn't kill anybody.

32

Somebody—a man named Roy Hoyt killed you!" A.J. declared.

"Killed me? ... I don't know ... all I know—I'm here in my house ... and my wife is gone. I can't find her. What have you done with my Wilma?"

It was the same endless merry-go-round. A.J. began to despair of ever helping Frank Bradley get his past straightened out. At this point, the mysterious Voice spoke to him again.

"This man doesn't belong here," said the Voice. "You are right. He didn't kill anybody. He belongs on the Second Plane with his wife."

"Well, is there any way I can help him find his Wilma?" A.J. asked.

"Yes, you can have Jason and the ladies take him to the Second Plane."

"Thanks, whoever you are. I'll do what you suggest. This man has been driving me nuts."

A.J. contacted Jason and told him what he wanted done. "You get the ladies and I'll have Frank Bradley ready for you."

Since the spirit of Frank Bradley was in the house, all A.J. had to do was to call his name and he responded. He could not see him but heard his voice. "Now, what do you want? Are you going to leave my wife alone?"

"Frank, I know where your wife, Wilma, is and I'm going to have you taken to her. Would you like that?"

"Where is she?"

"She is where *you* should have been. She is on the Second Plane. I repeat—you haven't killed anybody. You're not guilty of anything. Are you ready to go? If you are, my nephew, Jason, and the ladies are ready to take you to where your wife Wilma is. They are standing by. Do you see them?"

There was a moment's hesitation. Then, Frank's voice: "Yes, I see a boy and some women."

33

"Okay! Jason, and the ladies, this is Frank Bradley."

A.J. could hear an exchange of greetings. Then the voices died out.

A.J.'s Wilma, in the room with him, watching, able to see into the Next Dimension, said: "They're going, A.J. It'll take no time to get to the Second Plane."

In a few moments, Jason and the ladies returned with the report that they had been projected to a designated place where Frank Bradley's wife, Wilma, and his father and mother had been waiting to greet and to care for him.

"Since that time," said A.J., "Frank has been back several times to thank me. However, I haven't seen or heard from him now in about nine months and I doubt if he will feel any further need to come back to the house where he met his earthly death."

This reads, I know, like fiction, but it is reported exactly as A.J. told it to me. You will have to do your own evaluating, as we present more and more evidence which is strongly suggestive of survival after death.

Chapter 4

SPIRIT MESSAGES ON TAPE

One of the most experienced researchers who has been experimenting for the last few years with tape recording of spirit voices, is a dedicated woman, Sarah Wilson Estep of Severna Park, Maryland.

One of the functions of our ESP Foundation has been to act as a "clearing house" for different researchers, to put them in touch with one another so that they could exchange experiences and suggestions designed to improve methods of communication.

Sarah has kept us informed, regularly, of the results she has been obtaining and we have listened to a number of her tapes, wherein briefly worded voice messages have been clearly discernible. She has kept a careful record of all developments and we have encouraged her to write a book of her own, which she calls VOICES FROM BEYOND.

By arrangement with Sarah, here is what we consider to be one of the finest and clearest accounts of "Talks With the Dead by Tape Recorder," taken from her unpublished manuscript. I have not found it necessary to edit any of it. I am sure you will find it not only of great interest, but of great value.

The dead are alive and they try to prove it in many ways. One way they show this is by talking to us through our tape recorders.

Every morning, seven days a week, I sit down at my tape recorder and ask if I have unseen friends with me. For the last year, I have never ended a recording session without receiving one or more messages from the next dimension.

There are hundreds of individuals around the world who do the same thing and the number grows as others learn about the phenomenon. Professor Hans Bender, a noted German parapsychologist, has compared the taped voice to nuclear fission in its significance for mankind.

This significance cannot be overlooked. After serious study of the voices, many are led to the belief that man continues in a fully conscious state after death. It is also significant that anyone can record voices from beyond. We do not have to be a psychic super star to communicate with the dead. In the past we had to place our trust in mediums to put us in touch with the unseen world. Now each of us can be our own medium. We can call upon whomever we will and make our independent discoveries about spirit life and the nature of that world itself. This is the first time, in the history of mankind, that what has been considered paranormal has been placed within the reach of all who wish to explore.

The history of EVP (electronic voice phenomenon) began in the 1950's. Until the last few years a tape recorder was not something that was found in many homes and so, knowing this, we can understand why the advent of taped paranormal voices is still largely in its infancy.

When I first read in October 1976, that some individuals believed they were recording voices of the dead, I felt intense skepticism. As a psychic investigator, although I had met with some fraud, I discovered that people were more likely to be deluded than fraudulent. If claims of talking to the dead were not fraudulent, then surely the people making them were self-deluded.

As an investigator of the paranormal, I feel I have to be open-minded about situations that come to my attention. With something as important as the possibility of talking to the dead through a tape recorder, I knew I would only be satisfied if I could prove or disprove it to myself. Thus, the evening of October 24, 1976, I sat down at an old tape recorder that only partly worked and asked if I had friends with me. For six days it appeared I didn't. Since I wanted to give this unbelievable phenomenon a fair chance I worked two hours every morning and another two hours late at night. My requests for someone to say something, anything, met with silence. At the beginning I had decided to allow a week. If at the end of that time nothing was heard, I would forget it. On the morning of the sixth day when I asked them what their world was like I recorded the word "Beauty." Contact had been made! The word was clear, but I still couldn't accept that it had happened. From where did it come then? I didn't know, so I decided to extend my seven day deadline and see if anything else came through. Slowly, additional unexplained messages were recorded. I was never overwhelmed with voices. At times I would go days without recording anything, but more and more voices began speaking to me. Today, I have on file thousands of voices which I now accept as of the dead.

It is proper to ask why I believe this, and I welcome

the question. I have frequently heard from friends and loved ones who have died. They greet me by name; they say they still love me and are aware of my activities. My questions about how they find life in the spirit world are often answered. In addition, they show knowledge, sometimes precognitive, about other members of my family.

Recently, one of my daughters had a serious automobile accident. She told me the following morning that shortly before the accident she had a strong impression she should not continue on the highway. At the same time there was a purple light around the steering wheel. Ignoring both the impression and the light, she continued on her way. A short time later the accident occurred. When I went to my tape recorder later that morning and asked what the purple light was that my daughter had seen, I was told, "Mom Wilson was there." Mom Wilson was my mother.

Since I am acquainted with the characteristics of my own family members who have died, I am able to make a somewhat educated assessment as to how many of those traits, if any, they have carried over to the world beyond. With my mother and aunt who have both died within the last three years, this is especially evident. My mother retains her very strong love of music and becomes excited when she comes to talk to me. Aunt Jane knew about my work before she died and said she would try to contact me after death. She has, and shortly after her death said she was going to "rush" her healing. This was typical of her earth plane personality, for whom the days were never long enough.

In my own work I try, where possible, to substantiate the discoveries of others in post-mortem existence. There is a close relationship to what I have recorded and what researchers in the area of death-bed observations have noted.

For two days I was in contact with Paul, an unknown entity, who appeared confused as to what had happened. When he started talking about a white light and how big it was, I suspected he had recently died. I suggested that he look for someone who was probably near-by and was there to help him. He was able to do this, and the last contact I had was when he asked this other individual if he saw how bright the light had gotten and the helper replied, "Yes."

The take-away visitor is mentioned in death-bed observation work. The morning that my aunt died, her take-away visitors spoke to me and said they had visited with her and that she had seen the outline of them. Twenty-four hours after her death, Jane herself, came through and told me she was "Good. I'm back here now."

It is reassuring and comforting to hear from those we knew and loved before their death and to know that they still continue in a conscious awareness of us with expanded capabilities of their own. For many, this is enough and that is the way it should be. For others, such as myself, we want to know more. My questions have touched on all phases of spirit life and the spirit world. Although I have learned a great deal, I will never feel I have learned it all. At times, those on the other side have difficulty in describing to me something about their world. More than once I have been told I should "come back." Some months ago, a voice said to me, "You will learn great facts when you come back."

A little over a year ago, I had a spirit photography session. For a week before the session took place I talked to my unseen friends about what would happen and asked them to try and come. They assured me they would be there. A friend, who has the special ability to draw spirit entities to her, acted as medium. Her husband and another friend were the photographers. During the experiment, which lasted an hour and a half, twenty-three voices were recorded as well as six photographs which showed up on the commercially developed film. Like the voices, which are not heard until tape playback, we were unaware that we had been successful in getting pictures until the film was returned by the developer.

Those on the other side want to communicate with us for several reasons. They are anxious to let us know that death is not the end. From man's earliest history, this has been a question which to many has been unanswerable. In the past, they have tried to show us this through miracles which have chiefly originated in a religious context. Although for a number of people this was sufficient, for more it was not. Trance mediums have also claimed to be in communication with the spirit world. In some cases, evidence suggests that they were. Many times though, it has been difficult to be sure whether their claims were genuine and so we remained unconvinced. Now we have the miracle of the voices on tape, and to me it is just that, a miracle. How appropriate it is! Those on the other side meet us through our electronic equipment. Whether this is where man should be, could be debated. But since electronics are a fact of modern life, that is the level on which we are met. For all of his failures, man is loved, and it is conceivable that the most important goal of those who try to prove that life is forever, is that they hope once man becomes convinced of this he may start to live in brotherhood with the rest of the world.

The individuals who talk to me through my tape recorder have said that they want to teach us what their world is like so we will know what to expect when we die. Some researchers in post-mortem existence believe if any part of the human personality survives death it will do so in a kind of dream state. One time I asked if this was true and the clear answer came back, "Quite different. That is so different." The following day when I asked what life was like in their world, I was told, "There are obstacles. New arrivals are prepared for that. This is why the impediment. People are instructed for that."

The dead also want to comfort their loved ones, the bereaved. If we can be convinced our dead are not dead but are busy with a new life in another dimension, and we will in time see them again, then we can only wish them well and feel joy. At times visitors come to my home to listen to demonstration tapes and upon occasion will ask if they can try to communicate with a loved one. I will give one example.

Mrs. Evans, after listening to a tape one evening, wanted to speak to her mother who had died five years earlier. We made a short recording and at one point a clear female voice said, "I'm busy." Mrs. Evans was thrilled. She then told me she had dreamed several times about her mother since her death and in each dream the mother had told her, "I'm happy. I'm busy." We both felt that the "busy" message was evidence that her mother was with us.

When I ask those with whom I am in communication how they get through to us, I receive different answers. There appear to be Central Transmitting Agencies to which many go to speak. They also come into my recording room to be with me and to talk. I have dozens of Class A message segments in which they tell me they are: "Beside you," "Behind you," "In front of you," "By the clock," "By the books," "By the amplifier," and so on. Each time I start to record I invite them to join me in my office. They take me at my word and come. Two years ago when I first asked how many I had with me I was told "hundreds." At the time I thought this was an exaggeration but I am no longer sure that it is.

Styhe, whom I have never known, is my head monitor and has been with me for over two years. He and

41

his associates seem to have the special task of helping me with recordings. Styhe brings to me those with whom I wish to speak and he has answered many of my questions about his world. He also spoke at my request on a television program which was presented as a special news feature to describe my work. His voice was recorded, not only on my tape recorder but also on the equipment from the television studio.

Interestingly enough, the equipment on the other side seems to break down at times, the same as ours. On several occasions I have been aware they were having trouble coming through. One such morning, I asked if they were having a problem with their equipment. A loud, clear voice replied, "A problem."

For those of you who want to do more than read about taped voices and feel you would like to make your own contacts with the spirit world, there are certain things you will need.

First, if you already have some of the equipment that I will mention, use it. Secondly, if you must buy anything, it isn't necessary to spend a lot of money. Going on the assumption that you have nothing, you will first look for a tape recorder. I would recommend you stay away from the battery operated type with the built in microphone. They are usually noisy and the background sound will drown out the faint voices when they speak. A cassette or open reel tape deck recorder will give best results. Since both are tape decks you will need an amplifier to plug your recorder into so the voices can be heard. Some large AM-FM stereo sets have a connection for a tape recorder. Check to see if yours does. If so, you can save on the cost of an amplifier. You will need a microphone not only for yourself but also for some of those on the other side who use the mike as an entry point for their communications to you. Headphones are a must. The majority of the voices are weak, especially at first, and you will miss most of them if you don't wear headphones when you play the tape back. In buying headphones, I advise the earmuff type which snugly encloses the ear, rather than the flat kind. They do a better job in shutting out noise which may be going on around you. It is not-necessary to buy the most expensive tape. As long as it is quiet it should do a good job. For a cassette tape deck, I prefer sixty minute tapes. Longer tape occasionally gets wrapped around the spindles while recording or playing back and you may destroy some of it while trying to get it untangled.

If you continue working in the field there may be other things you will want to add later. An external speaker is convenient if you want a friend to hear what you have recorded. An equalizer also helps bring out some of the fainter voices. Many experimenters use a pre-amp but I have never found one necessary.

Now that you have your equipment you must decide where and when to use it. Voices will speak anywhere and at any time but it is best when you are trying to establish a channel with them to have a regular place and time to communicate. If you have a room in your home that isn't used, that would be a good place to do your recording. If not a room, perhaps there is a corner in the basement or somewhere else where you could set up shop. Your time to record should be at your convenience. The most important thing in finding a time, is to have it when the house is relatively quiet, and other family members will not interrupt.

There are different ways to record voices but we will look at the two which are the most popular and are used by the majority of experimenters.

The straight microphone method causes the least controversy. You simply turn on your equipment and begin to record. The microphone is used by you for announcements and questions you want to ask. The major drawback for the microphone method is that most

43

of the voices you record this way will be faint and barely heard. Occasionally you will receive a Class A voice but they are few and far between.

Since the paranormal voice uses sounds in the environment to help in voice manifestation we can deliberately provide these sounds. This is the second method we will consider. Whatever sounds are used must be kept faint so they won't overshadow those who are speaking from another dimension. A record player playing softly while you are recording can bring good results at times. I, and many others, turn a radio on while we record. Those who use a radio usually turn to a place on the FM or AM band where there is no program but only a soft hissing sound known as white noise. My contacts have told me they prefer the airband, 125–127 MHz, so I turn there. When I tune to a silent place on one of the other bands I will still receive clear voices, now and then, but since communications are reduced by at least ninety percent, I soon turn back to the air-band.

There is evidence that different groups on the other side come to speak to us with each experimenter having a basic group of communicants. I suspect that whatever group an experimenter is tagged by, adjusts itself to that experimenter and the particular method he uses. This helps explain why when an experimenter changes to another method than the one he normally uses the results, if any, will be poor.

Proper playback of recordings is important as well as frustrating. A five minute recording can take thirty minutes to play back. At first those who speak may do so in whispers. With headphones clamped tightly over your ears you will strain to hear if there is anything there. Suddenly you think you hear something! You will run the tape back and play the segment over, trying to decide if there is a voice and if so, what it says. Try not to let your imagination get the best of

44

you. If I am unable to interpret what I think may be a message, after playing it five or six times, I go on. Undoubtedly I miss some things this way but I would rather do this than create something out of nothing. In time, you will become more skilled at playback and interpretation of messages will be easier. The reasons for this are two-fold. First, the experimenter must learn how to listen to paranormal voices, and secondly, the voices themselves, learn how to speak louder and more clearly.

You will immediately notice that the paranormal voice does not sound like the human voice. It may be harsh, and at times speaks in a monotone. There is often an unusual rhythm to what is said. One of the many enigmas of this type of communication is the unique sentence structure that is frequently used and unexpected, yet basically correct, meaningful words in place of a sentence. Most messages from the other side are short. Three or four words are the rule and it is extremely rare to get anything longer than seven or eight words.

It is better to make one five minute recording each day, than to sit down once or twice a week to record for a half hour. Those on the other side soon learn when and where you will record and if you are dependable as well as persistent they will start to speak to you. Each experimenter must work out his own way to record. I always start each recording with the date, time and a welcome for those who come in love and peace. During a five minute recording I will ask three or four questions, allowing at least a minute between questions for the answer.

If you work to any extent in taping voices you will want to keep a log. This is a record of what you have recorded. Logs can be kept simple. I give each tape a number with a corresponding number in the log. In this way, I can relocate quickly any voice segments I want to replay. Along with the date and time the recording was made, I enter the message received, the question asked and at what number on the tape recorder it is heard.

As you progress in your efforts at communication, you will become aware that you are developing special relationships with some of those on the other side. For those who have been with me a long time and have spoken repeatedly, I feel a deep affection. When they say they love me, or look upon me as a friend, I reply in kind. I treat my known and unknown friends from the spirit world the same as I treat my earth plane friends. With both sets of friends I try to be courteous and thoughtful. I make every effort to be dependable. I am accepting them as individuals, and make allowances for individual differences. As much as possible, I attempt to understand those with whom I come in contact. If we keep in mind that the discarnate are still sensitive and intelligent, and retain their own personalities which respond psychologically to what they meet in their new world as well as here, we will be helped in knowing how to work with them.

A word of caution. After a certain length of time you may discover that you have a special guide that will help you with recordings, as I have Styhe. Your first inclination will be to call on him all the time for help. This is what I did with Styhe and he faithfully tried to respond. Finally one day he said in a slow, tired voice, "I weak." When I asked if my incessant calling on him was responsible for this he replied, "It does weaken." Since then I have been careful not to call on any one individual excessively.

Those on the other side operate at a faster vibration, a higher frequency than we, and it is possible that they have to change this when they enter our sphere to speak through a tape recorder. If they do this repeatedly without a proper rest period between, it could affect them adversely.

At times, you will hear from those on the other side who are lost, confused or frightened. As a compassionate human being you will do whatever you can. I try to explain as gently as possible that they are now a spirit and suggest they look for a friendly guide who will be happy to help them. Occasionally they will ask me directly for help and I will then pray for them and reassure them that they will be kept in my thoughts and prayers. Several times they have asked me to help them come back. I tell them I can't do this, but I feel that before long they will find happiness in the spirit world. We may feel inadequate to help those from another dimension but we can at least try.

Is it dangerous to come in close contact with those who have died? The paranormal, especially the dead and the world of the dead, has always been surrounded by mystery. What is unknown to us often appears fearful, and I am sure this is another reason the spirit world is trying to communicate with us. They want to break through the chains of superstition with which we have bound ourselves. Since that is the world to which we will all, sooner or later, go and call home, it is wise to learn as much as possible about it before we move there. Having said that, I must also say that there are some individuals who should not become involved in trying to make personal contact.

The highly impressionable, hysterical person who has many unresolved fears should leave the paranormal alone. We can never be completely sure what may come to us through the tape recorder. The very few threats that I have received have not bothered me, for I refuse to let them. I also think that good is a stronger force than evil and I place my faith and trust in the thousands of messages expressing love and good will from the other side.

Consideration must be given to those skeptics who say it is impossible to talk to the dead through tape recorders. Many parapsychologists give short shrift to the taped voice phenomenon. They have different theories as to where the voices originate but by and large, they agree they don't come from another dimension. They talk about the "psychokinetic effect" the experimenter has upon the tape. Psychokinesis is the ability of the mind to affect matter and has been proven under controlled laboratory conditions, but not in the matter of the electronic voice. It is also limited, and cannot be sustained for any length of time.

A careful study of taped voices shows there is too much coming through to be attributed to psychokinesis. The majority who speak to me are male. They break in while I am talking, so you have two voices speaking simultaneously, theirs and mine. Two or more voices will speak in brief conversation and because of the vocal quality and what is said, there is no doubt they are paranormal.

Another explanation which discounts the paranormality of the voices is that they are radio programs picked up by the tape recorder. Those of us who use a radio as a sound source for recordings are especially liable to hear this charge. I don't deny that this happens at times but I find it difficult to believe that the air control tower repeatedly calls me by name, says they love and depend on me, or comes back with answers to my questions usually in ten seconds or less. If I have any doubt about a particular message I never play it for others.

Some people who think spirit-human communication is possible feel we shouldn't become involved, that it is evil. This issue must be decided by each individual. Certainly, if you feel it is morally wrong, I would not advise you to go ahead. The Bible has been quoted to me, chapter and verse, as proof that it is wicked to have anything at all to do with the paranormal. Isolated passages should not be extracted from the Bible either to support or condemn psychical study. When one reads all relevant Biblical passages one can only conclude that psychic gifts are not to be condemned. My personal feeling is that the ability to talk to the dead through our tape recorder is a gift from God. Properly used it can benefit all mankind.

Some individuals feel more comfortable in keeping their feet firmly anchored in the hard facts of materialism. Others, believing life can and should be transcendental, look for the stars around and within themselves. As they start to explore these new worlds they learn that there is no beginning or ending of life. Our world and the world of the spirit interpenetrates at many points. We discover there is only Life.

Chapter 5

THE HARRISON HAUNTINGS

My wife, Martha, and I, had known Edith Harrison and daughter, Marion, for some years. (Not their real names.) They are both highly intelligent women of impeccable character, who, until they learned I was about to write a book in proof of "life after death," had never revealed their own ghostly adventure.

"This haunting, such as your friend, A.J. has had, is not an isolated case," they told me. "We would not have believed anything like this could occur until it happened to us. Now we know that such hauntings are much more common than is generally realized, because most people, like ourselves, will not talk about them, even to their own relatives, and close friends, for fear of ridicule."

When I heard their story, I urged them to let me publish it in support of other psychic experiences of like nature. After some deliberation, they agreed to let me do it on condition that I would not reveal their names. They felt that public exposure would reflect upon their professional standing and I had to admit, with still prevailing skepticism, this could well be true.

So here is the authentic account, now recorded in the words of mother and daughter, a report which carries its own conviction:

First, I need to give you a little background leading up to what happened. As I look back now, I realize that I have had what would be called "psychic experiences" throughout my life, without having really recognized them. I was always interested, as was Marion, my daughter, in ESP stories. They were entertaining but we never took them seriously. As for believing in ghosts, that was a humorous and perhaps scary idea, but utterly ridiculous. Having such an attitude, it can well explain why we took so long to accept different strange happenings as tell-tale signs that something beyond the normal was taking place.

I had come from a strictly religious family. My mother, particularly, in her earlier years, would probably have branded anything psychic as the "work of the Devil." Since Mama eventually played a vital part in the ghostly adventure, I feel you should know something about her. She was, in many ways, a most unusual woman, one of seven children, five boys and two girls, born to a poor family, living on the plains of Kansas.

From almost the time she had learned to walk, her father put her on the back of a horse. At the age of 5, she was quite an accomplished "horse lady" who liked to ride spirited animals that hadn't been broken to the saddle. I remember her telling me of her riding a stallion who had killed a man—who tried in every way to throw her, but her gentle persuasion and her stick-to-it-ive-ness prevailed. She was the only one who could safely ride him after that, and folks used to say, "that little girl certainly knows how to handle horses!"

One of the first memories of Mother was at the age

of three when she was attired in her party dress and was about to go out for the evening ... and I looked at her and said, with childish admiration, "Oh, Mama— you look so pretty!" ... and she turned back from the door and took me in her arms and put me on her lap and sat rocking me ... and I know this made her late for the party ... but somehow this show of affection made a deep impression on my child's mind ... and it stands out in my memory today as though it had just happened yesterday.

I guess this will tell you of the closeness between my mother and myself, which existed throughout life. It will tell you, too, of the gentle nature of a really determined and spirited woman ... but one who couldn't stand a quarrel. We never had cross words between us even in moments of disagreement.

Later in life, when mother was hit by physical adversity and lost her eyesight and broke her hip, she never complained or lost her spirit ... and when she couldn't watch television any more, she used to sit and play her harmonica ... and during her last illness when we had to put her in a nursing home ... she took her harmonica with her. . . .

One night, after midnight, when the hospital corridors were normally quiet, the nurses did not respond too quickly to a push-button summons, Mama took up her harmonica and started playing to call aid. She knew this would bring the nurses running to her, to keep all patients from being aroused.

When the nurses arrived and took the harmonica from her, she said, quietly: "I am getting cold. I don't feel very well. I'm going to die" ... and she was gone in three minutes!

Well, that gives you, I think, a little picture of my dear Mama ... except to tell you that, early in her married life, my father did something that mother felt to have been unfaithful ... and because of her strict religious principles, could not be forgiven. So, she picked me up, then a little girl of 5, and ran away, instructing relatives not to reveal our whereabouts, and I was deprived of my father's companionship until mother had gone on and he was near the end of his life, and mother and he had long since remarried.

Now, I am sure you are wondering why I should be telling you all this before I get to my ghost story—but you will see later how it fits in.

In Mother's later years, her brother, my Uncle David, was in ill health, needing constant care, so Mama took him into her home. As time went on, the care became a burden since Mother was not in good health herself. This prompted Marion and I, who were then living together, to decide to buy a larger house and move Mother and Uncle David in with us. This meant we had to go shopping for the place that would suit our needs.

After several near-misses, we came across a house with just the right floor plan—a house that our contractor friend said was well constructed, although it was more than fifty years old. The price for the house was beyond our means but we made the owners—a couple and two children—an offer anyway, considerably below what was being asked.

We had hoped they would come back with a compromise offer which we might be able to afford—but, to our great surprise, they agreed to sell without bargaining. We were shocked as well as delighted—but wondered why the owners seemed so glad to get rid of the place, which they had only occupied a little more than a year. Could there be something wrong with it which we hadn't detected?

When we got moved in, we found, while the house looked most attractive from the outside, the interior was in deplorable condition, needing repairs and re-decorating. The backyard, shielded by a high fence, was a shambles, looking like a jungle, a mass of weeds. Nothing, however, that couldn't be made attractive with a good cleaning out.

We moved Mother and Uncle David in as soon as we could and set to work to get the new home in shape. One of my first tasks was to clean out the closets and, in one of them I pulled open an old chest of drawers and found them lined with old newspapers, yellowed with age. This surprised me as the owners had appeared to be refined, cultured people, whom I would have imagined to be better housekeepers.

Under one of the papers, I came across an 8 × 10 inch photograph of a rather large man and an attractive young woman, with beautiful, big brown eyes. I somehow was drawn to this woman particularly and wondered who she could be.

Meanwhile, I had become acquainted with our next door neighbor, a widower by the name of Joe Thirlby. I took the photograph over to show him, to see if he knew who this couple could be. Joe said: 'Why, yes, that's a picture of the Kaufmans who built your house and who lived in it for 45 years, raised their two children there, until they were grown and married. Mr. Kaufman died first and Mrs. Kaufman lived there alone until her health failed and her children had her placed in a nursing home. She protested being taken away but it wasn't safe to be left there by herself, and the children didn't feel they had room for her in their homes, so they had no choice."

"Then, after Mrs. Kaufman died, the children sold the house to the people *we* bought from?" I assumed.

"Yes, but somehow they didn't seem to like it and they began talking about selling some months after they moved in," said Joe. Then he added: "But speaking about Mrs. Kaufman, a strange thing happened.

Some weeks after she had been put in the nursing home, with the house still empty, the electricity and gas and everything turned off, Mrs. Kaufman somehow got out of the nursing home, and must have walked miles across the town of Los Angeles, and found her place, and though the house was locked up, she managed to break open a window and climb inside. I saw her there and notified her children and they came and took their mother away."

Somehow, as my next door neighbor told me this, and I looked at the expressive eyes of Mr. Kaufman in the photograph, my heart went out to her. I could feel a hurt in her eyes and I said to myself: "Poor thing! This house was her castle. She and her husband had built it—had lived in it all these 45 years . . . apparently this house—this home—meant everything to her . . . she couldn't bear to be parted from it. How sad! How incredible that she would make this supreme effort, risking perhaps her life, to get back to it!"

I couldn't explain the compassion I felt for Mrs. Kaufman . . . the different feeling I had about the house—a house which the original owner had loved so very much. This feeling, rather than going away, seemed to increase with time.

But in the first few weeks of residency, most of my thoughts had to be given over to getting settled, and getting Mother and Uncle David comfortably situated. But, as much as Marion and I tried to help Uncle David, he passed on inside of three months.

Mother missed her brother a great deal and I felt I must spend as much time with her as possible. She loved to read in those days, and she would read to me by the hour, as I worked about the house or managed time to sit with her. She was an excellent reader and always selected books and subjects of mutual interest.

I occupied the bedroom in the back of the house, which overlooked the backyard. Mother was in the room up the hall. Her door opened looking down the hall, so I could often hear her as she sat reading, and exchange comments back and forth.

Reflecting now, I must have been blind or stupid not to have questioned something which began happening and which Mama was the first to notice.

One day, after we had been in the house a little over three months, after Uncle David had died, Mama looked up from her reading, with a startled facial expression, and called to me: "Edith, is Marion home?"

"No, Mama," I answered. "She's at the office. Why?"

"That's strange! I could swear I saw Marion go across the hall into her bedroom!" Mother answered.

"It must have been an optical illusion," I told her, dismissing the subject.

Every so often, thereafter, and I am chagrined to admit, for four and a half years, Mama, when reading or sitting with her door open so she could see down the hall, would remark about having "seen something." Why I had continued to think it was a trick of her eyesight or her imagination, and had paid only scant attention, is now beyond my comprehension. At times Mama would insist that she would get a glimpse of a dress on some form which crossed the hall quickly. "Oh, Mama, you've been seeing things again," I would say, or would comment to Marion that we must humor Mama because there was no sense in arguing with her over these visions.

Finally, after Mother had been with us approaching five years, she became ill and bedfast, requiring nursing day and night. I had developed a heart condition and my doctor said I could no longer take care of Mother at home, or I might die before she did. There was nothing to do but send Mama to the hospital while I went to bed at home. I had Mama constantly on my mind and both of us missed being together. Mama was so impulsive and so desirous of getting more freedom of action that we transferred her to a nursing home. We brought her home frequently on Sundays, but she was never to return to the house to stay.

Four days after Mother's departure, things began to happen. In our bathroom there is a vent that goes down to the basement. All of a sudden, while I was in the room, someone struck the pipes as though with a metallic object, two blows, followed by four more, which made the pipes ring like a bell.

It was a frightening series of sounds and I was sure some intruder had gotten in the basement, probably through a window, or even crawled through the vent. The door to the basement was locked and I was afraid to open it, for the moment, to go down stairs and investigate. When the sound did not repeat itself, I finally got up nerve to investigate, and, of course, there was no one there.

A few days later, when I was home alone, I heard footsteps in the hall—unmistakably the steps of a woman. I had the uncanny feeling of a presence and I suddenly recalled the times Mama had claimed she had had glimpses of a woman in the hall. I began to feel funny, now wondering if *I* had been imagining things.

One night when Marion was home from work, she called to me and asked: "Mother, did you just walk down the hall?"

"No," I said. "Why?"

"Because I heard footsteps!"

"Well, that relieves me," I said. "I've been hearing them, too! Marion, this proves it. Something's going on here."

We both fell to discussing what Mama had been seeing and wondered, since sound had been added to sight, what was going to happen next.

It wasn't long before we got an answer. Two heavy cabinet doors in the Vanity room opened and banged shut, causing Marion and me to almost jump out of our skins. Nothing had ever moved these door before. There were three great bangs.

This caused us to sit down and take inventory. There had been the sightings of Mama through the years, what Marion had heard, the footsteps we had both heard, the banging of the pipes and other noises—all leading to but one conclusion we were forced to make— we must be experiencing an *actual haunting!*

Some spirit entity, quite probably the original owner of the house, Mrs. Kaufman, was throwing temper tantrums over our being there and was trying to scare us out, as she must have done with the couple who had been so ready and eager to sell to us.

"If our assumption is correct," I said to Marion, "she must be greatly put out over not being able to get rid of us. I can't understand, though, why she waited all this while before raising such a racket."

"Do you think it might be," speculated Marion, "that because your Mother, when she was here, was about her age, she didn't want to make a disturbance while she was with us . . . but now that Mama is gone from the house, she feels she can deal with us more directly?"

"I couldn't say," I pondered. "But if this *is* Mrs. Kaufman, and I can't believe it could be anyone else, I can't help feeling terribly sorry for her. I only wish there was some way I could talk or communicate with her."

Two weeks later, when I was home alone, and in the vanity room, the doors to the cabinet banged open and shut. This time I knew the spirit of Mrs. Kaufman was there. Instead of being frightened, I was filled with a feeling of love. I just can't explain it but I wanted to reach out and put my arms around her and comfort her.

Somehow, though I couldn't see her, I just knew she was in the room with me . . . and a strong impulse came over me . . . and I started talking to Mrs. Kaufman's ghost. If anyone could have heard me talking to what appeared to be thin air, they would probably have put me down as an idiot. I began to speak out loud, and this, as nearly as I can recall, is what I said:

"Mrs. Kaufman, I know you are here . . . and I'm glad because I've wanted to tell you for a long time—I've wanted so much to be friends with you. I *do* understand how you feel. I'm living in your home and I know it's your home . . . When I was redecorating it, I've always thought of you and wondered and hoped that you approved of what I did.

"I want you to know that you are very welcome here with us . . . and to live here in the house with us. Can't we be friends? I'd like to be friends. But you know, I can't help but wonder if you went on and found your husband and the other members of your family . . . I wonder if you wouldn't be happier than you are here . . . and you wouldn't be so lonely?

"Don't get the idea that I am trying to send you away because I'm not. You're more than welcome to stay here with us!"

Well, I probably said some other things . . . I don't know now . . . said it with all the compassion and love I could command . . . I really did and I really meant it . . . and somehow I felt the spirit of Mrs. Kaufman was standing there in front of me and listening intently.

Two days later, when I was again alone in the house, I heard a man's footsteps go down the hall . . . so different from the woman's. They were long strides and they were very heavy . . . and they went straight like walking feet . . . and they stopped right about when he got to the south bedroom . . . he didn't come down to my back bedroom.

This never happened again but I have felt since that these footsteps belonged to Mrs. Kaufman's husband and that, in some way, he had come back for her . . .

because, two days after this, when I was in the bathroom, I heard tapping on the pipes in the basement—very soft and gentle, so unlike the loud banging of the other times . . . and the thought came to me that Mrs. Kaufman's spirit was trying to tell me something . . . and then, suddenly, I *knew,* she was telling me "Goodbye."

All phenomena ceased after that . . . and Marion and I are living in Mrs. Kaufman's beloved home yet today. Since then we have read books on experiences other people have had in haunted houses. In one of the stories, a man actually arranged to let a ghost occupy one room in the house, closing it off. There have been many cases of different manifestations and forms of communication. But Marion and I are still not ready to risk the skepticism of some of our doubting friends and business associates. We know, however, that you accept every word of what we have told you as true.

Chapter 6

A LIFETIME OF
SPIRIT COMMUNICATION

Able to hear and talk to spirit entities as well as to feel their presence, long-time North Carolina newspaper columnist, Gladys Childs (her real name) had kept a careful record of her communication with departed friends and loved ones.

In turning over her documented reports to me, she said: "I am making this information publicly available for the first time because I want to help people to know that death is not the end—that there is a great adventure awaiting each one of us when our time comes to leave this earth."

Mrs. Childs, a dynamic woman, has been psychic all her life. She was born in South Africa, the daughter of an official in the British government's highway department. Her mother, Helen Mason, was also psychic, able not only to see but to talk to what are commonly called "ghosts." She had ample opportunity, apparently, because three of the homes in which the Masons had lived had been haunted.

Gladys recalls, as a girl of five, a time when the Masons' Zulu gardener dug up two human skeletons in the front yard of their greystone house in Vryheld. She recalls being awakened in the night, hearing heavy objects like chains being drawn across the ceiling. Her parents searched the attic but found no trace of chains or rodents. The mystery was never solved but Gladys' mother had the psychic impression that the eerie sounds had been caused by the earthbound spirits of soldiers who were killed in the Boer War (1899-1902) whose bodies were buried on the premises.

On another occasion, the Masons had moved to a house in Estcourt which had formerly belonged to an old hospital unit. They had been in the house several weeks when Gladys, then a child of seven, was told by her mother of the ghost in her bedroom.

Said Gladys: "Mother would see this elderly man kneeling in front of one of the bay windows. He always wore a grey coat with large pockets, and was intent on sorting bits of string and pebbles on the floor in front of him. He never bothered anyone . . . Without telling a former hospital nurse of the ghost, she asked her if anyone had died in the house.

" 'Oh, yes,' said the nurse. 'Old man Pockets died in the room you are sleeping in. We called him 'Pockets' because he always wore a grey coat with large pockets and he was forever collecting bits of string and pebbles.'

"I know that a lot of people don't believe in these things," Gladys commented, who had recently returned from seeing her former homes on a trip to South Africa. "But you have to experience it to believe it. I grew up, as you can realize, in a psychic atmosphere and I soon found I could hear voices in my mind's ear, and that spirits could hear me or sense my thoughts. It wasn't long before spirit communication was a very normal practice for me.

"Let's put it this way:

"In this life, a friend comes into my apartment and we have a conversation. I can see this friend and the friend sees me.

"A deceased person's spirit comes into my apartment and we have a conversation. The friend or relatives see me but I can't see that person, because I am not clairvoyant, only clairaudient.

"It is as simple as that. BUT the spirit of the deceased person comes to me at its own convenience, not MY convenience. It is all mental, not audible.

"Relatives and loved friends who have died in my native South Africa find their way to me—by thought—after they have died.

"There are times when I am deeply troubled or concerned about someone or something, and a loved one in the After Life senses this and comes to me with an answer or comfort. Thought is the connection.

"Spirit communication is beautiful, a truly spiritual comfort. I am thankful to God for it because my American life would have been intolerable without it. Everyone who has ever loved me is dead.

"My awareness of spirit life came to me in my teens. My mother, as I have said, was clairvoyant. She could SEE the spirits of the deceased, was never afraid of them and discussed it freely with me.

"My father was psychic. He had a sister who was a clairvoyant.

"I grew up in three different haunted houses. My mother saw ghosts, some were violent. She talked to me about them, and it is still vivid in my mind, so that the two worlds were and are part of my life.

"I have read everything I could about the After Life and ghosts. I will be one, too, some day, and I want to be prepared!

"I had a deathbed message from my mother who died in the town where I was born. Six months after she passed, she was as close to me as breathing and brought me an urgent message to my father, which I relayed to him. I was 21 at the time. It was the last time I saw my father alive. My mother knew of his coming death which occurred a few days later. In fact she had predicted his death two years before it happened, exactly as it took place.

"I have had numerous spirit communications over the years in America. I hope, in the cases I report, that I can help people to understand death. It is so very important that they should know what to expect in order for them to accept their deaths when the time comes. It would ease the grief of the living to know their loved ones are still living in another dimension. My mother tells me there are places of existence after death, and one has to learn just as they learned in this world.

"Many people believe when they die they will go straight to heaven and be with Jesus. I don't believe anyone is that perfect. One has to make himself worthy—learn to listen to the inner voice . . . this is the way to make spiritual progress here and hereafter.

"Many of my spirit communications come to me while attending the funeral of the deceased. Sometimes they are only communications. Then, again, others come to me at my home, even from far off South Africa. Some come for many years, and some come from time to time, as far back as 22 years. They come, as I have said, at their convenience, not mine. I never know when they are coming.

"One thing I have especially noted is that everyone who comes by can't stay long, and always says: "I must go now."

"The presence is very real, only I repeat, I cannot see the person—but the person can see me.

"When someone dies, he or she is the same person

64

we knew on earth. Many can't accept the transition; many do accept it.

"Many people are too involved in the material world to listen when a loved one over there is trying to get through. Then, too, some spirits can't get through for some reason or another.

"We mortals must take time to listen, and to believe our loved ones over there are, and can be, close to us."

From the Spirit Communication
Records of Gladys Childs

Undoubtedly, many men and women have had the psychic capacity to receive messages, at times, from departed friends and loved ones, but have considered this ability of too personal and almost too sacred a nature to reveal to others, whom they feel would not understand or accept anyway.

In the case of Gladys Childs, she had the forethought to keep a dated record of most of her psychic experiences for her own reference as well as evidence. In giving me permission to choose such cases as I felt would be of significant interest, she made only one stipulation—that the identity of the friends and loved ones be protected, with the exception of a few instances.

As you read these cases, you will be impressed, I am sure, with the naturalness and humanness of the communications, almost the casualness of some of them, and Gladys' oft-repeated observation that "so-and-so came by" . . . or "dropped in for a brief visit" . . . or "had something he or she wanted to tell me, and knew they could get through to me."

What is also to be noted is the basic similarity of

comparisons between the psychic experiences of all people, independent of each other. These phenomena are fundamentally the same, giving them great evidential value—offering proof of the reality of the ordinarily unseen.

Here now are some of the cases, not always presented in chronological order, just as Gladys Childs has recorded them in her "Spirit Communications" notebook:

HE DID NOT BELIEVE
IN AN AFTER LIFE

Date of Death May 30, 1974

I had known WC for many years. He believed death was the end of existence. I talked to him about the After Life. He must have been listening. His health had always been good. However, a stroke lasting less than two weeks, ended his life on May 30, 1974, the day before his 84th birthday.

All during that month I had a strong feeling that WC would not live to see his birthday.

I could not get to his funeral so did not expect any spirit communication.

About 7:30 p.m., May 31st, my TV was on. The news had just gone off and I was reading the evening paper when, suddenly, I heard a distinct voice, clairaudiently, say:

"I am not dead. You are reading the paper, and the television is on. I am not dead!"

I knew it was WC—but I could not see him. He was standing in front of the gas space heater in my living room, next to where I was seated, reading the paper. He was very real even though I couldn't see him. My mind had been on the newspaper when the voice jerked my attention away from it.

He then said, "I like your apartment." (He had never been in it.)

After a moment, he said: "I don't want to go back to the funeral home." (Friends were paying their respects there at that time.)

He then walked across the room toward the television and leaned over to look at a picture of the late John F. Kennedy. (I had told him about the picture, saying that the president reminded me of him, WC, when I first met him.)

He then said: "My kids are all mad at me." I understood that remark. Then he vanished!

WC has come to me many times over the years, probably because he knows I am the only one this side of the Veil with whom he can communicate.

In the beginning of the visitations, he said he was "earthbound." The "greeters" had told him so. "Greeters," he said, "meet the spirits of the newly dead to help them make the transition."

It was not easy convincing the new arrivals, he said, and he, too, had to make them realize that they had died.

I always know when WC comes by. There is a special vibration that announces his arrival.

A DOCTOR AND HIS PATIENTS

Date of Death Oct. 16, 1975

One of the oddest spirit experiences I have ever had was while attending the funeral of a well known doctor, a long time friend, who died on October 16, 1975.

Before the service in the Funeral Chapel, I sensed departed spirits coming into the auditorium from every direction. There must have been more than a dozen of them. Each seemed to be coming with a specific purpose and heading for the casket.

It was simply fantastic. My long time friend, WC, who had died more than a year and a half before, was with them. When he saw me, he told me telepathically that our mutual friend, WV was still a little confused about his transition.

I was under the impression that the spiritual beings had been former patients of the deceased, or people he had brought into the world, as that had been his speciality on earth as a doctor, and that they had come to greet and to help him.

There is nothing more exhilarating than feeling a spiritual presence of someone who has passed over, even though you cannot SEE that person.

A STRANGER VISITS ME

About the Middle of March 1975

Only once has a stranger come to me in the spirit.

It was in the evening about the middle of March 1975. I was aware of my apartment being filled with a strong fragrance of a scented perfume powder.

I felt the presence of a woman. Imagine my surprise when she said: "Gladys, I love you. I have come to thank you for helping me. We have never met. I lived in another town and something you wrote, that was sent to me, helped me."

All I could think of was my weekly column, which is more of a potpourri type column, and I sometimes write about the after life in it.

She would not give me her name, saying it was immaterial, as we had never met.

However, she paid me a second visit the next evening, and this time she said her name was "Alice," and that she had died at the age of 58 with cancer. She said she had a daughter in Las Vegas who was in deep trouble. Again she

68

thanked me for helping her. Her visit has remained a mystery.

SISTER'S SPIRIT OFTEN VISITS

Date of Death Nov. 5, 1971

My younger sister, Ethel, died of cancer of the throat in South Africa. She was a beautiful person, physically and spiritually.

She has come to me many times over the years. I always know when she is here because my whole apartment is filled with the fragrance of a delicate French perfume which leaves when she goes.

She loves my television. If I am busy on my news work, she does not communicate. She just stays around. She has even come to church with me and I know she is seated beside me. She expresses her views on the minister who is different to the ones we grew up with. The American ministers intrigue her. She has a great sense of humor, always did have.

A FRIEND'S PRESENCE IS MISSED

Date of Death July 17, 1972

On July 17, 1972, a long time friend I met with his wife the first year of my arrival in North Carolina, died of a brain tumor. He had been hospitalized for several weeks. His widow and I are still very close friends.

I attended JF's funeral, never dreaming I would get a spirit communication from him. Just after the casket passed me, I felt JF's presence at my side and heard him say, mentally: "Gladys, I am glad you came to my funeral. But where is LG?"

LG was a school friend of his wife and had been close to the family all through the years. I said:

"She is at the beach and does not know of your death."

Then he said: "I was sorry, when I was at the hospital, I did not know when you came by. The pressure on the brain was too heavy." (He had not known several of us, prior to his death.)

JF was a jovial man, well liked, a great outdoorsman, a happy man. I asked him what it was like "over there." He replied, "Not bad, not bad at all."

TWO FRIENDS UNITED IN DEATH

Date of Death Feb. 8, 1974

JM was a long time friend of FS. Their friendship was exceedingly close and when JM died, FS said he didn't see how he could go on living without him.

On the evening of his fifth wedding anniversary to his second wife (Feb. 8, 1974), FS took his wife to a local restaurant to celebrate the event. On their arrival home from the restaurant, they watched TV for a while, then FS went into the bathroom and shot himself. No one knew why.

I had known FS and his wife for years. I attended the funeral. I was not sure, under the conditions of his passing, whether I would get a spirit communication, but I did.

FS called me by name mentally. He identified himself and said: "I know I am dead, as you who are living know me as dead. It had to be. There was no other way. You are the only one in this church or chapel, whatever they call it, who understands."

Then, to make sure he was getting his message across to me, he mentioned my full name, given and surname, and his full name and title, and repeated the message. This done, he wanted to tell me about JM. He said: "It was months before

JM could accept his *death*." This implied that JM had been trying to return to earth and be with FS.

FS said again that he knew he was dead and knew it had to be, and he had to pay, whatever he meant by that, but there was no other way. He said he was "at peace." He also said, "The force was too strong." He also mentioned that his young son, who had recently married, was grieving.

I have always wondered—could JM, the older man, have pulled FS over to his side of life? The relationship had been so strong on earth between them, is it possible they couldn't live, as FS had suggested, without each other?

HE DIDN'T WANT TO STAY DEAD

Date of Death Feb. 12, 1972

I had known BA for many years and had been his secretary in local government for quite some time.

We had often discussed the after life. He told me about "unknown footsteps" and the presence of unseen persons in his parents' home.

He was unmarried and 67 years of age when he died on February 12, 1971. I expected to get a spirit communication at his funeral but I did not. I had felt surely that, because of our many discussions during his lifetime, that some message would come through.

Instead, just before the funeral service started, I became aware of a "scuffling" in front of the casket, and heard BA's spirit say: "Let me go! I'm not dead! Let me go!" I could sense a struggle as if some unseen person was holding BA back. It was so real, almost like it was happening in the flesh. I got the impression BA was, or had not accepted his death.

71

Date of Death Aug. 24, 1973

The captain, a South African writer and farmer, and a friend of my teenage days, died in South Africa on August 24, 1973.

Before I learned of his death, he came to me in the spirit. He gave me the name of the person who would notify me of his death, and it was so, a few weeks later.

The Captain came to me many times, especially when I was troubled, and brought words of comfort. All through life we had kept up a correspondence. We talked of many things pertaining to our native land and our younger days, during these visitations of the spirit.

AN UNUSUALLY COMMUNICATIVE SPIRIT

Date of Death June 14, 1974

While attending an out of state wedding, RM, a long time American friend, was killed instantly when a car hit her as she started to cross the road.

I attended her funeral. We were members of the same church. Seated with me were my former editor and his wife, and a mutual friend.

Both the editor and the mutual friend died the following year.

Before the service started for RM, I was suddenly aware of her spirit before the pew in front of me and this is what she said:

"Gladys, I am glad you are here. I did not see the car when it hit me. I am glad I don't have to spend another night in that house alone. (She was a widow and had lived by herself.)

"Tell A and J (her daughters) there is no death."

I said, clairaudiently: "They won't believe me."

72

Then she said: "Tell CH (the editor) to stop crying. He still has some time."

As our mutual friend, JW, was seated between the editor and me, I had not seen the tears, until I leaned forward, and saw them after her remark.

RM came by my home several times after that.

Early in June 1975, RM literally bounced out of my kitchen into my living room and said enthusiastically: "Gladys, I have good news for you. Some of your articles are being published!"

I had mailed four historic articles to out of town papers and had not heard a word from any of them.

The next day, after RM's visit, I learned that three of the articles *had* been published.

RM is the happiest spirit I have ever communicated with. She is positively radiant.

She says that she is as free to come and go as she pleases. That in her world—a replica of this one—without the material—everyone has freedom of choice and one creates one's own environment.

RM comes to me when our mutual friend, EJ, has a problem, and she gives me a message for EJ, which I pass on.

In May 1975, RM came to me in her own breezy way, to tell me that I would receive recognition in the city "where the Governor lives."

That, of course, meant Raleigh, North Carolina. Toward the end of the month, I had an historic article, with several pictures, published in "State" Magazine, which came out of Raleigh.

On Tuesday, February 22, 1977, about a quarter to six in the evening, I was waiting for a phone call from Mrs. T., close friend and member of the same church we all attend, who was to pick me up to go to a church supper. Mrs. T. had been on jury duty all day and was running late.

One of my besetting sins is that I have always lived by the clock, and am always ready for an appointment ahead of time, and get fidgety when others are late.

Here comes RM who very positively started to lecture me on my useless worrying.

She said: "Gladys, stop worrying so much. You are only hurting yourself. I could slap you for it. The phone will ring in a few minutes, and you'll be on your way."

I thought, "Am I imagining RM is saying this?" Immediately she replied: "No, you are not imagining, This is RM" (giving her full name to convince me). She went on to name the friend who was to pick me up.

While waiting for the phone call, I asked RM to tell me more about her life in the spirit.

She said: "I am having a ball. I am as free as the wind and can come and go as I choose. I have also resumed my music studies here. I would not be fussing at you if I did not care about you. Please try and not worry so much."

Just then, Mrs. T. phoned and I said to my spirit friend: "You win!" RM stimulates my faith in the life after death.

The following are SPIRIT COMMUNICATIONS from the two friends, CH and JW, who were seated beside me at RM's funeral.

GLAD TO BE FREE OF SUFFERING

Date of Death April 19, 1975

CH, my former editor, died a very painful death of cancer of the throat on April 19, 1975.

I attended the graveside service held for him by the church we all went to as members.

I felt a sense of grief, which was sensed by his spirit because he said, mentally: "Do not grieve for me. I suffered torment in the last days."

He said that our mutual friend, WC who has passed into spirit, (as I have reported) May 30,

74

1974, had helped him through the transition, and that WC had said that I understood death.

The Editor and I had several spirit communications after that, relative to our newspaper work.

HAD TO LEAVE HER BODY

Date of Death June 25, 1975

JW, another old-time friend, died unexpectedly on June 25, 1975.

I was not able to attend her funeral but did get to the funeral home prior to it, with another mutual friend of the both of us.

It just happened that JW's spirit was there at the time. I felt her presence, and heard her say, clairaudiently: "Gladys, I am glad you came!"

I replied, sadly: "JW, I wish you had not left us."

"Hon," (an expression she often used in life) "there was nothing I could do about it."

It was said in a resigned way, and it has been the only communication I have had from her.

STANDING ROOM ONLY AT FUNERAL

Date of Death May 10, 1974

On May 10, 1974, in the late evening, JB, a prominent citizen, lost his life in a fire while trying to save the family business.

He was well liked in the community and held high office.

His funeral in a local church of which he was a member, was well attended. I was there, too.

I did not expect a spirit communication from him and was very surprised when I did.

He called my name three times, thanked me for coming, and expressed great surprise to see so many people attending his last rites. He seemed overwhelmed by it.

LOVED MUSIC AT HIS FUNERAL

Date of Death May 16, 1974

EF and his family were former neighbors of mine. He was head of a funeral home and a pillar in his church. He died on May 16th, 1974. As the church where services were held was near where I lived, I was able to attend the last rites held for him.

Not receiving a spirit communication, I tried to contact his spirit.

His reply was that he was enjoying the beautiful music in his beautiful church. His spirit was so absorbed in the music, I did not make any further comment.

SPIRIT WARNING OF A DEATH

Date of Death Dec. 13, 1957

Early in December of 1957, after having moved to my present apartment upstairs over a Doctor's Clinic, I was talking with JH, a lad of fourteen, who was waiting for his mother, the doctor's nurse, to ride home with her. We were standing in the car lot.

I was planning to do a story on the boy as he was very bright and intelligent.

During a pause in the conversation, these words came to me from a voice within me: "He is going to die, and it will be before the end of the year."

My first impulse was to dash into the clinic and warn his mother, and I restrained the impulse, thinking she would get the impression I was out of my mind.

Much to the shock of the community, JH shot himself on December 13, 1957.

No one knew why.

Date of Death Sept. 2, 1969

On August 11th, 1969, friends of mine lost their only son who was 16. I wrote them a letter of sympathy, explaining my views on death, stating my conviction that it was a transition to another dimension of life, but I did not receive a reply.

A few weeks later, the boy's father died unexpectedly on September 2nd, 1969. I attended his funeral. We were all members of the same church.

While in the church cemetery, during the burial, I was standing a few yards from the grave when I heard my name called several times, mentally, and the spirit of the deceased said: "Tell K (his wife) there is no death."

I replied mentally, "She won't believe me. *You* didn't."

"No," he said, "I thought you were crazy, but you are the only one in this cemetery who understands death."

AN AFTER DEATH FRIGHT

Date of Death May 7, 1980

On May 9, I attended the 3 P.M. funeral of a long time friend. The service was held in the First United Methodist Church, a block from where I live.

I had known Mamie for many years. She was 78, and I had also known her parents, long deceased.

Mamie had three daughters, the youngest married my youngest stepson, 33 years ago—a good marriage.

Mamie had four sisters and many relatives who were at the funeral.

Now this is something which had not occurred to me. That is how the DECEASED feels when the transition is made, and it is not what they expected.

At first I thought Mamie's spirit was not there as she had died before of a massive heart attack, probably brought on by nursing an ailing husband.

I made an attempt to contact her in the spirit, thinking she might not have known I was able to communicate this way.

Was I surprised to hear her say, mind to mind: "I did not think I was going to die. I have been so frightened as no one could hear me. I am so happy that I can talk to you. It is helping me not to be so frightened."

She kept saying she was so happy I had made contact with her, which helped her overcome her fear.

This conversation was taking place during the service.

I got the impression that a load of fear had been lifted from Mamie's spirit.

We could not say much more as the service was ending. It gave me a feeling of relief that I had, in some small way, helped her adjust to the new life she had so recently entered.

NO LONGER SO FRIGHTENED

Date of Death May 9, 1980

ML was a long time friend of mine. As her funeral was held in a nearby church I was able to attend it.

I did not think she knew of my ability to converse with departed spirits so I contacted her.

To my surprise she kept saying, "I've been so frightened, no one in my family could hear me. Now I am so happy, and I am not so frightened any more because now you can hear me."

Her husband, who had been in ailing health, died the same month on May 30th, 1980. I could not get to his funeral, but I know my friend is at peace now.

HAD NOT SEEN JESUS

Date of Death Jan. 15, 1981

I had known LW for a long time, and her husband who died in 1953. LW lived alone; she was a Christian woman, read her Bible every day, and was well liked.

I had transportation to her last rites but did not know if I would have a communication, but I did.

As the service started I heard her voice and felt her presence in front of me.

She said: "This is L—I did not understand. WC" (a deceased relative of hers and known to me) "told me you understood death. Tell my children 'their father' is here with me," (she said this twice). She said a couple of other "personal" things.

I asked her what it was like in the spirit world and had she seen Jesus.

She said: "No. It is not like the preachers say it is."

I did not continue the conversation as I wanted her to hear what the minister was saying about her.

REUNITED WITH LOVED ONES

Date of Death Jan. 16, 1981

JC was 67 when he died. I attended his last rites. He and his family had been known to me since my arrival in Lincolnton. I had Christmas dinner with JC, his three aunts and his niece. All were widowed except the one sister (his aunt).

I did not get a spirit communication from JC but one from his mother who had died a couple of years ago a day after her sister had died. I had

had a spirit communication from her sister, Winnie.

The mother said they were happily reunited, her son, and the sister who had died, and her husband who had preceded her in death some years ago.

She also said: "Tell her two remaining sisters, and named them, to stop grieving, that there would not be any more deaths for awhile." The remaining sisters are aged 80 and 87. Other members of the family had died in the past year.

There is so little time during a funeral service to get communications.

STILL TOO CONFUSED

Date of Death Feb. 12, 1981

GT was 84 when he died after a lingering illness. I did not get a spirit communication. WC, a relative of the deceased who has communicated with me over the years, was there and said that GT was still too confused and was having a problem accepting his death.

THE PRESENCE OF THE PRIEST

About six months ago I had just completed an interview with a local nun. Everything was quiet and peaceful. We were seated on the couch and no one else was in the house where the Episcopal Sisters are residing.

Suddenly everything was very quiet and the room was filled with a powerful spiritual presence that enveloped me, and there was a great stillness. I looked up and saw a tall priest standing between us. His right side was towards me. I could have reached out my hand and touched him. He wore a floor length black robe and a floor length gray stole about twelve inches wide and a priest's hat, and he was looking intently at the nun. He was there two or three minutes and then vanished. The next week the nun underwent surgery, successfully. I asked her later if she saw the Priest. She said no, but she felt the presence.

Summarizing Comments of Gladys Childs

I am often asked where I believe the higher planes of existence are; how spirits are free to visit anywhere they like; and what the "heaven world" or worlds are really like.

I am told the next dimensions are in a different kind of space around us, just as real to us there as this world is here.

Spirits are free to visit anywhere they wish by THOUGHT, they learn to transport their spiritual bodies by CONCENTRATED THOUGHT.

Here on earth, we mortals can "flash back" in THOUGHT to whatever part of the world we have visited or lived in, reliving and reviewing pleasant or unpleasant situations.

In this life, having the DESIRE to visit another state, or town, or a foreign country, we do so first by preparing in THOUGHT for same. THINKING, then PLANNING and then DOING!

You don't go anywhere, not even into the next room, before first THINKING to do so.

It is the same in the After Life. My understanding is that the spirits must LEARN to transport their spiritual bodies by the DEPTH of their concentration and the DESIRE of their MINDS. Remember, we first had to learn how to WALK here, to get any place on our OWN.

I am impressed, time and again, that the SPIRIT WORLD is a REPLICA of our world. The planes are similar to our earthly states, say in the United States for instance. People, like attracting like, find themselves with others of similar interests and environments.

Each plane has a place of LEARNING—arts, music, theatre, various professions and vocations, ad infinitum. One has the choice of what he or she wants to learn and do.

Of course, as in our world, there are those in the spirit world who are not ambitious, or just wish to stay around in their earthly homes or business places, or gather with other spirits of evil in the spirit world, as was their way of living on earth. UNLESS and WHEN they choose to CHANGE their THINKING, to give up on the evil and switch to a more constructive state of consciousness, they will remain in a low plane of existence.

Some spirits are EARTHBOUND for years. Then again, those whose deaths were caused by others, want to see justice done, and they try to get through to some psychic, to save an innocent person from being accused of something they did not do, or lead those in authority to the real culprit.

I believe we create here on earth our own HEAVEN and HELL by our THINKING. THINK miserable and you *are* MISERABLE. THINK happy and you *are* HAPPY. If we give our fellow man the POWER to HURT US, he can make us MISERABLE. Our fellow man also has the POWER to make us happy, if we let him.

Perhaps MY problem was that I gave my American husband and his children the POWER to hurt me. It was so difficult at the time not to be hurt, because I did care for him.

I hate friction. I usually bend over backward not to hurt anyone.

When my South African husband first came to me

in the spirit, it was in the evening and I was kneeling by my bed, saying my prayers, when I heard a "swishing" sound come swiftly through my bedroom window and semi-circle the room. I sensed the presence of three spirits.

Then a spirit voice came from an invisible entity standing in the center of the room, saying: "Gladys, I am here."

I knew it was my South African husband. He had been transported by the other spirits, but I did not know who they were.

Ted has come to me by himself, over the years, since that time.

I, myself, am trying to learn all I can about the After Life because I cannot escape it as it grows closer.

I will always be indebted to my beloved mother's knowledge and the early training and insight she gave me of spiritual things, which have seemed so normal to me in my advancing years. If there is anything to reincarnation, I'd like to say now that I have no desire to come back to another earth life, as this one has been filled with too many heartaches and frustrations for me.

I know there is such a thing as possession and many people get mixed up with the wrong kind of spirit influences. One has to be very careful experimenting with psychic forces. It is sometimes very difficult for people to get rid of evil spirits, once they become attached. I know there is a God Power within which can guide and protect you, once you keep attuned to it by RIGHT THINKING. I am sure that the reason I have been aware of spirit visitations all my life is because I grew up in that type of environment and it seemed so natural to me.

I feel I must repeat that I am not clairvoyant, only clairaudient. I cannot SEE the person, but they can see ME. It is a mind-to-mind communication, knowing the one I am speaking to is right there in front of me as I knew them in life. I wish I could see them. My mother and my aunt Laura were clairvoyant and could SEE the spirits of the ones who had crossed over.

I recall one evening when I was 17 years old, sitting with my mother in the music room of one of our haunted houses in South Africa. My two younger sisters, Maude and Ethel, had gone to bed. Mother was smiling at an unseen person standing in the doorway.

I asked her what she was seeing, and she replied: "A woman standing in the door entrance." Mother said she was wearing a *pink* dress and had the bluest eyes and sweetest smile.

At the time, it kind of scared me, as *I* could not see what she was seeing. People are inclined to ridicule what they can't understand. Death is awesome if you think it is the end. So many people today live at such a fast pace, thinking their physical lives will go on forever, never giving thought to what lies beyond, until too late.

I am often asked, "When a person dies, how does he know where he is, where to go or what to do?" My understanding is that we are met by relatives, friends or others known as "Greeters" (spirits familiar with the spirit world) who help the newcomers to adjust to the spirit world and the traumatic change from the physical, teaching them how to transport their spiritual bodies and accept the transition.

Let me state again that I don't do anything in preparation for a spirit visitation. No preparation at all. The spirits of loved ones come to me at their convenience. I never know when they are coming. The timing is theirs. I may be watching TV, reading the paper, or working on my news copy. I might be in church, or riding in a friend's car. I have had a couple of spirits come to me while enroute somewhere, walking or riding. I can be in a supermarket, or just anywhere. I never know. They come to me, I repeat, in THEIR TIME. That is, UNLESS I am at a funeral where I often get a communication as the spirit is still very close to its earthly life, and if the person has adjusted to the transition, since the time of death and the funeral service.

An Evaluation of the Childs Spirit Communications

Our Survival Research has revealed that an increasing number of men and women have had the psychic capacity to receive spirit messages, at times, from departed friends and loved ones. Many have been reluctant to report these psychic experiences which they have considered too personal, often almost too sacred, to risk the ridicule of skeptics or, even worse, those who would doubt their sanity.

Actually, we are getting evidence that the possibility of spirit communication is much more prevalent than has generally been supposed, and that thoughts between worlds can be exchanged by those, like Gladys Childs, who have come from home environments where members of the family have recognized and encouraged such psychic manifestations.

I am sure that you who have read these carefully organized and dated reports which Gladys has methodically recorded are convinced that she was not activated by her imagination or wishful thinking in documenting this material. She was motivated only by the desire to compile evidence for the further assurance to herself and others of survival.

It has long been my contention that evidence for "life after death" could not be established in the laboratories of scientific investigators with their present methods of research. Dr. J.B. Rhine, I was told, came to this conclusion years ago, and decided that he would devote his energies and research to other demonstrable phases of the paranormal. He died, as a consequence, without having achieved his original objective—the procuring of acceptable evidence that man survives death. This remained, to Dr. Rhine, with all his acknowledged contribution to the science of Parapsychology, an open question.

As you consider the personalized evidence contained in this book, add it all up and observe how the same manifestations are occurring in the lives of many different, sensitized people, who are reporting the same types of messages and the same types of experiences.

If a dozen people, for example, should visit California, never having seen it before, and came back with significantly similar reports of the landscape and activities of the people there—shouldn't you accept their reports as valid—and expect to encounter the same or similar experiences, yourself, when your turn would come to go to California?

Then why not take the words of the Gladys Childs and A.J. Plimptons and Edith and Marion Harrisons of the world, sifting out the reports of some as flights of fancy and imagination, but crediting others who have the solid ring of truth?

You can learn to tell the difference. Your own psychic experiences, if you have had them, will enable you to distinguish the true from the false.

Chapter 7

EVIDENCES OF SPIRIT RETURN

Countless evidences of "spirit return" are contained in the many psychic experiences which are coming to those who have lost friends and loved ones in every country in the world. It has not been a matter of belief, in many instances, nor a self-created image, or imagined or wishful or halluncinatory thinking.

True, apparitional appearances, voiced messages, visions and dreams, and sounds or rappings, and displacement of objects have occurred, often in response to a grievous yearning for contact with a departed loved one. However, an examination of many such cases will convince the investigator that a goodly number of such happenings have originated outside the ordinary realm of consciousness of the experiencer.

The average scientist either refuses or can't seem to realize that it is next to humanly impossible to set up conditions in a laboratory which will enable an exact duplication of different forms of psychic phenomena. I have been tested, on a number of occasions, under conditions charged with negativity and skepticism which I would have to combat before I could manage to fix my mind's attention on the experiment itself. For a sensitive person to be up against opposing mental forces is often enough to defeat his ability to demonstrate any extra-sensory facilities.

In spontaneous cases of psychic manifestation, the whole atmosphere has a positive charge, because the spirit entity is interested in making contact with a living person for whatever reason, and that person, once alerted, by the feeling of a presence, the hearing of a voice or the glimpse of a spirit form, unless frightened, usually will make every effort to receive and interpret the phenomena which may take place.

It is important to stress again and again that "feeling generates the power behind thought." Sir Hubert Wilkins and I early discovered in our long distance telepathic experiments, that the experiences which affected him the deepest emotionally, I picked up, in my mind, the easiest and clearest.

Imagine, then, the intensity of feeling which would often be generated by a person who has lost a loved one by death, in his or her desire for communication— a feeling which would likely be shared by the departed spirit. Under these conditions, energetic impulses dispatched by both parties, can often lead to momentary attunement one with the other, and visual or audible impressions result, on the part of the receiver.

In this chapter I am presenting case histories of manifestations which would seem to bear out this contention. In this first case, I should emphasize that Barbara Benson is an unusually psychic individual which helps explain the various types of phenomena which she experienced. I am letting her tell, in her own words, the pre-vision she had of the deaths of all members of her family in Hurricane Carla which hit the Texas coast, September 11, 1961.

"When Hurricane Carla was threatening the Texas coast in September of 1961, I was in Port Isobel, Texas. My mother, stepfather, three brothers, my oldest son and daughter, my mother's sister, her husband and their three sons were living in Bostrop Bayou, five miles out of Angleton, Texas. I had a little money but no car. I begged friends to take me to my mother and I would pay expenses. I warned them that my family was going to die but they said everyone had been evacuated. I told them, 'They are there and they are going to die.' But they would not believe me.

"Carla hit, September 11, 1961. On the night of September 12th, my former employer knocked at my door and asked me if I had a family living near Angleton. I told him, 'I did, but they are dead. The storm killed them.' He was shocked and asked me how I knew. I told him, 'I knew it was going to happen.' He took me to the mayor's house so he could inform me officially of the deaths.

"September 13th, I caught the evening train from Brownsville, Texas, to Alvin, Texas, where my father and elder brother picked me up. On the train, I was sitting, wide-awake, but with my eyes closed, thinking of my recently departed loved ones. It was a cold night and the rail cars were heated. I felt something like a cool, soft hand on my brow. I opened my eyes and looked around, thinking the conductor had come into the car, letting in a cool breeze from outside. The conductor was not present and all the other passengers were asleep, so I leaned back and closed my eyes again.

"Then I began to hear the voices of each departed loved one, speak to me in turn. They told me they were happy where they were; that it was lovely beyond description, and a very happy place to be. They asked me not to grieve over their passing beyond the Veil, but to be happy for

89

them. They assured me they would always be with me. I just would not be able to see them.

"When the conductor of the train came through the coach and I told him what had happened, he said he was supposed to be off duty when the train reached Brownsville but his relief help was stricken with appendicitis, so he had to remain on duty. He told me he felt he was meant to make that run, to try to comfort me and another lady who was bringing her husband's body home for burial."

AN AUTOMATIC WRITING MESSAGE
FROM BARBARA'S MOTHER

"In the fall of 1962, I was engaged to marry my present husband, Steve A. Benson. Having had an unhappy marriage before, I was worried about the chances for marriage with Steve. One day, I was sitting at the table doodling Steve's name on a sheet of paper, thinking of him and our upcoming marriage. Suddenly, I began to write rapidly, not knowing what I was writing. But the strange thing was, it was not my handwriting, but my mother's!

"When I stopped writing, I had a letter from my mother, nearly a year after she had died! She reassured me that I had made a wise choice and that we would be very happy. Everything she has said has come true. We have been very happily married, seventeen years as of January 16, 1980!

"I am sending you the letter my mother wrote after her death, and a picture postcard she wrote to her mother, several years before she died, so you can compare the handwriting."

NOTE: I have studied the handwriting and it is remarkably similar to the handwriting produced under Barbara's automatic writing influence.—HS

The MESSAGE from Barbara's mother:

"Baby, I think of you up here and look over you. I know that in days to come, you will get your happiness. Stick with Steve, he will make you happy. You are right not to hold it against Curly (Barbara's former husband) for the things he has done. He can't help being what he is. You will be married to Steve sooner than you think. You must try yourself if you want to be happy. He will make you a wonderful husband. Remember, I am watching over you and little Terry, from up here. Don't ever feel you are completely alone. Mommie is always with you. Kiss Terry and hug him for Nona (his grandmother's name to him). I'll always be with you, Lady Bird, so don't be impatient. We are all with you. Don't cry for us. We are happy here. No misery or unhappiness here. Little Tommie and Samuel are happy with us here, too. So rest your heart and mind for now. Trust us. The good Lord is taking care of you.

Love, Mother and Gang"

(EXPLANATION from Barbara: "Terry is my one living son, who was not quite 3 years old at the time. He called his grandmother, 'Nona.' September, 1958, a baby son, who lived only 11 hours, was born and we named him Samuel.

"February, 1961, another son, Tommie, was born, who lived only 13 hours. I told Mother before each child was born, that they would not live. I have had numerous other experiences as have several members of my family, involving ESP and precognition—but I am only telling you of the ones having to do with life after death.)"

AN UNCLE'S SPIRIT GUIDANCE

"I am recalling now communication I used to

have with my husband's uncle, Harry (Jake) San-
born. He was very dear to Steve and I was also
very fond of him. He was a trailer truck driver,
one of the best. After his death, a few years later,
I started driving a trailer truck, hauling steel.
Many times his voice warned me of oncoming
hazards, or advised me of the proper action to be
taken. He kept me out of many bad situations.
He had a sense of humor, too. Once when a police
car was dangerously close in front of my truck, I
heard Jake say: It's not recommended procedure
to run over Smokies (police). It was so funny to
me. I almost did run over Smokey!"

A MOTHER'S VISIT TO THE "HEAVEN WORLD"

While there is often no way to confirm reports of
psychic experiences related to the so-called "spirit
world" except to accept the word of the individual who
narrates it, it seems unlikely that so many would fab-
ricate these spiritual adventures.

Margery A. Gold of Salt Lake City, Utah, writes me
that her mother, aged 81, contracted pneumonia and,
on the sixth day, when near death, apparently lost all
feeling of pain and worry and sadness, while her face
took on the countenance of her deceased mother. She
became unconscious and the doctors and Margery felt
she was dying. After some hours, however, she rallied
and returned to consciousness, to tell of what must
have been an out-of-body experience.

She found herself in a beautiful garden where her
deceased mother resided. The flowers were unbelievably elegant, the ground covering like a heavy green
moss, velvety and soft to the touch. She wanted to take
some of the beautiful flowers with her, but couldn't
keep them in her hands. Her mother told her the next
time she came, she would be able to have the flowers
she wanted. She saw three small children who seemed

to know her and where she would reside, that is, what home would be hers. The fragrance of the flowers was indescribable. There were people working outside the walls of the garden. Regretfully, mother knew she could no longer remain. In the next instant she was back in her physical body and conscious of pain once more—but the crisis had passed and mother was left with the feeling that, for some reason, she had seen a glimpse, quite possibly, of her future life, but it had not been her time to go. Mother's mind is lucid and sharp and she has maintained a vivid memory of the beautiful garden and the happiness that shown in her own mother's face at sight of her. She has no fear whatsoever of death now, nor does she lack knowledge of life after death. She knows it exists.

SEES AUNT ATTENDING HER OWN FUNERAL

A case quite similar to the many Gladys Childs has described was related to me by Margery Gold, who says she has been psychic all her life.

"Several years ago, I attended my Aunt Susan's funeral, the deceased sister of my father-in-law. I was sitting toward the rear of the chapel, when two things happened simultaneously: Aunt Susan suddenly appeared, sitting on one of the chair seats adjacent to the pulpit; at the same time her casket containing her remains, was being wheeled to the front of the chapel to rest just below the pulpit. Her children, family and relatives followed the casket. Aunt Susan seemed utterly absorbed in looking at her family and stayed in the same sitting position until all were seated and she should again look at them.

"When Aunt Susan died she was in her early nineties. Her hair was gray and her skin was wrinkled. As she sat in this chapel she appeared younger. Her hair was black with only a few gray

93

streaks in the front. She was dressed in a bright royal blue print dress (I can see that dress now). The expression on her face was not one of sadness, nor was it one of joy, but just open concern for her family. She remained in the chapel about ten minutes and I watched her intently, certain it was her—then she disappeared as quickly and quietly as she had come!"

UNUSUAL PROOF OF SURVIVAL

I am indebted to Mary Horan of Los Gatos, California, for an account of a most impressive case which she accepts as absolute proof of survival.

She wrote: "I am 73 years old, worked forty years as a librarian. For the last sixteen of these years, I worked in the Philosophy and Religious Department of the Los Angeles Public Library; the last six years as the Department Chief Librarian. I have been interested in psychic research for about thirty of these working years.

"Now for my evidence which I shall present as briefly as possible. In my forties, I had a close friend named Estelle. We were both interested in psychic phenomena. We used to jokingly say, 'Okay—whichever one of us goes first, we will try to let the other know.'

"In 1954, Estelle died of cancer, and I was named her Executor. She had an illegitimate son (adopted out as a small child). He came back into her life a few years before her death, but only as a negative aspect. I settled her small estate, disposing the residue to this son whom I did not enjoy, and promptly ended the relationship.

"I had been living in Carmel, retired, for about ten years, with the Estelle episode entirely in the past. One day, I received in my mail box a pencilled envelope. The name and return address I did not recognize. I was about to toss it back into the return bin when I realized it had been forwarded from the Philosophy Department. I then opened it and read this brief message.

> Dear Mary:
> You may have forgotten me by now. (Richard, Estelle's son)
> Recently, I have become interested in automatic writing, and Estelle has come through several times.
> The last time, she said: "Please try to tell Mary as she wanted to know."
> That was all, and I don't know what it means, perhaps you will.
>
> Richard

"To say that I had goose bumps is putting it mildly. Of course, I knew what she meant. We had said we would let each other know *and she had done it!*

"For me this is rather fantastic proof! I wasn't trying to make contact; her son knew absolutely nothing of our mutual interest or our joking agreement.

"But she had remembered it, though I had long forgotten. It is my regret that I did not keep this letter, although I did write and tell him what the message meant to me. I do not even have an address for him now, although I still have her estate records. I hope this will be useful information.

Mary Horan"

It is, indeed, useful information. This is the kind of evidence that can never be demonstrated in a laboratory. You know, beyond any doubt, it could not be faked. If a test were to be set up to prove survival, you could hardly provide better conditions. There is evidence here, not only of the survival of Estelle's identity, but her memory. And she transmitted this message through a son who did not and could not know what it was all about!

NO TRACE OF EARTHLY ILLNESS

So many people have reported to me the spirit return of loved ones when they have been wide awake, in their normal state of consciousness. I have chosen one of these remarkable cases from the files of our ESP foundation. It is related by Nancy F. from Virginia who has asked that I not reveal her real name and identity because some of her friends and relatives would not understand or approve. They have expressed the opinion that she is imagining things, or still worse, that her psychic experience was the work of the devil.

Here is Nancy's account and I will let you judge for yourself.

Dear Mr. Sherman:
I have just read your book: "You Live After Death." I never really believed that people could make contact with loved ones in another world—until my husband died, April 23, 1979.

In August of 1979, I was lying in bed and the kids were asleep, and it was after 12 at night.

I heard my door open which was securely locked, and I saw my husband come through the door and sit down in a chair beside my bed. Then he reached down and kissed me, and I saw and felt the ring on his hand which I had left on him in the coffin.

He looked like he did when he was well. He had his hair and it was black . . . and he had no scars on his head and face.

Before he died, he had cancer. They had removed his tongue, part of his face, his neck, and he had no hair. His head had become loose from his shoulders because his body had rejected the skin grafts ... and he had lots of sores on his head and face.

But now his face looked *perfect*.

This is the end of a quote by Nancy. Now I would like to comment about it.

She said her husband, despite the devastated condition of his physical body at death, was returned to normal. He looked as he had when he was well.

He again had a full head of hair—and it was black. There were no scars on his head and face. His skin looked perfect ... and she actually *saw* and *felt* the ring she had left on his hand when he was buried.

If we accept Nancy's experience as genuine—and I personally do not doubt it—then it has to be reassuring to many who have lost loved ones as the result of some debilitating disease—to *know* that they have left all this behind on entering the Next Life.

THE FURTHER EXPERIENCES OF NANCY

Taking up Nancy's letter once more, she goes on to say:

"There have been several times that I have wakened up during the night and felt my husband's presence with me. I have thought I have seen him standing in the doorway, watching over me.

"My son, who is 12 years old, said he woke up one night and saw his father standing over his bed, smiling at him.

"The last time he appeared to me was when I was awake a few weeks ago, and my grandmother, who has been dead 28 years, was standing with him, beside the bed. This surprised me because my husband had never met my grandmother. She had been dead for 5 years before I had even met my husband. Both of them told me

97

things I had been worrying about were going to be better in a little while.

"I know these visitations were not dreams. My *son* wasn't dreaming and he also saw his father. He was right there looking after him as he used to do in life.

"So, you can understand, Mr. Sherman, that I have reason not to believe—but to *know* that people survive death."

HE HELD HIS SPIRIT WIFE IN HIS ARMS

A heart-touching case has the ring of truth in it. It was recently sent to me by William B. (name withheld by request) from British Columbia, who writes:

Dear Mr. Sherman:

It is now just two and a half years since the deep emotional experience which I have finally decided to report to you.

First, I should tell you that I am living in my son's home who is a bachelor and an architect by profession.

My sleeping arrangements are in a bedroom on the ground floor, which overlooks the back garden. This room was occupied by my dear wife and myself.

She was an invalid and I gave her day and night care for four years. The last two, she was in a wheelchair, and was badly confused.

Finally, my son suggested that his mother be sent to an "Extended Care Unit," where she was looked after for three more years.

In April of 1978, I had just visited her the day before, when the doctor called me at 4 a.m. to tell me of her passing. Her body was cremated and the ashes sent to me by the crematorium.

What I am now to report happened on Monday, April 17, 1978, at approximately 4:30 A.M. I had retired at about 11 p.m. and, not being able to sleep, was reclining in bed and reading your book, "You Live After Death," which I often refer to, many times, for the comfort it brings me.

The next thing I was aware of, was that I was sitting on the side of the bed, facing the garden window, and the "love seat" in front of it.

Lying on this small sofa was my darling wife, Thelma! She had her legs drawn up and was partially turned toward the window, so I could not clearly see her face. She appeared to be dressed in a sort of nebulous garment of a light color, reaching to her mid-calf, similar to a negligee.

I rushed over to her, exclaiming, almost hysterically: "Sweetheart! . . . Oh, my darling! I have you here!" at the same time turning her towards me.

Her hair was thick, luxuriant, long and black—and it cascaded down over her shoulders, as I turned her toward me. She looked at me and her face was beautiful to behold—young and radiant—as when she was seventeen! (And she had been 68 at the time of passing!) Her eyes were full of love and she looked at me without speaking.

"Can you walk, my darling?" I asked, and I turned her limbs toward the floor. She smiled and swung her legs out as if to rise up. I swept her into my arms, holding her closely . . . and pounded the floor with my bare feet, calling to my son, Christopher, who slept in the room below.

I had forgotten that he had remained in town over the weekend . . . and I kept calling: "Christopher! . . . Christopher! . . . I have Mom here! . . . Come quickly!" In my state of ecstasy, not realizing that Christopher was not home, I kept calling, thumping again and again. "Christopher! Come quickly! I have dear Mom here!"

My wife felt real, warm and solid in my arms

and we gazed at each other. Realizing now that my son was not at home, I also became conscious that my darling wife seemed to be shrinking ... and I spoke to her, saying: "Oh, darling, I have you here with me!"

She looked at me with an expression of utmost love, and said, very softly: "No, Daddy—I died!"

"No, darling," I replied, holding her closely. "I have you here with me again!"

She said, once more: "No, Daddy—I died!"

The tone of her voice was as a mother explaining with great tenderness to her child. Nothing more was said by my wife, as she kept becoming less and less in my arms, with me frantically calling: "No, no—don't leave me!"

And then she was gone and I found myself sitting on the side of the bed again, shaken and completely distraught, looking at my clock at the bedside. It was 4:30 A.M. and a faint dawn of light was coming up.

This is my complete experience, word for word, exactly as it happened to me over two and a half years ago—as clear to me now as when it occurred. The experience was utterly real.

There are many cases similar to this. Apparently, when the energy which enables these spirit entities to manifest, plays out, their forms dissolve and disappear into the Next Dimension. There is still much we do not understand about this psychic phenomenon. The difference between Dimensions of existence seems to be a matter of frequency.

≈≈≈≈≈≈≈≈≈

Chapter 8

≈≈≈≈≈≈≈≈≈

AN AMAZING EXCEPTION

It would seem that, once a departed loved one has succeeded in demonstrating to grieving loved ones on earth that he or she had survived death, that they go about the business of existence in the next Dimensions knowing that those remaining here will be joining them in time.

But, having made this observation, I am now compelled, in the light of a remarkable case I am about to report, to admit that there are rare but definite exceptions to this "psychic rule."

Fortunately, for purposes of research, the man to whom these amazing multiple "Spirit visitations" came, lived only some 200 miles from our home in North Arkansas and was ready and willing to submit to full questioning and examination as he sought, himself, to understand how the first psychic experience he had ever had, could be happening.

Arlis Coger, who owned and operated a drug store in Huntsville, Arkansas, for many years, related how he had never had anything more significant happen in his life than being able to fix his attention on the back of the head of a school-mate and causing him to turn around and look.

His wife, Anna, to whom he had been married almost 45 years, died of a kidney ailment. He loved her dearly and was having a hard time making an adjustment when he awoke one night, two months later, to find her in bed beside him. Her body was warm and solid—so real that he reached over and stroked her forehead twice before she suddenly vanished.

In Arlis' words, "This was not a dream. I, like others, have dreamed all my life. This was different. I am not a fanatic and am of a sound mind. *Anna actually returned from the dead!* Nothing can convince me otherwise."

This proved to be only the beginning of Anna's thirteen return spirit visits which came, at irregular intervals, over the period of a year. The first time, he did not have the presence of mind to record the hour, but later kept careful records. There was no consistency. He would be awakened just after falling asleep; sometimes during the night; and sometimes in the early morning.

To indicate how unusually real and substantial these "visits" appeared to him, here are some excerpts from his records:

"The first time, it was almost terrifying—but I do not think that is the right word to convey my feelings."

"The second appearance, unlike the first, was a joyous occasion. We embraced each other and, all of a sudden, she disappeared and left me wide awake."

"The thing I noticed most was that her body was warm. Mind you, this was not a dream. I actually embraced her and I was awake."

102

"This appearance was unlike the others. She was standing by the bed. I had always thought an angel was dressed in white. She was not. She had on a long, soft, golden robe. I reached out and took her by the hand, and my hand slipped down on her fingers and they were firm. She passed from my left to my right and communicated with me. I do not think it was by voice but it was perfectly clear. She said, 'Things are not what they are cracked up to be up here.' I sensed that she wanted me to be with her up there. But the next time she appeared to me in bed, and when I asked her if she was happy now, her answer was a simple 'Yes' and I felt much better."

"Tho I scarcely dared hope, Anna was back again last night. It was brief and sweet as I embraced her and communicated that it would be nice if she would visit one of our children who do not believe in her returns. She did not answer . . . but gave me a wonderful lip to lip kiss."

"Two nights in a row . . . four minutes to 1 A.M. As far as I know, I have never had any contact with her in her spirit world."

"All of a sudden the sheets over me raised up in the air above the bed and Anna was there. It was only a second or two but she was definitely there."

"I drew her close to me and she laid her head on my shoulder. I was conscious of her luxurious hair against my cheeks."

There have been numerous incidents in the lives of countless people giving evidence that loved ones who have departed this life often return on the dates of remembered earth events. Arlis Coger, as almost a climax to his wife Anna's remarkable series of spirit visitations now reports:

"Today, Oct. 6, is my 75th birthday and the 1st anniversary of Anna's passing. I expected to be depressed but I am not because Anna came back last night. She was standing by the bed! She took me in her arms and lifted my upper body up and put her arms firmly around me and kissed me solidly on the lips. Then she let me back down. The thing that is so outstanding is her strength. *She bodily picked up the upper part of my body.* In her physical body, she would never have been able to do this. There are tears in my eyes as I write this but it is not from grief. There is joy in my heart *knowing that some day I will be reunited with her for eternity.*"

"This is Nov. 1st 1982. Yesterday was the 46th anniversary of our marriage. Some time between two and three A.M. I was suddenly aware of Anna in bed with me under the covers. I took her in my arms and told her of my great love for her and she seemed to go away a few moments and then return and the process was repeated seven times for at least 30 minutes. I hope she continues to come back to me until I can be with her in her spiritual world. I have absolutely no fear of death. I know there is another life beyond the grave."

Further Proof of the Truth of Spirit Return

In one of his reports to me, Arlis Coger enclosed a clipping he had taken from the October 18, 1982 issue of the "People" Weekly. It contains a portion of an interview with Anwar Sadat's widow wherein she tells about an unusual dream she had about her deceased husband, who seemingly returned in spirit to her and the children. Mr. Coger, accompanied this clipping with the written comment. "Anwar's widow thinks it is like a dream, but, to me, it is real. I have had over thirteen occurrences like this, of Anna returning to me. They are as different from a dream as daylight and dark. She actually came back to me."

"Do you realize that you often speak of your husband as if he were still here?"

Our religion says that when the body dies, the soul continues to live. Yes, I still feel he is with me. Even now, I, the children, we feel him. My son, Gamal, heard his voice one morning. It was dawn. He woke and was sitting up in bed when all of a sudden he heard his father's deep, loud voice saying: 'Why are you so sad, Gamal, and why is your mother sad and why are your sisters sad? Tell them I am extremely happy and relaxed.' My son said he felt goose pimples all over him. He jumped out of bed and actually looked for his father but did not see anything. Only the room was filled with the echo of Anwar's voice.

"Did you have a similar experience?"

Not exactly like that, but I was surprised by him after he died. *I was sleeping in bed and found him beside me as if he were still alive. It was so real that I asked: 'Anwar, are you here?' I stretched out my hand to touch him and ensure it was really his flesh. And he lay there and smiled at me.*

"It was a dream, of course?"

Of course, but it was not like the usual dream that goes away when you open your eyes. I opened my eyes and could still see him next to me. I reached out and actually touched *him and then, suddenly, he was gone. It was a shock.*

105

Arlis Coger was greatly heartened as well as inspired to learn that a personality of the world renown of Mrs. Sadat had spoken publicly about the spirit return of her husband, Anwar. "It's very evident that I am not alone in the experiences I have been having," he commented. "As I have stated, I have never had any psychic happening before, and then to have it repeated so many times, let alone once, I can't explain. But, I am deeply grateful for whatever has made Anna's spirit returns possible."

ARLIS COGER'S SUMMARIZING TESTIMONIAL

Every individual who has reported the spirit return of a loved one is convinced of the reality of the experience. that it was unlike any dream they had ever had . . . that they often emerged from a sleep state into full wakefulness, to find the spirit entity either with them in bed, or standing or sitting in the room . . . sometimes able to make physical contact . . . to receive a voiced message . . . or to sense an invisible presence.

In the case of Arlis Coger, he has had the unique opportunity to study the phenomenon repeatedly, at close range. This is his description:

"The body Anna was in was not the one lowered into her grave. For one thing, she was somewhat younger. It had the power to go through material things. There was a sheet and a blanket on the bed. When she would leave me, she would just disappear without even a ruffle of the bed covering which she was under. Her body was firm to the touch. It was warm. We could communicate, although I do not think there was any voice. Anna had some kind of a spiritual body, different

106

from her former physical body. I have seen her
full figure several times as she stood by my bed."

ANNA'S SPIRIT VISITS
COME TO AN END

Absolute proof that Arlis Coger had nothing to do
with, or no control over the spirit visit of Anna, that
they were not the result of vivid imagination or self-
induced hallucinations, is contained in the fact that
Anna's materializations have stopped.

On December 21st, 1982 I received a Christmas card
from Arlis, with this brief but significant message:

"Anna has not returned since October 31st. I
hope she comes during the holidays. Pray for me
that she will return again."

Arlis

But Anna has not returned and Arlis has about decided that he will not see her again until he joins her
in the Great Beyond ... that she has accomplished
whatever purpose she had in establishing the fact of
Survival ... both for Arlis and for all others who might
be seeking such assurance that there actually is no
death.

Chapter 9

THE DAVE SAALFELD STORY

Much has been written about Near Death Experiences but, impressive and convincing as many are, some skeptical researchers still remind us that these seeming out-of-body projections do not necessarily prove Life After Death since all those who have been pronounced clinically dead have not actually been testifying from the After Life.

It is for this reason that I have tried to present evidence only about those who have actually departed this life. I have received an increasing number of case histories of Spirit Return from men and women who, no longer afraid of ridicule, or charges of imagination or unbalanced minds, are willing and eager to speak out publicly in the hope that they can bring comfort and assurance to those who have had deaths in the family or are facing the possibilty of death themselves. They have reported occasions when departed loved ones have appeared fully materialized, in daylight as well as dark, and have not only been able to communicate by actual voice or in a "feeling type" of telepathy, but have also touched, embraced and even kissed those living!

The kind of evidence I am presenting can never be demonstrated in a scientific laboratory, but you know beyond doubt that it could not be faked. The men and women to whom these experiences have come have no motive for fabricating them. The happenings are spontaneous, totally unexpected, and came to them either in the waking or emerging-from-the-sleep-state.

Just recently, I received this highly evidential report from Dave Saalfeld, a former combat pilot in the Second World War. He explained that with all the interest in death and dying today, he had finally decided to make public the psychic experience he had had which he had been afraid people would not believe before. Here is his testimony in his own words.

"One day, I was sent on a bombing run on Berlin and had this strange occurrence. We were twenty miles from our target. I had the bomb bay doors open and settled down for a level run. We had not reached a flak area yet and all was serene. Then the *voice* came as loud as anything and said, 'Get out of your seat!'

"I thought someone was fooling but it became more insistent. I took my helmet off as I thought it was on the inter-phone but the voice persisted and became very impatient so I had the co-pilot take over and I got up and stepped down into the tunnel area. In no less than ten seconds, a tremendous burst of flak tore the steel seat to bits and half the instrument panel. I still can't explain it."

Who can explain it? This raises the question: *Is it possible that there exists what are called "Guardian Angels" who occasionally sense what is coming toward*

109

us in time and try to get through to our point of aware-
ness and warn or protect us? But why, if this is true,
are some of us so favored . . . saved from serious injury
or possible death, while others, just as deserving, are
not alerted? Are some of us more *psychically sensitive*
than others? Perhaps this may be a reason.

Dave Saalfeld now tells us of another experience . . .
again in his own words:

"I was severely wounded and carried from the
plane to the 231st station hospital at Wyndom,
England, an army hospital.

"I awoke about 2 A.M. all trussed up . . . in a
hospital ward . . . and only one other patient was
there.

"I hurt so bad, I was wishing for a doctor to
obtain a shot. Not even a nurse was there.

"All at once, a very distinguished looking
gentleman, in a white jacket, appeared through
the ward door. He was grey-haired and wore a
moustache. He walked right over and sat upon a
chair beside me . . . and said, 'Hi Dave—looks like
you were in the wrong place!'

"I asked him for a shot, but he said I wouldn't
hurt in a moment. I thought that was funny.

"He talked about this and that for about 5 minutes. Then he said he had to go . . . but that his
name was 'Dr. Moreau,' and that I would make
it *FINE* through the war . . . and that I would be
back flying soon. With that, he said 'Goodbye' and
left.

"Ten minutes later a nurse came in and I noticed I was feeling warm and pleasant and didn't
hurt anywhere.

"I told her . . . that was a nice Doc they had
there . . . and she said, 'What Doctor?' I told her
his name and what he looked like, and she said:
'We don't have a doctor like that here. There is
no one but me on duty.'

110

"I thought someone was a little crazy, but I knew it wasn't me!"

Then, as if this wasn't remarkable enough, Dave Saalfeld went on to say:

"Thirty-six years later ... when I was sitting in a psychic class, conducted by an elderly lady medium ... her spirit control suddenly announced; 'There is a David here, and someone wishes to speak to him ...'

"This was only my second time in this class, and I hardly knew anyone in it.

"This man's voice came, speaking through the entranced medium, and said: 'Hello again, Dave, we meet once more—'

"I asked who it was, and he said, 'Surely, you remember me—I'm Dr. Moreau. I told you that you would make it through the war.'

"Needless to say, after 30 some years, I had forgotten the incident."

You figure it out! May I say here that I have had some 60 years of investigative experience and there is MUCH ... VERY MUCH ... that I STILL can't figure out!

Nor do I have an answer for one more psychic experience that Dave Saalfeld relates ... except to testify that it really happened exactly as he tells it.

It seems that this elderly woman medium goes into a trance and that her body is taken over by spirit entities who speak through her ... in much the same manner as this mysterious Dr. Moreau apparently did. On this particular evening, at a seance Dave attended, he reports the following unusual happening.

"The spirit guide who was in control of the medium said to me: 'I have someone here whom we

111

are unable to comfort or convince that he has died . . .

" 'He says he knows you. He refers to a time during the war when you switched aircrafts one morning, at the request of headquarters. You let your co-pilot take your aircraft that day, while you flew with another crew to help out because of a lack of pilots.

" 'At any rate, the spirit control continued, . . . your aircraft flown by co-pilot, Lt. Gazelle, was blown up and all were instantly killed.

" 'This entity is really wild and agitated and wants to talk.'

"It was Lt. Gazelle and he said to me: 'How come you are not still fighting, Dave?'

"I said, 'The war's over, Jack . . . and you didn't make it . . . and you're no longer in your physical body.'

"He said, 'I'm not dead, Dave, I'm still fighting!'

"I told him he was *fine* and that he should go along with the gentleman . . . the spirit guide . . . who had brought him.

"He said: 'I sure am fine! Just look at me—the mess I am in!'

"Evidently, he still thought he was in his badly injured physical body . . . he was still carrying the image of it within him. Because, the way he was acting in the body of the medium, he had the entranced medium thrashing about and gesturing wildly.

"The spirit control said they would have to take him away . . . that he was unmanageable."

"Mr. Sherman, no one else could have known any of these things. The lady medium is a beautiful soul. She passes into a complete trance, and can remember nothing. She has many entities talk through her . . . and I am convinced that my old co-pilot, Lt. Jack Gazelle did come through.

112

"I believe he's long since been straightened out, and has been freed from the in-between world, and has let go of his images of his war experiences. He obviously had been living these over and over in his mind . . . even after he had died. But now, I believe he has gone on to higher dimensions where he has found other friends and loved ones awaiting him."

The earthbound conditions which Dave Saalfeld has been describing are VERY REAL! We are learning much about them in the research we are doing . . . and on the tape recordings of spirit voices from the OTHER SIDE.

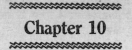

Chapter 10

ASTOUNDING PROOF
OF LIFE BEYOND

As many Workshoppers know, who have been attending our ESP Foundation's Body, Mind and Spirit Healing Workshops for some ten years, President Al Pollard and I decided, after our 1978 Workshop in St. Louis, successful as they are, featuring many of the most outstanding psychics and authorities on the higher powers of mind, to suspend these meetings so we could devote a major portion of our time to Survival Research.

It has been my life-time ambition, before I should leave this earth, to help provide research which would establish solid evidence of "life after death." As I have pointed out, I long ago discovered, as did the great pioneer investigator, Dr. J. B. Rhine, recently deceased, that a laboratory was not equipped to produce this proof. It would require a different kind of research out in the field of human experience. I have always felt that an abundance of evidence was there, waiting to be properly collected, organized, and evaluated. The book you are now reading is a step in that direction—but it is only a forerunner of things to come.

If you have not had occasion to be exposed to some of the psychic phenomena which is now being studied, what I am to present in this chapter should be mind-boggling.

Let me introduce you to a remarkable, psychically endowed man, P. KALUARATCHI, of Sri Lanka (Ceylon), who has been engaging in a most unusual type of Psychic Research. He has been hypnotizing two young children, a girl and a boy, ages 13 and 11, placing them in trances. Then, with the aid of his spirit guide, Klevin, he permits earthbound spirits to enter and use the body of the medium as though it was their own, while they relive their last tragic moments before death on earth.

These discarnate spirits, most of them, do not know they have died. They have been wandering about, clinging close to home and business places, not understanding why they can no longer get the attention of those around them or communicate with friends and loved ones.

Once they find themselves in the body of a medium, which they take to be their own body, they experience the same pains and sensations which led up to their death. It is as though they had a recording in consciousness of what had happened to them, in imagery form, and when returned to exist in a flesh and blood body, had played this recording back through it, suffering the same feelings as they had had originally.

It has been P. Kaluaratchi's assignment to interview these spirit entities and to explain to them the predicament they are in and how to be released from it.

Time and again, he will say something like this: "You are under the impression that you still possess the body you had the last day you lived on earth. You

115

have left that physical body. But spiritually you have not died. You survived as a discarnate spirit. Now you are possessing our medium who is a healthy young woman, so you cannot have the pain you are imagining. Take a look at the body you are now in. Does it look anything at all like the body you had while on earth? Is it even of the same sex? (if this should be the case.)

When a true realization is brought to them of the nature of their new existence, a transformation takes place in the consciousness of the earthbound spirits. They are able to detach themselves from the traumatic hold that the images of their usually tragic deaths have had upon them, and can then "look toward the light," to a "higher plane" of existence where friends and loved ones, who have not been able to reach them, can now greet and extend help.

A. J. Plimpton discovered this same need in his encounters with the earthbound, and how to help them get free of their fixations, as I have previously reported. Due to this developed telepathic ability, he is now able to communicate with the earthbound directly and send them on their way, whereas P. Kaluaratchi is communicating with the earthbound through mediumistic channels—each accomplishing the same objective.

Of course the work that P. Kaluaratchi is doing is of immense interest because he is able to get the name and address and specific circumstances in the death experience of each earthbound spirit. The medium can re-enact through his or her body, whatever experience the possessing entity has had, which is often as harrowing as it is startling, as some of the case histories I have chosen to present will indicate.

The documented material is so extensive, so significant and so well worthy of study that I am preparing a book with Mr. P. Kaluaratchi on this subject alone.

116

(Fortunately, as you can see, K. speaks English fluently.) My working title of this book is to be: THE GREAT DRAMA OF EARTHBOUND SPIRITS—HOW TO ESCAPE AFTER LIFE ENTRAPMENT.

Plans are underway, as I write, to bring P. Kaluaratchi and two of his mediums to the United States for a duplication of this psychic work here—as there are vast regions for the earthbound spirits in every country and I am told there will be no difficulty establishing communicative contact.

Says Mr. Kaluaratchi: "With regard to our psychic ability, we are willing to face any scientific investigation to prove the truth of what we are doing. So far we have faced many eye specialists and boards of doctors who do not know what to say about the ability of mediums to read and to see while blindfolded, through a power I am able to transmit to them with the help of my guiding spirit. It is a form of electrical energy.

"The mediums remain blindfolded during the time they are possessed and the eyes of the earthbound spirits see through them and talk to us as though they are actually physically present which they really are, in the medium's body.

"There are three ways the dead persons, earthbound spirits, communicate with us. The first is through control of the medium by entering into his or her electrical field around the body. The second way, they are not in the earth vibration, but come to us from higher mental planes. They do not control the medium as earthbound spirits do. I am unable to explain how these miracles take place but we can see and have to accept their happening. We leave it to you and others to scientifically determine how this is done. The third way, sometimes the guiding spirit shows the medium a board containing written records, which she reads with blindfolded eyes, X-ray vision. There are many other ways through which knowledge is brought to us. We have talked to spirits living in the higher mental planes who have been there over 500 years. I have my doubts on hypnotic regression for establishing facts about a past birth. But with respect to mediums giving unbelievably accurate information—I think there is much to be found in genetic memory extending through generations.

"As long as an earthbound spirit remains in his disturbed, confused state of mind, he will have a feeling of hatred and other destructive thoughts toward his enemies and others he has not liked for one reason or the other. But once these feelings are removed, his or her state of mind changes and they no longer harbor ill will toward even the person who may have killed them or done them harm.

"On the other hand, we have come across earthbound spirits who have influenced persons living on earth to kill others because these spirits have had malicious thoughts toward them. The persons who can be influenced in this manner are those who can be aroused emotionally, are strong willed, and act on impulse. In this way, lower spirits can do bad deeds to those still living on earth. Whenever we encounter such spirits we give them an understanding of their position and this usually brings about a change in them.

"Earthbound spirits of different nations speak different languages, of course, but the consciousness of the spirit is transferred to the medium and she gives out impressions in her own words.

"Since, with the aid of my guiding spirit, I am able to give X-ray vision to my mediums, I have found I can do this to many people, and I estimate that at least 10,000 persons in Ceylon can be given X-ray eyes under this induced trance. I should like for us to test if we can also give vision to the blind through this method, since when people die they leave all their illnesses and handicaps behind."

A Sample Case History
of Kaluaratchi's Work
A Tamil Victim of Communal
Disturbances Natale

On August 4, 1979, a public seance was held at the Buddhist Hall, Natale, under the auspices of the District Judge, Mr. Semarasinghe, and other prominent citizens. A demonstration was given of the medium's ability to read selected papers, currency notes, with her eyes blindfolded and sealed. The District Medical Officer, Natale, examined the medium and satisfied himself that she cannot read blindfolded under normal conditions by normal means of seeing. Then a demonstration in Spirit communication was given for the edification of the public gathered in the hall.

After the medium was put into a trance, the guiding spirit brought in an earthbound spirit and allowed it to control the medium. The medium lay on a mattress on the stage. She struggled in pain and cried out, lamenting.

> P. Kaluaratchi: Who are you?
> Spirit: I am a male.
> PK: What is your name?
> SPT: I can't remember. I am a Tamil by nationality.
> PK: What happened to you?
> SPT: I was shot.
> PK: Who shot you?
> SPT: They shot me.
> PK: How did they shoot you?
> SPT: They broke into our house and shot me.
> PK: When did this happen?
> SPT: On 18th of August, 1971. They first came to our house and asked me for the gun. I said

119

I did not have it. They came again in the evening. We refused to give the gun.

PK: Where is your house?

SPT: Near Aluvihare at Natale. So they went away angry. Then on the 18th of August, 12 or 13 persons came, wearing masks. They broke in and assaulted my father. They pushed him down violently. They kicked my mother and forced her to get under the bed. My elder sister, Manehari, tried to run away from the house. At that time, they shot me. Sister heard the gunshot and came to see me.

PK: Who was this sister?

SPT: She was Manehari. They asked her for some water and dragged her into the kitchen. One of the intruders smashed the lamp. I heard a gunshot.

PK: Where were you at this time?

SPT: I had received a gunshot and was struggling for life. Finally, I left the body. The shot fired in the dark hit one of the intruders. He was burnt by the lamp also. On account of this confusion, they left the place.

PK: What did you do?

SPT: *I went up.* I chased them to hit them. They went and dressed their wounds at Dr. Silva's Dispensary.

PK: So, did they receive medical attention?

SPT: Dr. Silva suspected them and reported the matter to the police. When my sister tried to inform the police, the GramaSevaka (Village Headman) prevented her. His name was Tikiri Banda. He obstructed her from going to the police.

PK: Why was that?

SPT: I do not know.

PK: What was your name?

SPT: I can't remember.

PK: You remember your sister's name well?

SPT: Yes.

PK: How was that?

SPT: I loved her more than my life.

PK: Where did you reside?

SPT: Near Aluvihare of Natale.

PK: Were you married?

SPT: Yes.

PK: Who was your wife?

SPT: I remember only a part of her name—Greta. I have forgotten the other part.

PK: Were you employed?

SPT: I was employed in a ship.

PK: Did you have any children?

SPT: Yes, two, I remember.

PK: Did your sister have children?

SPT: Yes, I remember that she had five children.

PK: Who did this harm to you?

SPT: I can't remember them properly. That day, they wore masks. The previous day, one Gamini called over. There was a case in the Kandy Courts. I remember the Sansoni Commission referring to this case.

PK: After you departed from this life, you chased your assailants. After then, what did you do? Did you re-enter your body?

SPT: No, it was badly damaged. I watched my sister weeping. I tried to console her. She ignored me. She kept on weeping and lamenting. I stroked her head and tried to console her.

PK: Did your wife not weep?

SPT: I was near my sister.

PK: Did you not get back to your former body? It must have been buried.

SPT: Yes.

PK: That body was injured and damaged. The injuries sustained cannot cause you pain now.

SPT: But I can't remove them from my mind. Every time I think of the incident, I receive gunshot wounds. I fall down. Darkness over-

121

comes me. My sister weeps. These happen as it happened on that fatal day.

PK: Now, it should be clear to you that today is not that day.

SPT: Yes.

PK: Now you are a discarnate spirit. So you can live without suffering the pains of your former body.

SPT: Yes.

PK: Do you have anything further to say?

SPT: No, if I remember any further details, I will come back and tell.

PK: Then I wish you farewell.

SPT: Farewell.

DOCUMENTATION

On this day, there was a large crowd in the audience, comprising Rev. Buddhist monks, and laymen and laywomen. But there was no one who knew of this incident or the Dr. Silva referred to by the spirit. There were over fifty Buddhist monks, some from the Aluvihare area. Only one elderly gentleman said he faintly remembered such a Doctor. The majority said no such event had occurred in Natale.

I was sad that none of the fifty-odd Buddhist monks could confirm this case. I decided to investigate myself. The following day I went alone with Mr. Sarath Kodisinha, the Pallewala Correspondent of the DAVASA newspaper to Aluvihare, and made inquires.

We learned that Dr. Richard Silva had run a Dispensary in the area about a year ago and that he had died. His orderly is now running the Dispensary in Dr. Richard Silva's name. We went and met him. The Dispensary is now being run by D. G. Charles who was an employee of the Doctor. The address of the Dispensary is: Palapathwela Dispensary, Dr. Richard Silva, Palapathwela. D. G. Charles said he was aware of this murder case and confirmed the facts divulged by the communicating spirit as true.

He narrated the following facts: On the 18th of August, 1971, a person came for treatment, saying he was injured while creeping under a barbed wire fence. He saw something resembling gunshot injuries. He did not dress the patient but reported the matter to Dr. Silva, who informed the police. He said that Manomani and the other members of the Tamil family lived near the 1½ mile post off Aluvihare. The house was near the home of Mr. Want. A report of this case appeared in the Psychic newspaper, SITUMINA in April 7, 1979. (The distance from my home in Wilawatta to Natale, is approximately 92 miles.)

The Case of Reuben Perera-Kotte
Fall From the Mango Tree

On May 28, 1978, at 5:15 P.M., a session was held in the presence of a party of visitors. The medium was blindfolded and made to read books and the numbers of currency notes produced by the visitors, who were amazed at this ability. The spirit who came in this day had a strange story to tell. It is possible that none of the visitors believed this story. Even I (Kaluaratchi) did not believe it, till I verified the facts and found them to be correct. Here are the details:

I invited our spirit guide, Klevin, and his spirit friends, to introduce a suitable spirit for his edification and to eliminate false concepts. The electro-magnetic field of the medium was being adjusted and the sitters could see how changes were taking place in her physical form. The sitters were watching with intense awe and interest as to what would happen next. The medium started struggling in her bed as though she were

123

being attacked by a swarm of ants. The sitters thought that actually ants had somehow got there and were biting her. Uttering groans and "Ah, Oh, Alas—biting, biting, biting—burning sensation—biting, biting!" she started to brush off her hands and feet, all the time uttering cries.

P. KALUARATCHI: What is this?

MEDIUM: Some creatures are biting! (Having struggled vigorously in bed, the medium falls off to the ground. She still cries: "Some creatures are biting me!" For two to three minutes, she continues to utter pathetic groans and say, "Alas—burning sensation, burning, burning!" She ignored Kaluaratchi's words addressed to her, as she suffered intense mental discomfort and pain.

PK: Who are you? (The spirit now possessing the medium was so confused and overwhelmed by his discomfort and distress that he was in no position to reply. Now, as usual, Kaluaratchi endeavors to explain to the spirit that he is in a new body, and that the discomforts of the former body are no more physically existing; that they are only mind-made by the spirit's inability to understand that he has died and is now in a new plane of existence . . .) You are some person who has died. Our spirit friends have brought you here to help you. (The medium, now possessed by the spirit, is silent. Seems to be thinking over something.) Tell us who you are.

SPIRIT: I am a man (a male person).

PK: What happened to you?

SPT: I climbed up the tree to pluck mango fruits. Red ants attacked me. I climbed down and applied kerosene oil on my hands and feet, lighted a torch made of rags soaked in oil and climbed high up the tree.

124

PK: Then . . . ?

SPT: My body caught fire by contacting the flame of the torch. Burning, I fell off the tree. With great difficulty I put off the flames. Then I was taken to Columbo hospital. My name is Hettiaratchige Reuben Perera.

PK: When did you meet with this mishap?

SPT: In May, 1978, the date was the 20th or 30th—I can't remember exactly.

PK: What is your age?

SPT: 39 years.

PK: That day, you, Reuben, fell off the tree, got burned, and died as a result.

SPT: No, I did not die.

PK: I do not see Reuben. I can see only our medium and I hear what she speaks. A female medium is lying on the bed in front of me. She is a female, not a male. Look well, you will see her wearing a jacket and cloth. (The medium looks well at her body—the spirit possessing her is seeing.)

SPT: But still, I am here.

PK: Yes, Reuben is not dead. He merely lost his physical form that day. His soul or spirit is not dead. But physically, he died, and hence his former body is no more.

SPT: Here are the wounds, here are the wounds! Medicines have been applied. Although I am in the hospital, the doctor does not give me any medicine to give me back my body.

PK: Now, Reuben, you have a good body. You can get up—raise your head and get up. (The medium is still sprawling on the ground.)

SPT: I can't get up. My hand has a burning sensation. I can't get up. (The medium attempts to get up. She sits on the ground. She trembles and sits in discomfort. The spirit possessing the medium is still under the delusion that he still is in the former body, suf-

125

fering its pain at the time of death. Hence the spirit is going through mental agony. Gradually, however, the spirit has partly begun to realize that he is dead and is no longer in his original body.)

PK: Now, you have no pains ... get back to bed.

SPT: No, I feel a burning sensation. (He thinks over something. The medium gets up and relaxes on the bed.)

PK: Reuben, you have physically died. Is that not so?

SPT: Yes.

PK: Well, from where are you—where is your home?

SPT: At Kotte-Etul Kotte.

PK: Reuben, when did you die?

SPT: 1978—May 20th, or somewhere near.

PK: What happened to you, Reuben?

SPT: When I climbed up the tree, I got burned. I was bitten by red ants. I fell off the tree.

PK: Was an inquest held on your death?

SPT: Yes.

PK: Who was the Inquirer?

SPT: Inquirer into Sudden Deaths, Columbo, Mr. Walter D. Perera. (There were some visitors in the audience, some of whom were from Kotte. They were unaware of such a death in that area or closeby, so I questioned them.)

PK: Reuben Perera, what is your address?

SPT: Hettiaratchige Reuben Perera, Etul Kotte, Kotte.

PK: Was there a house number?

SPT: Can't remember. (I, Kaluaratchi, don't know whether the sitters were satisfied.)

Reuben Perera finally realized the true position regarding his death and that he was now in a spirit plane. He got over the fixed impression he was laboring under and the consequent suffering it entailed. He

126

left the seance room under the guidance of the Control
and other spirits, saying he would come back with further details and information if he could manage.

He came back again, in May, a year later at a seance
session then held. I put the medium under trance and
questioned whether there was any further information
available. Our spirit control, Klevin and other friendly
spirits brought back Reuben to our seance room.

> MEDIUM: (reporting) Now Reuben is in the
> Lecture Hall.
> PK: Has Reuben possessed you?
> M: No, he is now evolved spiritually and un-
> derstands things better. It is not necessary for
> him to enter into my body.
> PK: Then, where is Reuben?
> M: He is standing by the spirit friend. (The
> Control)
> PK: (explains) A Spirit who comes for the sec-
> ond time after realizing his true position, and
> still remains earthbound, behaves in 3 differ-
> ent ways:
>
> 1. Some enter the magnetic field of our
>   medium and give further details.
> 2. More evolved beings come and stand
>   by the control and give information
>   without actually possessing the me-
>   dium.
> 3. The third group never come to us after
>   their edification and full understanding.
>   They spend their time in studies at the
>   spirit lecture hall. They indicate what-
>   ever they wish to transmit to our spirit
>   control and pass the information
>   through him.

That night, Reuben did not give any further details.
He merely repeated his name and the information pre-

viously given. He said he could not recall anything further.

On the following day, I went to my school to teach (as I am a teacher by profession. I entered a tea-kiosk to drink some tea. I chanced to see an old newspaper wherein I saw a news item under the caption: "He fell down from a Mango tree and was burned to death." It was dated June 6, 1978 in the Dawasa newspaper of the Independent Newspaper Co., Ltd. I recall the report is as follows.

By Staff Correspondent—Indrani Fonseka.
There is a report from General Hospital, Columbo, of a person who climbed a Mango tree after applying kerosene oil on his hands and feet to avoid being bitten by the red ants in the tree. He carried a lighted torch to burn off the attacking ants. He sustained burn injuries, fell off the tree and died. The unfortunate person was Reuben Perera of Mahawelarama Road of Etul Kotte, aged 38. Mr. Walter D. Perera held the inquest into his death at the General Hospital, Columbo.

Alfred StinSuwaris Perera of Etul Kotte gave evidence at the Inquest. He was led by P. C. Mandasena of the Mirihana Police. He later said this: "Mr. P. Kaluaratchi of Wilwatte has written an article in the SITUMINI Psychic newspaper on the information he gathered from the surviving spirit of Reuben Perera. It is entitled: "Reuben Perera of Etul-Kotte, who died from a fall from a Mango tree, speaks from the spirit world."
I, Kaluaratchi, also called at the Court of the City Coroner on June 15, 1979 and, with his permission, checked the record of Inquests. We found that this case was recorded therein at the approximate date.

This information was given to us by the spirit of the dead before it was published in the paper. The spirit communication took place on May 28, 1978, and my newspaper article was published August 11, 1978. The distance from Wilwatte to Kotte, where Reuben Perera had lived was approximately 40 miles.

Many of these earthbound case histories are not too pleasant reading but the experiences that the spirits relate explain pretty much why they are where they are in the Next Dimension. The P. Kaluaratchi cases are not the only ones although they are among the best organized and authenticated. However, we have cases in this country of like nature, offering proof of the reality and universality of these earthbound conditions in which untold numbers of spirits have become temporarily entrapped.

The length of time that earthbound spirits remain in "detention" because of their fixed ideas, their feelings of guilt; their desire for revenge for some wrongful act, including murder; the earth-binding pull of "unfinished business," a compelling love of someone left on earth; and a number of other mental and emotional ties, varies in days, weeks, months and years.

Time seems to stand still for some who remain attached to locations and scenes of their past, causing them to relive many things that have happened to them, usually of a tragic nature. Eventually, contacts are made with other living mortals or some spirit helpers from higher dimensions who are able to get through to them, and cause them to realize that they no longer possess their physical bodies, that they have, long since, been free to leave these dismal, confused earthbound conditions and join friends and loved ones in a higher plane of existence.

Recently, Mary Martin Bacon, President of Truth

Center Foundation in Seattle, Washington, and a sensitive who has taught others how to develop psychic ability, sent me some unusual case histories, all carefully documented, furnishing more evidence in support of communication with earthbound spirits. These communications have come through an entranced medium, Duane Bennett, whom Marry trained, and who is aided by his gifted wife, Nila, acting as the "lady of the records." She not only records what communications are received, but interviews the Spirit entities brought to the medium by Mitchele, the French-Canadian spirit guide. Duane Bennett is a businessman, an accomplished actor, and a good healer who has been practicing mediumship for the past ten years. He was concerned, for a time, when he discovered that he possessed psychic abilities and that he slipped into trances and was possessed by different spirits, who were seeking an outlet to relieve their minds of some past life experiences that were weighing heavily on them. Duane felt more assured when Mitchele appeared and volunteered to be his spirit guide and when his wife agreed to keep a record of his trance experiences and to check them for possible verification. As a result, nothing has been accepted that has come through unless it could be validated.

One of the mysteries is that, on occasion, earthbound spirits manifest and want to report and talk about experiences that are still on their minds after some years have passed, such as the case of John R. Waldo, who asked permission of spirit guide Mitchele to use the medium and speak about an incident which took place in June of 1908, in Tacoma, Washington. In introducing this spirit to Nila, Mitchele said: "There is someone here to tell you a story. It has a meaning behind it. You'll be unable to help him. He just wants to get it off his chest."

130

The story, exactly as it came through the entranced medium, is as follows:

"My name is John R. Waldo. I want to tell you how an incident or an episode can destroy a young and impressionistic person's life, when he is not directly responsible for a life-taking act.

"I was an observer and partial participator in what happened. It was a little after ten o'clock on the morning of June 6, 1908. I was standing on the third floor of the Chamber of Commerce Building in Tacoma, when the elevator door opened. A Mrs. Albert Toczer or Rockzen, oh, I can't remember her name (it was later determined to be "Tozer") came out. She had two little children with her. One was four and one was six. The four-year-old was Albert, Jr. They'd come to see their father.

"As they stepped off the elevator, the mother said: 'Oh, dear, I'm on the wrong floor, children.' She grabbed her six-year-old boy by the hand, while the four-year-old turned and scooted back to the elevator which had gone and already started up and out of sight, although the door had not yet closed.

"The lad plunged into the elevator shaft and fell thirty-two feet and died instantly. The horror-stricken mother ran down the stairs. I tried to save the little boy, but I only have one arm and I had an umbrella and package.

"I followed her down, found her at the base of the elevator shaft with her four-year-old cuddled and cradled in her arms. His cheek was laid wide open. She was in hysterics. I went to get the Building Superintendent, but couldn't. I rang for the elevator to come down, then I got to thinking the elevator could crush the two of them, so I ran up a floor and pushed the elevator button so it would stop before it got to the bottom floor. Then

I ran up to where the six-year-old boy was, and got him.

"The six-year-old boy had pushed the floor button and Chauncey, the eighteen-year-old elevator boy stopped and wondered what was the matter and we told him. By then the mother's screaming had attracted the attention and another elevator had taken them to the fifth floor to a Dr. Hill.

"When Chauncey heard the story, he screamed out his innocence: 'It's not my fault ... it's not my fault!'

"As tragic as it was for the family, the tragedy was Chauncey's. I lost touch with everybody but Chauncey in the following years, and saw him demoralized and declining at an early age. This incident ruined his life.

"I found later the buildings were trying to work out a code system where these doors would close before the elevators would go up. The elevator operators had been instructed not to leave a floor until the doors had closed. How wrong it is to pre-judge."

Just WHY the spirit of John Waldo should have felt compelled to tell this tragic episode after all these years and to moralize upon it, when one would think it might more logically have been poor Chauncey's to tell, is difficult to understand.

Nevertheless, Nila felt it had the ring of truth in it, so she went to the files of the Tacoma DAILY NEWS and after quite a search, found the account of this tragedy in the June 6, 1908 edition, under the following headlines, photostatic copy of which she sent to me:

LITTLE BOY KILLED IN SHAFT

Albert Tozer Falls to Instant Death
in Chamber of Commerce Building
MOTHER SEES THE ACCIDENT

Tot in His Haste to Reach His Father, Darts into
Open Door and Plunges 32 Feet to The Bottom—
Merry-Making Turned to Terrible Grief.

Many of Duane Bennett's spirit communications
have taken place late at night or in early morning
hours, when he has passed from sleep into a trance
state and his spirit guide, Mitchele, has awakened
Nila, to announce that he had an earthbound spirit
needing help. This case occurred at 3:20 A.M., January
20, 1974, after the couple had gone to bed.

M: Nila, this is Mitchele. There is someone
   here named Emil Eggert. He wishes to speak
   with you. You'll have to check on this. Re-
   member, I told you the "absence of evidence"
   is not that "evidence is absent."
N: Yes, I remember.
SPIRIT: This is Emil Eggert. Are you there?
N: Yes, I'm here.
SPT: I can hear you. Can you hear me?
N: Yes, I can hear you. (Spirit has great trou-
   ble breathing)
SPT: I am so startled, surprised.
N: Is this the first time for you?
SPT: Yes, it is. I was summoned to you by
   Mitchele Laurens. I'm a Californian. I left the
   earth through death ten years ago, with a
   broken neck.
N: Oh, dear!
SPT: (Still troubled with heavy breathing, re-
   flected through the body of the medium.) I was
   so startled at being able to talk to you like this
   . . . I forgot about my emphysema until now.
N: Oh, is that why you're breathing like that?
SPT: I didn't know I did.
N: Just a little bit at first.
SPT: I loved my car. It was a blue Corvette. It
   had orange and black license plates . . . I

didn't like it because it didn't match. There were 1963 plates. The top on my Corvette. I guess it was too short for me. My head was only two inches from the ceiling ... You're Duane's wife, Nila, aren't you?

N: That's right.

SPT: May I call you Nila?

N: Surely.

SPT: I want you to do me a favor. My wife, Dorothy, lives in Sonora in the County of Sonora in California very near the Sonora County Hospital. (We found there was no Sonora County and decided he must have meant Sonoma, and found, on investigating that this was correct. Many spirits make these minor errors, due to fuzzy memories or excitement.)

SPT: I'm worried about Dorothy. She is near to destroying herself.

N: Oh, no!

SPT: Would you relay a message to her and say to her that I don't want her to do this. I want her to find another output for her energies and her monies, turn to the ways of life, not to the ways of dying. My sudden death left me floating here for quite awhile until the adjustment came, but if she destroys herself, I'll never see her here. Please let her know that.

N: I'll try.

SPT: This is all so unusual, getting to talk to you this way. Our marriage was pretty stormy, at times. I want you to let her know that I love her and want her with me for our studies and so we can progress together. (He has more trouble with heavy breathing.) Tell her for me, please, Nila, for her not to remember me as she does, but remember me as I was. Thanks to you for this.

M: Nila, this is Mitchele, Emil Eggert is gone! (We found his wife, Dorothy Eggert, at 1-707-996-1959, 362 Andrieux St., Sonoma, Califor-

134

nia. We called her and have it on tape. Of course it was a great shock to her but she verified it all to be true. Some eight months later, Nila went to California to get Emil Eggert's Death Certificate, which further verified his story. He was killed October 31, 1963.)

That memory lives on in consciousness after the change called "death" is evidenced by this case history of a young seaman, Burney Burns, who has never forgotten a beautiful young lady that he met and was courting in a park when fate took him away from her, followed by a disaster. After all this time, since the early 1900's, he has been carrying thoughts of endearment for her and would like her to know, wherever she is, what had happened to him. His mind has been fixated on this moment and experience. He can't get away from it, and wants to live it and tell it over and over. Here is what he told to Nila, through her entranced husband:

"Nila, I've always been called Burney. In my late teens and early twenties, I went to the Park every Sunday afternoon and just walked around and enjoyed things. As I lived in a big city, I liked the trees and grass. This particular day, this little mongrel dog came up and I petted him and we were immediate friends. We walked along and I played with him, when he went running after this beautiful show dog on a leash, being held by a very attractive girl.

"We began to talk about the dog. Her name— I have never forgotten—was Wilma Lanauer. We talked friendly for a while. You might say I was right smitten with her. The next Sunday, I saw the same dog there, again playing at the same time. There she was and we got to talking some more, walked a little further, talked a little more.

"The next Sunday, the dog wasn't there but I

135

befriended another kind of a mutt dog, as I recall, and she wondered about it, but we talked and the dog stayed with me. The next Sunday I had still another dog. Then she began to see through me, and called me 'Tricks.' She always walked her dog at that time. Our friendship grew quite deeply to the point where I couldn't think throughout the week of anything but her.

"I knew she liked me, but she made no overtures and I was about to pursue. The next Sunday it was another dog and she laughed and we were very much at ease with each other as I had determined that the next Sunday I would let her know of my intentions and my feelings.

"I was anxiously awaiting that Sunday when I received notification to ship out and then I ended up on the armored Cruiser Tennessee off the California coast. My duty called for me to be below deck. If I recall right, it was on the sixth of the sixth month, eighth year of 1900, when a steam pipe blew up in the boiler room and six were scalded and burned. I was one of them; four died and one died much later.

"We were transported to Los Angeles and we were put in the baggage car of the Pacific Electric Company and taken into Los Angeles at the intersection of 29th and Long Beach. There were six ambulances there waiting for us to take us to the Angeles hospital which was only eight blocks away. We were all moaning and groaning with piteous agony. There were about two hundred people crowded into the intersection with cameramen taking pictures as we were put in the ambulances.

"Despite my suffering, my mind was on Willie as I had started to call her. I've never seen her since. Would it be possible for you to find her for me and tell her what my intentions were, no matter where she is or what she is doing today?"

* * *

136

N: Burney, what was your last name?

SPT: Burns—Walter Burney Burns ... (We could not locate Wilma Lanauer ... but we found a headline account in the San Francisco CHRONICLE of "Death in the Fireroom of the Cruiser Tennessee" and the name of seaman Walter J. Burns as one of the badly burned survivors. The story went on to say that "Men are Literally Cooked Alive When the Steam Pipe Blows Out.")

It seems that when a person leaves this life and can look back upon his past life on earth, he can plainly see, perhaps for the first time, himself, his conduct, and the experiences he has had, in proper perspective. This often leads to remorse, regret, and the wish that he might find some way to atone for his sins of omission and commission. This no doubt accounts for the hope he might return to earth and live life again, when he feels he would have done differently.

On the night of July 26, 1974, after medium Duane Bennett retired, he slipped into trance and his guide Mitchele, spoke to his wife, Nila.

"Nila, you have heard the expression, 'he has seen the light' ... I have one here with me who has 'seen the light.' I have told him that you are 'a woman of records.' He has been disturbed for a long, long time over his past conduct on earth ... and wants to talk to someone about it. I have told him you would be willing to listen and help all you can. He tells me his name is Loftus Keating."

The voice of the spirit entity, giving the name Loftus Keating, began speaking to Nila through her entranced husband:

"Lady of Records, I have seen the light. Mitchele suggested that I talk to you. I am here to apolo-

137

gize for a lost life that I led. I have been burdened with it since I came here years ago. I was born in Cincinnati, Ohio. My brothers and I, since I was fourteen, chartered boats for River trips, pleasure trips and fishing, for tourists and city folks. My folks then moved to Louisville, Kentucky. I was the only one of the boys to go with them. We lived there quite awhile. The boys stayed behind and tended their boats.

"This is where my story begins. I need to tell you this so you will understand. Back in Ireland there was an ambitious young man, who was a Lord, with a common physical failing—he fell in love with a commoner, whom he married. Their marriage was supremely happy, but they were disowned by their parents and dismissed by the Lords.

"This young man stole money from his family and came to America to start the new life, and settled in Louisville. His name was G.G. Lenny. He never let me call him anything but G.G. L-E-N-N-Y. He established a brewing company in Louisville which became the biggest in the country. He enjoyed extreme wealth, and all he wanted at his disposal. He had two sons and a daughter, whose name was Rachael—Rachael Lenny.

"One day, during an extremely bad electrical storm, his sons were at the window, the father was in the room, and also Rachael, all enjoying the sight of the lightning flashes. Suddenly, a terrific bolt of lightning hit the side of the building. One boy was seared to death by the window sill; the other was knocked across the room and his head split open, an unsightly thing for a father and sister to see.

"This father never went back to his factory. He was sure that it was God's wrath that had brought this thing down on his head. He spent the rest of his life declining in remorse for this.

He thought it had been due to his doings and his thievery.

"It was at this time in his downhill slide that fate put us on the same path. I was just then around and about over the puberty stage when he discovered me. Our acquaintanceship was short-lived, but he introduced me to acts of sodomy and sexuality which opened a whole new world for me, exciting at first, but I learned to hate him, hate him with an intense burning hate, and a desire to get even with him. I did it by marrying his daughter, Rachael.

"Her father became very vicious with me. He would get fits of insane temper. I once saw him choke the life out of a friend of mine. To get away, Rachael and I moved to Davenport, Iowa. We had one daughter, Marion, who was an angel disguised as a human being. While there, I lived off Rachael's earnings as a seamstress. She is the one who made the money that I spent on liquor, carousing and whoring. I was very untrue to her, a very distasteful type husband. Here again, she was angelic as was her daughter, and for this I am suffering great remorse.

"I cannot find Rachael where I am. I want you, as a Lady of Records, to do what you can to let those know how I regret the hateful life I led . . . the terrible times I gave Rachael . . . the terrible youth I had. Seeing the light now, I want to make progress. Mitchel brought me to you to help me in this. You'll find the records about me in Scott County, Iowa. They go back quite a few years . . . I cannot remember how many."

(Mitchele reported that the contact with Loftus Keating had been broken. The DOCUMENTARY EVIDENCE follows. Neither Duane nor Nila had ever been in Iowa. Some time later, while visiting relatives in Indiana and on the way to visit others in Illinois, they

139

went about 120 miles out of their way to spend an hour in Davenport, Iowa, and found in the city Directory PROOF of LOFTUS KEATING'S existence. This was in August, 1974, just before Labor Day.)

NOTE: I have been furnished, and have in my files, photostatic copies of the names of the Keatings, dating back to the years of 1858-59-60, up through 1887.

A sample of the listing:

Keating, Loftus, brick layer, res. Second ss 2 w Rock Island.
Keating, Rachael, Mrs. dress makr. Second ss 2 w Rock Island, res. same.

(HS)

If we accept these communications as genuine, it would appear that individuals who have lived dissolute lives, arrive on the Other Side with such a low grade of spiritual development that they remain in an earthbound region for an indeterminant period of time until some manner of release comes to them. Obviously, Rachael, wife of Loftus, had apparently gone on ahead of him into a higher plane of existence. He hoped, somehow, by finding a sympathetic ear, to free himself, as he said, so he could make progress.

Chapter 11

MIND-TO-MIND COMMUNICATION

It has long been my conviction since the existence of telepathy—mind-to-mind communication—has been pretty well accepted by those researching the Paranormal, that—if man survives death with a retention of his identity and memory—he should be able, under the right conditions, to transmit as well as receive thoughts from the Other Side of life.

I came to this firm conclusion as a result of my pioneering experiments in long distance telepathy with the Arctic Explorer, Sir Hubert Wilkins, when I found I was able to accurately record impressions of his thoughts and feelings over a distance of between two and three thousand miles, for a period of some five months. During that time I became increasingly capable of zeroing in, so to speak, on Wilkins' mind, distinguishing a difference in *feeling* from my ordinary awareness or imagination, when contact was made.

The feeling was so strong, at times, that I would see vivid mental images in my mind's eye of happenings

Wilkins had experienced that day, somewhat like strips of film from a movie. When pictures would not come, I often would get feelings of Wilkins' thoughts and what adventures he and members of his crew had been having, in their search for the lost Russian fliers.

When each night's recording session was over, in the study of my New York apartment, and I took my notebook into the living room, to review and discuss what I had received with my wife, Martha, I was always tormented with doubts by my Conscious mind. It seemed impossible to me that I had been able to pick up such a variety of impressions, many of which were eventually confirmed by a check against Wilkins' diary and log, as well as witnessed by Dr. Gardner Murphy, in Columbia University.

The significance of such a demonstrated phenomenon lent itself to wide and growing speculation. While I had studied the work of psychic mediums who purported to be able to hear spirit voices and, on occasion, to see spirit forms—there was so much room for self-delusion and fraud that, if actual telepathy had been employed, it could be contended that so-called messages from the dead had resulted from reading the minds of the sitters at the seance, and not to genuine spirit communication.

How could an investigator really prove that there would have been no physical way that certain information could have been received, of such a specific nature, other than through a spirit entity?

Certainly, it seemed reasonable to me that, a known identity or celebrity, now in the spirit world, should be able to discuss subjects of which he or she had been authorities on earth. But the majority of "spirit messages" from such personalities were usually of such a trivial and noninformative nature as to be suspect. If any of them were genuine, the best that could be said for them was that these messages must be coming from

142

masquerading spirits in the earthbound realm. It would be embarrassing, even degrading to suggest that a John Wayne or a Bing Crosby or an Elvis Presley or a Hubert Humphrey or any other reputable individual would have been reduced to such juvenile and often ridiculous utterances as some psychic mediums were attributing to them.

Headline-hunting reporters from different tabloid newspapers have asked me to try to contact the spirit world and to get interviews with big name people who have gone on. Admittedly, this would provide great copy if communications made sense and offered proof of survival. But one could easily be accused of trying to trade on these names for self-exploitation purposes, and in many instances this could be true.

I am not suggesting that genuine communication cannot be established, at times. I believe we are getting closer and closer to more accurate tape recording of spirit voices and to certain forms of telepathic communication with those in higher dimensions but much that is being reported cannot be verified and should not be taken seriously.

In the unique case of my telepathic experiment with Wilkins, I had an established record of successful mind-to-mind communication while both of us were alive. Thus, when Wilkins left this life on December 1, 1958, it was logical to assume, if man survives death, that Wilkins and I should still be able to communicate on a mind-to-mind basis.

We had discussed this possibility, as I have reported in my book HOW TO MAKE ESP WORK FOR YOU, but had made no pact in the event one or the other of us should embark on the greatest adventure of all. However, Wilkins was conditioned to think of me as I was of him, and I sent out the thought that my mind would be receptive to any transmission from him, at any time.

From what little I have come to know about the Life Beyond, I feel that those who have gone on are busy there as they were here, that they have the advantage of knowing they have survived, and that it will be but a matter of time before their loved ones will join them. For this reason, I have not attempted to bring any of my loved ones or friends back, while still remaining ready to respond if I sense that any of them may have a special reason for trying to get through to me. This is the way I have felt about Wilkins.

And there have been several notable times when I am sure Wilkins *has* reached me, on which occasions I have dropped everything I was doing and made my mind receptive as I used to do during our telepathic experiments. When these contacts with my mind were made, I felt Wilkins' presence as though he were in the room, and was able to relax and dictate to Martha, word for word, what came through. In this way, I was not troubled by the mechanics of writing, and could keep my entire attention upon the impressions of his voice, which appeared to be talking to me in my mind's ear.

The first contact was made when I was in Hollywood, California, on a writing and lecturing assignment. The date was April 25, 1959, about five months after Wilkins' demise. I was working on a book manuscript when, suddenly, my thoughts were blotted out, and I seemed to hear a voice in my mind's ear, which said: "Hello, Sherman—this is Wilkins!"

The feeling was exactly the same as had often come over me when Wilkins and I had been communicating telepathically back in the years 1937 and 1938. I put everything aside, calling to Martha: "Quick—get your notebook . . . I think I'm hearing from Wilkins!" Martha had long been accustomed to taking down impressions of one kind and another which had been coming to me from time to time, so she was almost instantly ready, as I placed myself in an easy chair, relaxed, made my mind receptive.

This done, Wilkins began immediately, my memory of his physical sounding voice, echoing in my consciousness as I commenced repeating his words. What Martha transcribed and what we are reproducing here, is a word-for-word account, as incredible as it may seem. I am sure, had Wilkins and I not had this previous earthly telepathic experience, we would not have been prepared to communicate in this manner. I, of course, had no idea of what was coming next but the flow of words continued, unbroken, except one little interruption, late in the communication when someone came to the door. I think you will find Wilkins' message of deep interest and significance.

Hello, Sherman!

It is not easy to get through. I have been trying for some time. I find that each mind is like a miniature universe, a collection of magnetized ideas or concepts, revolving around a nucleus or center which represents the entity itself.

The entity holds these ideas or concepts in what the world calls, today, its orbit, and it is difficult to get through this magnetic field from outside. I can realize now what a monumental attempt you made to receive what you called "thought impressions" from me during our experiments.

The universe is not at all like man has described it in his books and scientific treatises. It is difficult to get away from a planet on which you are born because of the hold its energy particles have upon you. That is why I am glad I had the body the world knows as Wilkins returned to the fires, so that its ashes might more speedily be freed from any identification with me.

It was a source of profound satisfaction to have these ashes released at the North Pole, and to have it done by these new under-ice pioneers. They are going to realize my dreams—dreams, I find, which no single entity really completes in any life, but leaves for others to carry on.

I am watching you reach out for my thoughts with your mind as I dispatch them through the magnetic field of your consciousness. It is interesting to me to see how thought impulses travel through your mind circuits to your point of awareness, where you put these impulses which become feelings, into words. It is quite a process.

Once mental contact is made you have to hold to it by a sort of fixation and I can perceive that receiving is more difficult than transmitting. I have only to concentrate my forces on you, but you have to stop temporarily, the machinery of your own mind to let me through to the point of awareness. You have to picture me as I *was*, not as I *am*. But no one ever sees the true entity. It is always surrounded by form in any dimension, and apparently remains an eternal mystery to itself.

(At this point the persistent buzz of the apartment doorbell broke in, and Mrs. Sherman had to answer the door. It was the houseman with a package. The communication was then resumed.)

I perceive you are getting tired and have just had an interruption, which requires a displacement of energy.

You are now resisting the word I am sending through to you because you think it sounds so bromidically English. It is simply a sign-off and the word is "Cheerio," and my name as you have so often seen it, I am writing in your mind as . . .

"Wilkins"

On June 13, 1959, while we were still in Hollywood, I had a second and longer communication from Wilkins, and again Martha grabbed up a notebook and recorded word for word what was dictated to me.

Hello Sherman!

I have been making a study of the mind circuits with others who are interested in opening up reliable and provable channels of consciousness.

I now can realize why more contact has not been made between the two worlds of "the living" and "the dead." You have a language barrier on earth which means if you do not understand a language it is only a series of unintelligible sounds to you.

Because the mind of the average human is centered upon his existence in the flesh and his attention is fixed for the most part, on his outer rather than his inner life, he automatically rejects thoughts and impressions which he might otherwise receive and identify from the minds of those who have "gone on," as they say.

It will require the establishment of what might be termed *listening posts* on the interior levels of mind, on the part of those interested in and capable of reception of thoughts, and of regularly prescribed intervals such as we set up in our experiments, for any dependable results to be obtained. Trained sleeping subjects are the best in many ways because the machinery of their minds is at a position of comparative rest.

But when all circuits of mind are engaged in ordinary conscious and subconscious activity, it is extremely difficult to reach and impress the entity. This is a hard point to get across but perhaps I can illustrate it by reminding you that different organs of the body are utilized to perform different functions at different times, but never together. Nature closes off one function to permit another to be performed by the same organ, as the occasion demands. In the case of the sexes, dual utility is obvious. One function must be slowed or largely stopped before another can take over and use the same channel for another purpose.

Since every mind circuit operates normally in what might be called a closed circuit, this circuit has to be opened, either consciously or unconsciously, before contact can be made with the thought current from the mind of another, either fleshed or unfleshed. This is the problem and it is not without dangers because thoughts carry a charge with them, and have a tendency to influence whatever consciousness wherein they find lodgment, either for good or for ill.

We are existent in a field of constantly changing what you call electromagnetic phenomena. This is as good a description as any since no words can really describe it. If you could sense the wheels within wheels within wheels in the interrelated activity of all minds on the human creature level, it would be overwhelming. The activity is ceaseless and ever-changing, and no mind remains exactly the same in consciousness, as it reacts to experiences from one moment to the other.

Body forms are changing from the instant of conception, and every particle in them changes, as do the minds in control of these bodies and particles. Your own mind is now resisting the names recognizable to the world, and entities interested in attempting to establish communication, some of whom I have been brought in touch with here, simply because you feel these names might be obvious and induced by your imagination. You are so desirous of screening out everything which might seem like a machination of your own mind, that it is difficult to introduce or mention recognizable personalities to your consciousness.

I guess this will have to wait until you feel more assured that this may be a genuine contact.

Again, "Cheerio," and this is "Wilkins" signing off.

Much was given me over which to ponder. I said then, and I repeat today that I am still studying and experimenting in an attempt to find and develop ways to make my mind a clearer channel through which to receive impressions. I have had a vast experience in the years that followed these communications from Wilkins, and I have made some progress. But there is so much that remains a mystery, so little yet known, so much to be known.

Now, for the first time, I am releasing in print, a third communication from Wilkins, received by me on January 10, 1960, and which contained a SERIOUS WEATHER WARNING CONCERNING RUSSIA, YEARS BEFORE THIS WARNING WAS CONFIRMED!

Hello, Sherman! This is Wilkins!

You recall, Sherman, my studies of the climatic conditions in the Polar regions and my often stated contention that, if we could develop effective enough meteorological instruments and observational posts in the Far North, we could pre-determine the kind of weather various areas of the world would have, weeks and months in advance. It is and has been my feeling that the weather of the world is formed at the Poles, due to the motions of the earth, the electro-magnetic conditions there, and the constant inter-play of forces which bring about vast changes in the atmosphere.

It is even more apparent to me now from my new vantage point—that frictions develop in and around the earth body which evolve into storms—just as frictions develop in and around a human body—itself a molecular formation—which produce barometric changes with a consequent raising and lowering of air or blood pressure.

Air under pressure—or feelings under pressure—have to expand—have to find release—to move out from any center of disturbance. Now, if man could artificially create a friction in space which would alter or upset the electrically charged particles given off by the spinning of the earth on its axis, these turbulences could bring about great weather changes everywhere on the globe.

This is the project, Sherman, that the Russians are hard at work on. They are confident that, should they be able to control the weather, they could cripple any portion of the world they wished with great snows, severe cold or heat, cyclonic winds or cloudbursts, leading to vast floods and untold loss of life and property; or cause a withholding of rains so that great droughts would occur, destructive to all crops.

The Soviets are even now experimenting with certain weather-control methods—the seeding of the atmosphere with a variety of elements designed to have an electromagnetic influence. They are seeking a plan by which they can combine an atomic explosion in the atmosphere with the expulsion of a chemical or powder solution that can have far-reaching and even directional influence on the weather, utilizing the prevailing jet streams at different levels.

They are also experimenting with the airstreams as a means of releasing certain poisonous or nerve gases which could have a devastating effect upon the U.S. and Canada in particular.

I give you this information as a warning. You will see evidences of these experiments in freak weather conditions in the months and years to come. Such tampering with the oceans and the air surrounding the planet can produce chaotic conditions in time.

This is all for now . . .

"Wilkins"

As recently as March 10, 1979, in the newspaper SPOTLIGHT, some nineteen years from January 10, 1960, when I received this warning from the spirit world of Sir Hubert Wilkins, came the following head-line article:

U.S. HIT BY SOVIET "SNOW JOB"?

Did America suffer its third straight devastating winter because the Soviet Union is manipulating the weather in a new type of war?

There is strong evidence that the Soviet Union has mastered the ability to manipulate the weather, thus increasing its own growing season while inflicting chaos, death and heavy financial losses on the U.S.

This was first examined in The SPOTLIGHT on Feb. 14, 1977, and a year later, on Dec. 13, 1978. Despite the fact that much information has been developed by the government and in the private sector, the Establishment media has *covered up* this story . . .

Perhaps no one in the Next Dimension would have had a more intimate knowledge of "weather fixing" than Wilkins who had studied such conditions during his explorations while on earth. I hesitated about making this information public because of my concern that few would believe it, least of all government officials.

As I have previously stated, I believe that those who have left this life, once they have become acclimated to the New Existence, do not ordinarily try to return unless they have an impelling reason to do so. And if and when they can find a channel of communication, I feel that they, like Wilkins, would and should have something specific and pertinent to say consistent with their personality, background and intelligence. Just to come back with the message that they are "well and happy," unless associated with some identifying information, can hardly be accepted as proof of their claim that they are who they say they are.

In the instances when friends have tried to communicate through me, they have always had an understandable reason which has later been verified in most evidential and convincing ways. I have reported some of these cases in other books, such as HOW TO MAKE ESP WORK FOR YOU and am repeating one of them here as an illustration:

In the year 1958, Martha and I were motoring to Phoenix, Arizona, where I was to deliver a series of lectures. While driving, a strong impression came to me that the spirit of a long-time friend, H.C. Mattern, was with us in the car. He and his wife, Mary, were a unique couple, conducting as they did, a nation-wide business for cleaning and preserving leather upholstered furniture, for big city banks and other companies and industries. They were using a chemical solution invented by H.C. and employed crews of men to help them in every city they visited.

H.C. had died the year before, leaving Mary to carry on the business. She had taken one of their best workmen on tour with her to help manage the cleaning crews. I didn't know anything about this and had not been in touch with her for some time.

Now, while driving, I said to Martha: "Honey, I feel that H.C. is here and has a message of some sort for Mary. Will you please get your notebook out and write down what comes to me?"

It seemed as though, at least I had the feeling, that

H.C.'s spirit was watching our actions, even though I couldn't see him, because, as soon as Martha had her notebook in hand, I heard him say in my mind's ear:

"Harold—tell Mary that man is no good! Kick him out!"

As I spoke these words out loud, Martha wrote them down. Then I waited expectantly for more particulars. Instead H.C. repeated: "Tell Mary—that man is no good! Kick him out!"

With that, I felt H.C.'s presence disappear.

"I guess that's all," I concluded. "But how am I going to write Mary anything like this—and make her believe it has come from H.C.?"

We continued on to Phoenix where I lectured that night and had put this experience out of my mind. But H.C. was not going to let me forget. I was awakened in the night psychically hearing him say: "Tell Mary, that man is no good . . . kick him out."

"H.C. wins," I told Martha in the morning. "I've got to write and pass this message on to Mary, for whatever it may be worth. I don't know where she is at present. Think I'd better write her in care of their permanent address, "Grand Central Station, Box 395, New York City, and have it forwarded."

This I did, and felt instant mental relief at the doing.

A week passed when I received a long distance phone call from Mary, from Atlanta. She was crying.

"Oh, Harold," she said, "the most unusual thing has happened! Last night I was awakened and saw H.C. standing by my bed. I saw him as clearly as I ever saw him in life. I felt as though I could have reached out and touched him! Then I heard him say: "Mary, that man is no good! Kick him out!" . . . And just half an hour ago, the mailman brought me your letter, forwarded from New York, with your message from H.C. and the same words: *"That man is no good. Kick him out!"*

Mary went on to explain that a man she had hired to work with her had been wanting to buy an interest in the business and she had been considering this offer—but now, after H.C.'s double warning, she thought she had better investigate. She *did*, and reported back to me that the man she had trusted "had been stealing her blind," so she had done as H.C. had ordered: "kicked him out."

You can see from this that Telepathy can be a means of communicating, mind-to-mind, between those on the "earth plane" and can also be used, on occasion, for the transmission and reception of thoughts between the "living" and the so-called "dead."

A.J. Plimpton, Gladys Childs, Edith Harrison and others mentioned in this book, have demonstrated not once but many times their "other world" communicative abilities. While there may be a percentage of error in reception of some messages and "interference" from "earthbound spirit entities," the evidence seems overwhelming in support of the reality of a life beyond physical death.

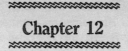

Chapter 12

WHAT THE AFTER LIFE IS LIKE

Some pollsters claim that fifty percent of all peoples attest to a belief in "life after death"—and many are now willing to describe highly personal experiences wherein they feel they have seen and talked to departed friends and loved ones.

This being true, my wonderment is why those on the Other Side have not given us a more comprehensive and realistic description of what the Next Existence is like.

In the case of A.J. Plimpton, not having been interested in Psychic Phenomena until the loss of his wife, Wilma, he had little or no basis of comparison for the experiences which began happening to him. At first, when voices commenced coming through on tape and he finally felt he had established contact with Wilma, by tape and then by telepathy, A.J. was assailed with doubts. It seemed too good, too impossible to be true, especially when Wilma and others told him, from time to time, what existence was like on the Other Side.

His initial jolt came when Wilma chided him for having given up his organ playing and selling his organ. "You shouldn't have done that," she said. "I have created a home like ours on earth, complete with a duplicate of the organ, for you to use when your time comes to join me."

"How did you build your house?" A.J. asked her.

"I visualized it," Wilma told him. "I just pictured it in my mind the way I wanted it and it came into being, including a duplicate of your organ . . ."

"That's hard to believe," said A.J.

"You've already seen it," said Wilma. "You've often left your body in your sleep and visited us in what you call your astral."

"I have no memory of it," said A.J. "And until I do, I'm sorry, I just can't buy that."

A.J. was willing to try anything that might improve his means of communication. He asked me if I knew any authority on astral projection to whom he could go who could teach him a technique for leaving his body. I recommended a long-time friend, John Mittl, who lived in Allentown, Pennsylvania, who had been giving OOBE classes. A.J. lost no time in getting in touch with him. It was while visiting Mittl that he had his first and only out-of-body experience.

"It was while I was meditating on what Mittl had told me, that it happened," A.J. reported to me. "I was wide awake, filled with an intense desire to see Wilma, and all of a sudden the room and bed my physical body was in, vanished and I found myself standing in a beautiful green field. There, about a hundred feet from me was my wife, Wilma, dressed in slacks and a blouse. We saw each other at about the same time and began running. I grabbed her in my arms and kissed her and she felt just as real and warm as she had ever felt in life. We talked and she took me by the hand and led me, we actually glided to the home she had told me about—identical to the house we had had in Oklahoma, except the living room was in the other end. There was my organ, in its usual place, and all the familiar furniture, and a duplicate of my clothes, suits and everything as I had remembered them. I noticed that the doors and windows had no locks and I remarked about this. And I recalled Wilma telling me that locks were not needed—that no one would dare go in any home without permission. Then I have a vague recollection of being taken to visit departed friends and relatives who seemed to know I wouldn't be able to stay long. All of a sudden, everything blanked out and I was back in my hotel room in Allentown, Pennsylvania, in my physical body. It was a great experience which I have tried to repeat time after time, but somehow I haven't been able to set up the same conditions. However, after this happened, I no longer doubt what Wilma tells me—because this one time, I knew I had been there."

A.J.'s account opened up many questions I hoped he could answer.

"If Wilma says you leave your body many nights, and are with her and your nephew, Jason, and the 'Ladies' and others, what do you look like to them?"

A.J. laughed. "That's a good question. I worried about that because I always sleep in the nude, but Wilma assures me that when I enter the astral, I have my clothes on. She doesn't see me put my clothes on but I have them on just the same. So I guess modesty is observed on the Other Side, just as it is here."

Jason has been a continuous source of information for A.J. He has told A.J. that he is staying with Wilma much of the time; that he can go and come at will; that he often visits his parents who are still living—but they have not known he was there.

He says he is going to a tremendous school where everything is taught in pictorial form. He guesses he has the intelligence of an average adult on earth. There is lots he doesn't know . . . lots to learn . . . and he likes it fine.

No one needs any cars or planes to go places. They can fix their minds on where they want to go—and they are there—except they can't go higher than the Second Plane. When they get up near it, they are separated by an invisible electromagnetic barrier . . . and they can't go higher until they get higher development— something to do with higher frequency in consciousness.

Those on the First Plane need help—because, as has already been pointed out their development is so low, they aren't ready to go higher. But lots of people coming over from earth are developed enough to by-pass the First Plane completely . . .

A.J. asked Jason what church he went to and Jason said he hadn't seen any churches. He guessed they weren't needed because people couldn't lie to one another as they had telepathy . . . and could read everyone's mind. And no one could hurt anyone in this Second Plane, since all feelings of hate and violence had been left on the First Plane.

People didn't talk about a God Power but there was a Power behind everything, that you didn't see it but you felt it. All these things and more, Jason told A.J., and Wilma said they were all true.

As new knowledge is gained of the nature of the After Life, new names and terminologies will have to be invented to describe conditions more accurately. Today, different delineations are being designated by different investigators, requiring different interpretations. For example, while there is no actual proof as yet, A.J. has been told that there are 25 Dimensions in the First Plane and the 16th Dimension is populated by the most contactable of the earthbound spirits, whom A.J. calls the "troublemakers." Below this Dimension, down to the First, lower and lower grades or levels of consciousness are supposed to exist.

Sometimes, A.J. says he is so exasperated by the interference of these earthbound entities that he has threatened to have Jason and the "Ladies" shepherd them down into lower levels of existence.

One day, as an experiment, A.J. reports that he called upon Jason to take a group of five of these "pestering entities" (who are easily led) down to the First Dimension and leave them there for several days. Jason wasn't eager to go, because he had heard that this Dimension was a pretty dismal place. He returned to report: "Uncle Amour, it's terrible down there. It looks like a jungle. There is water dripping from ghostly looking trees; there aren't any houses or buildings; it's dark, hardly any light at all, and people are sitting around on rocks and logs; no one is trying to talk, they just sit and stare at one another; they're not doing anything. They don't seem to know who and what or where they are. When I took those earthbounds there, they didn't want to stay. When I left them they were hollering and screaming. I guess we'd better not let them stay there too long."

The next day, when A.J. was in touch with Jason, he sent him down to the First Dimension again and found the group of five only too anxious to be returned to their 16th Dimension, which, by comparison was "paradise." They told Jason the people were all crazy down there. That they were glad they didn't belong there. That they wanted to do all they could to go higher.

Jason told A.J. that no matter how much a person might want to punish or beat an offender, or do something to teach tormenters or pretenders a lesson, it wasn't permitted. Those in the lower dimensions were allowed to punish themselves until they had a desire for self-improvement, when help would come to them, eventually and always from higher sources.

Once A.J. found he could communicate telepathically, he was able to ask questions of Wilma and others and get direct answers. This didn't mean that he always obtained the information desired but what was not known was freely confessed. Quite often Wilma would say, "there is lots we don't know over here. I'll have to try to find out, and report back."

A.J. was amazed to learn that when he thought of someone in the "spirit world," they heard his voice, telepathically, as though he was speaking to them. Wilma explained that she heard A.J.'s thoughts twice—first as he was forming the words in mind ready to speak . . . and then as he actually spoke these same words—so that when his thoughts became audible, they sounded like an echo of what had been formed in his mind.

Occasionally spirit entities will break in on A.J.'s consciousness and engage him in conversation. He hears their voices in his mind's ear. They always express wonderment that he can hear them and A.J. is just as astounded that they can hear him.

"How did you locate me?" A.J. will ask.

"I heard your voice and I followed your voice vibration and it brought me to you," a spirit entity will reply, as though this form of communication is a new experience for them.

160

Experimentally, A.J. has concentrated his thoughts on different well-known personalities who have recently passed on to see if he could get a response. Some of them have replied, asking who he is and what does he want with them, and how is it possible they are able to hear his voice when he is not on their Side of Life?

This phenomenon is so fantastic that A.J. will not permit me to use the names and experiences he has had with them, because so many psychics are claiming that they have been communicating with John Wayne, Jack Benny, Bing Crosby, Elvis Presley and others and he feels that all of them cannot be true, and he has a measure of doubt himself.

For example, he has been told and has evidence that there are what might be called "Rest Homes," situated about thirty miles apart around the entire surface of the earth, to which the spirits of all who die are transported, for care and attention, before going on to different dimensions and planes of existence. Depending on their individual development, they either pass through the Rest Home almost immediately or are permitted to sleep while adjustments are made to the new life experience they have entered.

A.J. has let his nephew, Jason, act as messenger, visiting "Information Centers" to learn where certain personalities may be at the moment. They always appear astounded, when contact is made, to learn this communication is coming from the "Earth Plane." It is A.J.'s opinion that many men and women, willing to devote the time and effort, can develop this form of "between worlds" telepathy, and that he is by no means the only one.

Wilma has told A.J. that many people who have died in any community, have remained in the area for a time, and that he or anyone who possessed "psychic sight" could see them all around, on the city sidewalks and strolling in the midst of highways, paying no attention to cars which seemingly pass right through them.

This reminded me of an experience I had as a young man in Detroit when my heart momentarily stopped during an operation, due to an overdose of chloroform. I found myself floating against the ceiling, looking down on the operating table, where I was joined by my brother Edward, who had died some six years before. I was, of course, surprised to see him and asked him what he was doing here—since he was supposed to be dead. Edward simply smiled and said he had come to take me with him. This shocked me and I asked: "Does this mean that I am dead, too?" I got no answer. Then I said: "Edward, I can't die now. Why, Dad and Mother don't even know that I'm being operated on." (For the lancing of a gangrenous toe.)

As I said this, I blacked out and found myself walking down Front Street in my home town of Traverse City, Michigan, three hundred miles away. I was headed for my father's men's clothing store, passing people on the street, and I felt as physical as they looked to be. As I turned in to the "Sherman & Hunter Company," and started down the center aisle, I saw my father's partner, Fred Hunter, waiting on a customer. I waved at him. He seemed to be looking my direction but he didn't see me.

Dad was in his office at the back of the store, working on the books, his back to me. I came up behind him, calling, "Hi, Dad, this is Harold. I'm home!" I put my hand on his shoulder and my arm passed right through him. I couldn't understand this—it gave me a shock reaction. As I repeated my greeting to Dad, I bent over so I could look him in the face. He pushed his chair back, unseeing, stood up and stretched and walked over to the window, overlooking Grand Traverse Bay. I followed him, still trying to attract his attention. "Dad, this is Harold. I'm home!" Once more I put my arm around him and it again seemed to pass through his shoulders. Now I was deeply concerned. Something was wrong. I thought of Mother in our family home, 439 Webster Street, six blocks away . . . and I immediately blacked out and found myself in the living room. It was late afternoon, I could hear mother in the kitchen, getting dinner. No sooner thought of the kitchen than I was there. Mother was peeling some potatoes at the sink. I crossed over to her, put my arm around her, and said: "Hi, Mother . . . this is Harold. I'm home!" My arm went right through her.

That did it, this time. I pulled back, blacked out and the next thing I knew I was in the Detroit office of Dr. Garner. He and his assistant, a dentist friend who had administered the chloroform, together with the nurse, had been trying to revive me . . . I was breathing heavily and the room was going around crazily. But I was beginning to get my bearings . . . and was able to recall vividly my out-of-body experience which had taken me to see my folks in Traverse City . . . and also to seemingly know what had been happening to my body on the operating table. When I recovered enough to tell Dr. Garner about it, he said since I had had such an accurate knowledge of the time they had had restoring me, how could he doubt that I had actually had an astral projection? A letter to Dad and Mother confirmed their whereabouts and actions at the moment I felt I was with them.

I feel that this out-of-body experience has been worth re-telling because it has helped me, through the years, to understand and accept many similar experiences others have had. I am presuming the feeling is not too different when death of the physical body occurs and one finds himself in the spirit body.

Realizing this, it should not be too difficult to imagine that we are probably surrounded by invisible spirit entities who are going about the business of living in a dimension closely akin to ours. A.J. is told, and has evidence, that he is seldom alone—that earthbound spirits who are attracted through the vibration of his voice, are passing through, making momentary contact with him on subconscious levels, exchanging thoughts and feelings, often without conscious awareness.

In a remarkable book named OAHSPE, purportedly dictated to Dr. John Ballou Newbrough, American psychic medium, in the year 1881, by Higher Intelligences, an account is given of the lower and higher "heaven worlds" and their relationship to living mortals on planet earth. Do not let the form of expression disturb you. Read for the knowledge contained which seems to confirm what we have come to know since this book was written, with respect to higher dimensions of existence and especially the earthbound conditions.

"The Lower Heavens travel with the earth around the sun, called by some 'the intermediate worlds' . . . through which heavens all souls must pass, being first purified and risen in wisdom, before they can inherit the emancipated worlds in the Higher Heavens of Etherea.

"Nor are these revelations for mortals only, but to thousands of millions of the spirits of the dead, who know not the plan of Ascension to the Higher Heavens; but who wander about on the earth, not even knowing the organizations of the kingdoms in the Lowest of Heavens.

"For many who have died believe the heavens

to be an unorganized wilderness, void of government and instruction and discipline.

"And by virtue of their presence with mortals, though *invisible* to them, do inspire mortals with the same darkness.

"The time shall surely come when all things will be revealed to the inhabitants of the earth . . . who will then be able to read the books in the libraries of these heavens and learn to know of their own knowledge."

Wilma and Jason have told A.J. that they have visited these libraries and have seen, projected on vast screens, in pictorial form, scenes of past events on earth, knowledge beyond description, which they do not possess the capacity to describe, and which must await the arrival of any spirit to begin to comprehend.

Many religious-minded people have reported out-of-body experiences to me wherein they feel they have had glimpses of the "heaven worlds" and have been comforted and assured by them. Their minds can easily have been conditioned by their Bible studies and beliefs so that some imaginative coloring may have resulted—but there still seems to have been little doubt that the psychic experience was basically involved.

Here is a typical such case described by a long-time friend, Rev. Harold Hayward, retired Methodist minister, in this own words:

"As a young minister I was afraid of death. So I began to ask God to reveal to me what death was really like, so I could help other people.

"It was the 12th of August, 1946, at four o'clock in the morning, that I was sitting in my chair meditating on this question of death, when I found myself becoming very heavy. Every part of my body was like hundreds of pounds of weight. The only thing I could compare it with was when a person was dying, they would say that they were so very, very tired. So I said to the Lord, 'Okay—if this is death, I am ready.'

"Immediately, I was out of my body and as I was going through the ceiling, I looked back and saw my body lying in the chair. A hand seized me and I went through the air at terrific speed. The only way I can compare it with is like a Genie in a movie, going through the sky.

"A voice said, 'shut your eyes,' but I didn't and found myself going through a tunnel which was very dark, coming into a gray color, then to a lighter shade, into green, brown to gold, then into WHITE which grew and grew in intensity, but it was not blinding.

"I found myself in a meadow, with all kinds of flowers, up to my knees. In fact, I was walking on flowers, but did not crush them. In the distance there was a great city, but the ecstacy was so great, I could not contain it, so I cried: 'I can't take any more of this!' and suddenly came to in my physical body in the chair.

"On the way, I had seen enough of the Life Beyond to know that there is no death, and the glories which I encountered were beyond anything that my eyes had seen or my ears heard, or had ever entered into my mind.

"Since I am a Bible student, I wanted to find out if there was any place in the Bible that could confirm my experience, and I came upon this passage from the writings of Apostle Paul:" (2—Corinthians, 5-1, King James)

"For we know that if our earthly house of this tabernacle were dissolved, we have a building of

God, an House not made with hands, eternal in the heavens."

"That satisfied me as far as Body and Life in the After Life was concerned. As a result of this spiritual experience, I have had no fear and have been able to help many, many people when loved ones were gone from their presence. I am absolutely convinced there is no death."

I have respect for my friend, Rev. Harold Hayward's convictions and this may well be the interpretation of many of the more orthodox Christian believers. However, our Survival Research goes beyond the evidence represented by religious experience, in an attempt to bring Science and Religion closer together.

There seems every indication now that survival from physical death is a universal plan of Creation which applies to all grades and levels of human consciousness, irrespective of religious faith. Even so, higher spiritual development appears to dictate or determine the quality and character of life in the Next Dimension.

If you can visualize landscapes somewhat similar to those on earth—beautiful countrysides, mountains, lakes, waterfalls, flowing streams, forests, flower gardens, pastures, and areas containing great auditoriums, outdoor amphitheatres, libraries, rehabilitation centers, laboratories, unusual industries, educational institutions, information halls, a variety of homes—almost anything mind can conceive—perhaps you will find them all in the dimensions awaiting you in the Next Existence.

Certainly, more and more people in every country, who have had near death experiences, are returning to tell of realistic spirit adventures in surroundings of this nature. Can it all be imagination?

Quite often people are reporting dreams which they feel have been more than dreams—quite possibly out-of-body experiences wherein they have been transported to some "place of learning" or some "inspiring event" which they have a vague recollection of having attended in company with a friend or loved one.

NO DEATH, ONLY TRANSFORMATION

Another minister, Rev. William E. Achor, Founder of the Science of Spirituality, Inc., P.O. Box 2202, Winter Haven, Florida, 33880, shares with me the same concepts of "life after death" and has provided a fitting climax to this chapter, in his inspired and logically presented words:

Many questions have come my way recently regarding death, death experiences, and life beyond death. So often death is considered to be a morbid subject, something *not* to talk about, something from which we need to shield our loved ones.

How much more harmonious it would be, if we could but recognize that death is another step in the process of living, a natural and necessary step in our soul's progress in life—eternal life.

It might be compared to entering school for the first time, like going away to college, and like leaving our family home to start our independent life. Each of these changes is a metamorphosis in the progression of our earthly life.

These steps in living are very traumatic experiences for many children; those who have been closely bound to their home, to their family dependency; or who have been shielded from their

168

growth of independence, sheltered from responsibility and from the natural life changes. With each of these transitions, the former self dies, although the characteristics are carried on, the individual is the same, but with new freedoms and responsibilities.

If we have been taught of death as a natural release from a particular limited existence; if we were taught to expect it as a freeing experience; then that is what it would be. Then perhaps we would not fear this experience of transition and would not then pass this fear along to our loved ones. Then all of us would find the transition to be an easier and more peaceful experience.

If we truly accept the continuity of life, then there is no death, only transformation. If we truly accept the unity of all being, then there is no separation with death—only a different mode of living—and a different mode of communication. I understand that the loss of communication may be the main source of regret, the major sense of loss in the death of a loved one.

We are basically oriented to communicating only through the five physical senses and this mode of communication is mostly lost with death. There are higher, more expanded, octaves of the five senses, however, through which we may perceive and communicate non-physically; and this happens more frequently and to more people than you might think.

When I chose to leave the company where I was working during my final years in industry, one of the men in my department came into my office to talk. He knew the kind of work I was to be entering. He asked me what I would do if my dead mother kept showing up and telling me what I should do about this, that, and the other thing; telling me how I should live my life, really nagging me about it.

I explained to him that when a person dies, they are still alive and are still the same person. If a woman was trying to run her grown son's life when she was in the physical, then, if she could get through from the next realm, she would still be telling him what to do. I further explained that I believe a maturing man—or woman—should tell a "living" mother who is persistently meddling, to stop it. "Well ... your mother *is* still living," I told him. "She just isn't in the physical body anymore." Then I told him that if it were *my* mother, I would tell her, "Mom, you've lived *your* life here. Now it's time for me to live *my* life here, as I choose to live it. You are welcome to visit, but I want to make my own choices, my own decisions; so please get on with what you have to do there and stop interfering." My associate said, "That's what I finally did, and she has left me alone; but I've felt guilty about it ever since, and that was several years ago."

I suspect every one of you have had communications with someone who has passed beyond the physical earth plane of existence. It may occur as simply a feeling of their presence; it may be prefaced by a particular scent that you associate with that person, so that your awareness of their presence may be aroused. They may appear to you in dreams and visit with you in that media, because there it is most acceptable to you. (Dream visits are most complete because our inhibitors seem to sleep, too; at least some of them. Besides, we *can* pass it off as "just a dream" if we are not ready to acknowledge its reality.) Or, they may "appear" to you in a form of physical being; almost always happier, healthier, and usually younger looking. Or they may communicate through thought transference or in audible voice (audible only to you). But it *is* the one you knew (know). They are communicating, or trying to, and your aware-

170

ness of them may be as real as though they were
alive. **THEY ARE ALIVE, THEY ARE HERE,
THEY CAN AND DO COMMUNICATE.**

CLEARING OLD DEBTS

Many people say, 'If only I had treated him
differently . . . If only I had forgiven him . . . or
sought forgiveness . . . or visited with him . . . expressed my appreciation, *etc.* . . . and now it is too
late. He's gone!'
IT IS NOT TOO LATE! HE IS NOT GONE!
Those of the realm just beyond our physical earth
presence have not lost touch with the world in
which we find ourselves. They are far more aware
of the things and people of this world than you
and I; if they choose to be. They have more flex-
ibility of movement through time and space, and
through thought perceptions, than we have in our
earthly existence. They are in no way blocked
from seeing us, or communicating with us. It is
we who cannot normally see them, or hear them,
or sense their being.
So if you have felt badly about not having communicated something to someone who is now
dead, stop feeling guilty about it and simply tune
in to that person in your thoughts and, in
thought, express your feelings, your love. Forgive
them, or accept their forgiveness, as the case may
be; and *know they are hearing you.* They perceive
more than your thoughts; they may also sense
your true motives and attitudes, so they really
receive and understand your communication. If
you do this in a meditative state and have established a close attunement with that person, you
may very well sense their response. When you
know you have communicated, you can then let
go of your sense of guilt. That memory is healed.
You have freed a block, released a burden, from

within yourself; and at the same time you may have released a similar block within the consciousness of the person with whom you communicated. It is a blessing and an added freedom to both of you.

FINISHING OUR ASSIGNMENT

We had best respect our physical existence here in this earth realm; and not be overly anxious to transform into the world beyond; lest we stunt the beauty of our butterfly self, and restrict our next phase of living.

Some tend to look on death as an escape from their circumstances—*it's not!* Since life is on-going, since life continues, then the circumstances we have drawn to us continue to be drawn to us. *Life truly is on-going!* We leave the physical body behind, but we retain our attitudes, beliefs, and emotional patterns; we are still the same person! We are neither more saintly nor more evil; we are the *same* being! Our consciousness is our being, and the consciousness is intact, we simply do not have a physical body as we understand it.

If people really understood this, there would be a lot fewer suicides. Suicide is an attempt to escape from life; which is impossible. The progress of the Suicide's soul evolvement is deferred for some time as a result. (The time involved is dependent on the motives and the magnitude of the inharmonies that we created.) That person is then bound to the experience and environment of his suicide. His emotions and feelings remain, but now he will need to observe the consequences of his act and suffer whatever agonies he created in the lives of others. At the same time he is helpless to communicate his feelings, helpless to change the scene. Loving forgiveness and prayer can help free these Suicides from their suffering, so that they may more quickly proceed in their process of learning, so they may once more take up their path for Spiritual growth.

SPIRITUAL LIVING

There are some who do not experience death; not even dying. Their continuity of life is so well accepted, their focus on living is so complete (regardless of outward appearances), that they pass easily and peacefully from this realm to the next with no loss—no gap—in their consciousness. These are spiritually aware people, people unafraid of living. HOPEFULLY I AM ONE ! JC

Suicides I have known !

Bill Friedman PISTOL
Chuck Pranlee — PISTOL
Winn Strickland * AIDS
Ben Shomphers * alkie
Guy Curtis VW - ALKIE
Danny Carroll AIDS
Ryan carroll MC

Chapter 13

MY ASTRAL PROJECTION
EXPERIENCE

Everyone dreams at one time or another, and there are some dreams which cause us to wonder how they could possibly have originated. They are so vivid and so real with sound and feeling and sight, that they appear to be more than dreams, and quite possibly they are.

On some occasions, we may have actually left our physical bodies and been projected astrally—in our spirit form—into another dimension. Once there, we have seemed to be attending a school of some sort or participating in an experience taking place at that moment, surrounded by other people, either known or unknown, but usually in the company of those who have left this life.

For some years, I have privately kept a little notebook which is filled with recordings of such "beyond-the-usual" dreams, which, upon awakening, I have dictated to Martha. I have found that, if I remain in the "twilight zone of consciousness" and do not let my-

174

self fully awaken, and if I can arouse Martha so that she can get out of bed, grab our notepad, and let me start describing what has happened, that I can re-dream it and recall most of it. Sometimes I can remember whole conversations as well as scenes.

It is one such "dream" that I have decided to relate to you now and let you judge whether or not, this time, I had actually been out of my body. So that you can get the full significance of it, I need to fill you in on the character and background of the deceased personality involved.

His name was Harry Barnhart. He was a large, magnificent figure of a man, with a dome-like, bald head, impressive features, great natural poise, broad-shouldered and broadchested, with a powerful baritone singing voice—so powerful that when he was called upon to Open Soldiers' Field in Chicago and lead a crowd of one hundred thousand people in a "community sing," he cut off the microphone, stood a lone figure in a white suit on the stage and projected his great voice by itself into the farthest reaches of the stadium!

In the early 1900's, Harry Barnhart, then a steel worker in the Carnegie Steel Mills in Pittsburgh, had organized and trained and conducted a mighty chorus of 200 steel workers, who toured the country, under Carnegie sponsorship, presenting concerts which thrilled the nation.

Later, this inspired song leader went to New York City seeking the fulfillment of a vision, "I Hear America Singing," and secured permission of the Mayor to place a piano on the bandstand of the Mall in Central Park, and with the aid of a woman pianist, invited the strollers in the park, each Sunday afternoon, to join him in singing old, traditional folk songs like "Auld Lang Syne," "Battle Hymn of the Republic," and "Home Sweet Home."

These "community sings," embracing people of all

175

races and colors, were an immediate success and soon developed into Sunday night musicals which attracted thousands who sang with great and joyous spirit.

I first met Harry in the early nineteen-twenties, when I came to New York in search of a writing career. I was later to serve as manager of his Great American Eagle Band, comprised largely of ex-Sousa band members, during the days of the Great Depression.

It was while I was associated with Harry; on a part-time assignment, that I wrote a little published pamphlet, which I titled: "This Must All Come to Pass," describing a tremendous vision that had come to Harry at the height of one of his "Song and Light Festivals." The vision has proved to have been prophetic, applying, as it does, to conditions in the world today, and because it relates to my "out-of-body experience" which took place some years later, after Harry had left this earth, I am reproducing it here:

A man of prophetic vision stood upon a platform in the center of Central Park's lagoon near Seventy-second Street, New York City. All about him was the soft, inky blackness of a warm summer night, the blackness dotted by vari-colored lantern lights, strung from the trees around the rim of water, hung from the lamp posts along the walks and by-paths, and adorning boats that drifted about the mirrored surface of the lake like lazy fireflies.

This man raised an electrically-lighted baton and from out of the darkness swelled the music of a hundred piece orchestra. He turned in another direction and the baton, as if by magic, brought fifteen hundred human voices into being. The lagoon, a gigantic sounding board, sent the harmony of sound reverberating into the consciousness of a hundred thousand people, massed under cover of the night on every surrounding elevation down to the very edge of the water itself.

Harry Barnhart, originator of singing in the army camps and first to introduce community singing in America, had begun the conducting of his famous "Song and Light" Festivals in Central Park.

But tonight, the tenth of September in the year nineteen hundred and seventeen, was to mark the final Festival of the season. It would also mark the last occasion for some thousands of soldier boys who were grouped on the plaza at the north end of the Mall across the lagoon from the host of singers.

On the morrow, these sons of America would embark for France on a voyage from which many would never return. And the atmosphere seemed charged with a tremendous, heartfelt something ... an inexpressible inner emotion that went out to these men beneath the influence of this eery-throated music. It seemed as though the mantle of night had glorified the invisible singers, giving them the quality of heavenly voices, and enabling them to lift the consciousness of the vast unseen audience until a hundred thousand human souls felt themselves to be in the awe-inspiring presence of the Infinite.

Quite unconsciously these hundred thousand had been blended into one ... and the at-one-ness had blotted out all ungodly thoughts of hate, greed and passion—the unspeakable inhumanity of man to man. For this most precious of moments, Eternity kissed the upturned face of beggar, thief and saint—recognizing no essential difference—and making each tolerantly aware that all were indeed God's children ... mere mortals clumsily seeking the door to Immortality ... a spirited release from this world of sorrow and striving—a world created by themselves.

177

A few there were amid this assembled throng who sensed and were capable of interpreting this mighty heart throb . . . but for the great majority there occurred a buoyant lifting up—as though an almost overpowering electrical current had been closed, which, when released, left within an indescribable hunger . . . a hunger for higher and finer things . . . a peculiar unsatisfied attitude toward themselves which, in the light of this new soul experience amounted to self-condemnation.

Music, the true language of the soul, was delivering its profoundly moving message to each human heart, cleansing the sordid thoughts of men, opening up the dried up well springs of the spirit and awakening individuals to the existence of a vital, unearthly something within . . . a force which properly nourished and developed might transform and radiate their lives.

And Harry Barnhart, directing genius of this soul-stirring phenomena, alone on his platform in the middle of the lagoon, was charged with the ebb and flow of the vital current being generated by the hundred thousand vibrating to one harmonious unit of expression. The program had risen, by transcendent degrees, to the last number, the deeply loved hymn, "Nearer, My God, to Thee." And this number was to be sung, not alone by the trained chorus of fifteen hundred voices, but by the entire multitude of one hundred thousand.

Like a mammoth organ, pouring forth its majestically pulsating notes, came the response to the movement of his lighted baton, appearing as a rhythmic spark in the blackness of the lake . . . "Nearer, My God, to Thee . . . !"

But now, between the swelling words of the hymn, there came to Mr. Barnhart's sensitively attuned ears, a new sound . . . the sound of marching feet . . . terse military commands . . . "One, two, three, four . . . Hip! Hip! . . . one, two,

178

three, four! . . . Still all my song shall be Nearer, My God, to Thee! . . . one, two, three, four . . ." The soldiers were leaving . . . leaving ahead of the crowd . . . his boys . . . boys he had schooled to sing in the army camps . . . boys, singing as they marched, "Nearer, My God, to Thee" . . . going forth to war.

It all suddenly seemed so incredible . . . so fantastic . . . so humanly inconceivable in that uplifted moment . . . that humans still hated and sought to kill one another. . . . The great soul of Harry Barnhart was suddenly torn by an overwhelming emotion. An agony of feeling possessed him as he strove to balance the higher spiritual attainment of the instant against the pull of marching feet . . . the realization that his boys were disappearing in that black void before him—vacating their reserved section, guns shouldered so that bayonets glistened above heads that could not be seen—bayonets gleaming through the spray from the lighted Bethesda Fountain . . . water leaping and playing in the myriad rays of color as if to soften the sharp points of steel . . . boys marching off to ships that would carry them into a hell on earth . . . and, quite possibly into another kind of darkness . . . "Darkness be over me . . . my rest a stone . . . Yet in my dreams I'd be . . ."

Footsteps—rank on rank—the muffled, rhythmic shuffle of feet—an old rhythm now—a worldly rhythm . . . the old rhythm of hate . . . "Nearer, My God, to Thee" . . . marching feet . . . growing more faint . . . "Sun, moon and stars forgot" . . . distant voices, one, two, three, four . . . Hip! Hip! . . . one, two three . . . "Still all my song shall be . . . Nearer, My God, to Thee . . ."

They were gone, his boys . . . fearless, resolute . . . passing out and on with a song on their lips . . . "Nearer to Thee!"

And with their going, as the last echoes of the

hymn died out, leaving an awesome God-like stillness, the lighted baton fell from Mr. Barnhart's hand. He was caught up and held, rigid, as though by an unseen force. Before him, the blackness melted into a dazzling light ... and there came to him a vision—a vision so vivid, so detailed, and so awe-inspiring that, when it was over, the conductor of the "Song and Light" Festival pitched unconscious on his face.

Friends, reaching the platform, placed his body in a rowboat and bore him ashore, thinking that he had collapsed from exhaustion ... the strain of leading so great and so thrilling a song program. But only Mr. Barnhart knew what had occurred as he lay, scarcely conscious, for two whole days ... living and re-living the vision he had seen. And because there were few who placed any credence in visions, Mr. Barnhart has revealed little of what he saw, except to several intimate and understanding friends. These friends, however, have been able to confirm different events as they have come to pass and are now witnessing happenings throughout the world depicted by Mr. Barnhart, years ago.

The result of this vision was to change Mr. Barnhart's entire trend of life. Since nineteen hundred and seventeen he has prepared himself for the new work that he saw himself doing in the great world crisis ... a work so important and so crucial that it dwarfed anything he had done heretofore.

Just as in the "Song and Light" Festivals, Mr. Barnhart dealt with a quality of musical appeal which reached the heart of humanity. Now—in the New Day he felt to be dawning, he was equipped, through the Great American Eagle Band to rally a dismayed and unsettled people, helping them build and sustain a new consciousness which would give them the strength to meet whatever was to come.

Believing profoundly in not only the wisdom but the necessity for a "singing people," Harry Barnhart had introduced a singing property in the band music which characterized every number and lended to it a symphonic effect. One of America's outstanding music critics, hearing the band in rehearsal, was so carried away by it as to declare: "Harry Barnhart has developed not only the greatest band in America, but, without doubt, the greatest band in the world." A well known English composer ventured the prediction: "This band will be an instantaneous sensation, once introduced to the country. I know of no band this size or quality in the world today."

THE FULFILLMENT OF THE PROPHECY

Harry Barnhart's vision had foreseen the coming Stock Market Crash in 1929, when banks were closed and the Great Depression followed with panics and suicides and searing hardship suffered by all classes and the WPA was instituted to put millions back to work. It was in those days that I, as a much younger man, came to know Harry Barnhart and marched with Harry, in his resplendent white suit, at the head of his Great American Eagle Band of a hundred pieces, which led the mammoth WPA parade up Fifth Avenue, New York, witnessed by several million hopeful citizens who were trying to recover their economic morale.

But Harry had seen beyond the Great Depression and the looming of a Second World War to days when conditions would be even worse before they could get better, and I had written about this vision in 1933, when the little pamphlet, "This Must All Come to Pass," now yellowed with age, was published.

The premiere of this band took place in the Grand Ball Room of the new Waldorf-Astoria Hotel, in a series of hour long, Sunday afternoon concert nation-wide radio broadcasts, sponsored by General Foods, with White Eagle, famous Indian baritone as the featured singer.

It was Harry's dream that this would be followed by "community sings" in the great stadiums of the country, with hundreds of thousands participating, but Harry did not live long enough for this to be achieved.

Harry had said that, "A nation and a world that is spiritually sick cannot solve its material problems until the spiritual ills are corrected. Man-made laws have only served to further involve and entangle man. Our mechanical world has been thrown in reverse gear. Mother Nature has yielded abundant crops and yet millions are starving. Civilization has made a mockery of its supposed cultural advancement. If to 'civilize' means 'to reclaim from savagery,' what greater savagery can be imagined today than the universal distrust of our fellow man, the savage conquest for money which leaves millions destitute, the savage preparation to take wealth by violence, if it cannot be attained by financial manipulation, all of which points to more savagery in the form of another great war."

It should now be clear in this present day, that Mr. Barnhart's vision of a coming cataclysm is not without foundation. The evidence of an imminent debacle is upon every hand. It does not take a prophet now to read the signs of the times. Human greed, piled up and intensified through centuries of like greed, will not die of its own accord. It is becoming more and more evident that it must be expurgated by a calamitous happening, so terrifying and so devastating as to bring about in human consciousness, an entirely new standard of values. Then, only, can this standard of values be made to exist in the world. Until such a time, the well meant efforts of politicians and educators are destined to fail since the success of any New Era depends upon the will of the masses. And if the consciousness of the people is not prepared and elevated to a new plane of living, the people cannot be made to accept any new standard of values or put them in operation.

These thoughts came to Harry Barnhart in the early years of this century. He responded to them as best he could, foreseeing a time when money would take on a different and a higher valuation ... and when the medium of exchange would lift instead of submerging humanity ... when the real spirit of man, hitherto unreleased throughout all the ages of history, would be liberated. Real joy has, in itself, never been known to the world. Real joy cannot be known, according to Harry Barnhart, until this real spirit of man is liberated.

History, in the main, has thus far been a recording of wars and rumors of wars, with humanity in one part of the world or another, undergoing great tribulation. The history of the future, will, however, record a day of genuine peace and good will among men. It is this day that Harry Barnhart has envisaged ... a day not so far off as present world conditions would make it seem.

MY VISIT WITH HARRY BARNHART
IN THE WORLD BEYOND(?)

In the early morning of December 6, 1965, I had one of the most unusual psychic experiences of my life. My remembrance of this spiritual adventure is just as vivid and real to me now as my memory of any physical happening I have ever had. I think, when you have read the account, that you will feel it is not likely I could ever have imagined it. Here it is, in the exact words as I dictated it to Martha:

Harold awakened Martha at 2:30 A.M. having had one of his unusual "dream" experiences.

He seemed to have been taken to a vast amphitheatre which could accommodate untold millions of people. Some great event was to take place and there was an air of great expectation on the part of those assembled. But it was the most unusual assembly of human creatures H had ever seen.

It was made up of the down-and-outers, the misfits, the degenerates, the insane and psychotic, the crazed, the confused, the dazed, the religious fanatics, the hate mongers, the primitives, the embattled, the alcoholics and dope addicts of every race and color, known and unknown. All were there, held by some strange spell that had been put upon them.

H was in the company of some friends who had "gone on," whom he regrets he cannot recall. They seemed so familiar and so well known at the time, and were so interested in his observing this event. They said he had been brought there for that purpose and to meet one person he knew, in particular.

H looked about him at this strange and ghastly assemblage, but he saw in each face, however carnal or distraught, a look of deep yearning, as though each entity was somehow seeking release from conditions it had either brought upon itself or had had imposed upon it. No one was paying any attention to H. The interest of this multitude had somehow been captured by the impending event.

H saw before him a stupendous arena bathed in vari-colored light which seemed to billow like a mist. Suddenly, he heard music in the distance, and as it grew in volume, marching figures became visible. The curtain of clouds lifted. A great band was playing, but in advance of this band, H beheld a horde of flag-bearers. There must have been thousands—and each flag was different—flags H had never seen before—flags of nations and rulers long since vanished from this earth.

The flag-bearers separated, right and left, and formed a mammoth circle around the great arena, so the tremendous band of musicians now could be seen. It was all so tremendous in size and H saw a variety of instruments he could not recognize.

The ranks of the band now parted and H saw the personage he had been brought to see approaching. He was a resplendent figure of a man, attired in a dazzling white suit and, accompanying him in full regalia, was a handsome Indian. The man was Harry Barnhart. He continued approaching H in the company of his Indian friend, and H saw behind him, a mammoth chorus following.

But now the scene appeared to be close-up and H was in the presence of Harry and the Indian. Harry's face was radiant and he greeted H with all the oldtime affection. He said: "Well, Harold, you finally made it. I've been looking forward to your visit for a long time!"

Then it seemed that H became aware that this was Harry's mission—conducting these gigantic "Community Sings" as a part of a tremendous rehabilitation program that was continually taking place.

Harry explained that the Indians who had played such a part in the earth's history were assisting in the rounding up and assembling of these earthbound souls. The Indian who accompanied him was "White Eagle," the Indian who had sung as soloist with Harry's Great American Eagle Band, which had been composed largely of ex-Sousa members and which H had previously managed.

Harry said that the only way many of these souls could be reached was through the vibration

185

of music which established a new rhythmic tone in their consciousness and helped remove the discords of past life experiences.

H became conscious that there were many experienced helpers and associates working with Harry—great numbers of them—intermingled with the vast assemblage which contained millions who had passed from earth life thousands of years before, but who were represented, in one way or another, by the flags and standard bearers in the arena.

H was led to his seat of honor where he could behold the program. Harry parted from him after an affectionate bear-hug and was whisked away to a beautiful, elevated platform where he appeared to be magnified to gigantic size—a tremendous white figure with baton, easily seen by the millions upon millions present. The music swelled and the opening chorus of praise and adoration to Jehovah struck instantly into the heart and soul of everyone present.

The music was too transcendent, too moving in its effect upon all present for H to stand, and he awakened with the memory of this experience which he has now recounted.

Chapter 14

SPIRIT COMMUNICATION
BY TELEPHONE

My first knowledge of the Spirit medium, Freda Fell, came to me through the scientist, Dr. L.K. of Palos Verdes, California, who wrote me, as follows:

Dear Mr. Sherman:

With interest I read your book YOU LIVE AFTER DEATH. Answering your request to write you about the cases which support the hypothesis of "life after death," I have to describe to you the following.

My very dear wife passed away five months ago. We loved each other so very much and I had several very colorful dreams since her death when I seemed to be with her—but dreams are dreams.

Yesterday, however, I attended a symposium, given by known medium, Freda Fell from Canada (previously England). I never saw her before. I did not even know anybody in the audience. At once she interrupted her talk and looked at me.

187

"Did you lose somebody near to you during the last couple of months?" "Yes," I answered.

"There is a lady here who shows me a ring ... she is your wife ... She said she was not suffering by dying ... and now she is okay—and very happy."

It was a big surprise to me. Because it stirred me so deeply emotionally, I left the room. When the meeting was resumed, she again said to me: "The lady is still here. She says that January was the difficult month ... the operation. In February her parents from Yugoslavia came and the sickness was getting better. In June, when they left, the sickness turned worse, and at the end of August, she passed over, without pain.

"She shows me for some reason her hair—and asks me to tell you it is now okay. She also says you have someone playing the violin. She is very happy now ... she died from cancer. You can be assured she is here with us."

I understand why she pointed to her hair. During her sickness, due to medication, she lost her hair completely. *She was buried in a wig.* Everything Freda Fell told me was perfectly correct. There is no doubt that this medium could not have known all the details ... and certainly nothing about myself. A friend of mine, an M.D. who was present, was equally as surprised as I was. We both are studying unusual psychic phenomena these last two years. *The violin reference* had to do with my sister.

To me it proves that the soul not only survives, but also found energy to come to me and to tell me she is okay. You are right in your book when you state that this is the law—and life has no borders or limits. Please excuse me for my bad English—it is not my native language and I do not have the time to correct this letter with the dictionary.

Sincerely,
L.K.

You can be sure that I lost little time making contact with Freda Fell and learning more about her unusual psychic background. She told me that she had been born in London, England, now living in Vancouver, B.C. and had always been psychic since a little girl. She thought that everyone had a communicative ability—able to *sense* and *hear* and sometimes *see* those who had gone on. She just seemed to know, lots of times, what her parents and others had been thinking and doing—and often surprised them by remarking about things that she shouldn't have known about.

When her grandfather and Aunt died, their spirits often joined the family at tea time, and Freda talked to them as though they were physically present, and also played with children, whom she insisted were there. This usually caused her to be charged with a high imagination or lying.

During the Second World War when London was being bombed, Freda, then between eight and nine, would refuse to go to the air raid shelters. One night in particular, her mother and neighbors tried to force her to go to the shelter in Kensington Park with them but she struggled against it, claiming she was being told it would be safer to remain at home. Her mother finally stayed out of the shelter with her and that night the shelter was subjected to a direct hit and many were buried and killed.

Freda has been married twice, divorced the first time, mother of three children, a daughter and a son, now living in England. Her first baby, a boy, died after four and a half months; is now fully grown and matured in the spirit world, a son who communicates with her occasionally, and recognizes her as his earth mother.

A saintly elderly woman, famous trance medium, with whom Freda around the age of 28, conducted healing services, told her she was a "natural medium," who was destined to be of help to humanity after she had completed her family raising responsibilities, gave her the courage and confidence to enter public life. Freda has traveled various parts of the world since then bringing inspiration and comfort to thousands who have sought the assurance of life after death and communication with departed loved ones.

Freda has trained herself to give expression to whatever feelings come to her or whatever the spirit entities say to her without reservation. She is insistent that people who come for "sittings" must be prepared to accept whatever spirits choose to appear, whether the visitation is welcome or not.

For example, a young woman made an appointment with Freda, having certain deceased persons in mind from whom she hoped to hear. The first spirit to manifest was her grandmother on her father's side, to whom she was violently opposed. It seems that this grandmother had made life miserable for her mother and she did not want to have anything to do with her "alive or dead."

"If you don't want your grandmother to speak to you," said Freda, "there is no use going any further. I have no control over the spirit friends or loved ones who want to come through me, and I won't close the door to any of them. They each have the right to have their say. So, if you are opposed to your grandmother, for some family reason, we might as well terminate this session right now."

The granddaughter reluctantly agreed to go ahead, whereupon the grandmother proceeded to unburden her long pent-up feelings of regret and remorse for the way she had acted toward her mother, asking forgiveness. A long-standing family feud was not only cleared up but a personal problem which had been troubling the granddaughter. When she left the "sitting," she was relieved in mind and heart.

"So often," said Freda, "when people get on the Other Side, they see their past life in another light, and yearn for the opportunity to right certain wrongs or make amends for what they have done. Usually, this chance isn't afforded, because not many channels of communication are open to them.

"I get many suicide cases, and I am asked if persons who take their lives are not punished or penalized in any way. Yes, quite a few regret their acts and wish they had their lives to live over again—but others are happy to be free from the pains and crippled conditions they may have suffered. I feel each individual suicide should be judged by the motivation behind it—and that we should never condemn. We just cannot tell what combination of forces have brought on a tragic ending."

One of the most astounding things that Freda does is to communicate with spirit entities on radio and TV programs in answer to telephone calls coming in from all parts of the country, some as far as several thousand miles away. Time and distance are apparently no barrier. All she needs is to hear the sound of the caller's voice—and this contact with the "voice vibration" is sufficient to place Freda's consciousness in touch with all the family links necessary for communication.

Here is the introduction to one of these live radio broadcasts, made by Interviewer Terry More of station CJOR, Vancouver, B.C.:

"Our guest today is Freda Fell. She is a clairvoyant or spiritual medium, if you will. She is a woman who is able to ... I don't know, though, what powers or ability she has . . . she says . . . to communicate with the Spirit World. Certainly to make contact—in some way or other—to reveal to people some things about themselves . . . and about the people who have been in their past lives—or people who have maybe passed away.

"Now, something I want you to understand when we do the program this afternoon—Freda Fell is not a fortune teller . . . she is not the type of person to whom you phone and say, 'What shall I do with my stock?' . . . Or, 'Shall I sell my house?' . . . No, she is a spiritual medium . . . and she deals with things that have gone on in one's life . . . people that have affected one's life . . . but she is NOT a fortune teller. So, don't phone her, ask her to give you any advice about what you're supposed to do or how is your health, or anything of that nature. That's not what she does. I really don't know what she does . . . but it certainly happens, whatever it is . . . Now, after all this, we come to you, Freda . . . Are you ready to go to the telephone?"

    FREDA: Yes, I am—but you know, Terry, there are a lot of people out there who have had their own experiences . . . and sometimes it can upset them because they don't realize what is happening . . .

    TERRY: I realize that, for sure.

    FREDA: This is sad because they cause themselves an unnecessary lot of anxiety . . . and I think if it were explained to them in a rational way, they'd realize there is nothing wrong with them . . . that they were perfectly all right when these things did happen.

    TERRY: A lot of people are very afraid of this kind of contact that you make . . .

    FREDA: Exactly.

    TERRY: It's amazing. Even the people who state that they don't believe in it, are the ones who are the greatest opponents of it.

FREDA: You are so right.

TERRY: I have come across many people who I thought were reasonably rational human beings ... who had a degree of tolerance in many areas ... who hear of the kind of things that you do—or talk to people who are involved in the area of spiritual medium work ... or whatever ... and they immediately turn around and say: "What a bunch of garbage!"

FREDA: Yes, yes—I know ...

TERRY: They are directly opposed to it and part of the opposition is the fact that there is a degree of fear on their part ...

FREDA: This is true, but as I say—I don't think there is a person living who has not had some form of experience ... or something in that way ... that they have not been able to explain ...

TERRY: The old instinctive response ... All right—let's go to the phones. They are all lighted up like Christmas trees!

Characteristic of this fantastic type of spirit communication by telephone which Freda Fell has conducted for so long, in so many countries and cities—the moment she hears a person's voice whom she did not know existed until that moment, the connection has been made and she starts talking, reporting her impressions of friends and loved ones which come flooding in. She talks without hesitation, with quiet but positive authority, not permitting her listener to say anything but "yes or no" to her comments, and often describing experiences that were associated with the spirit friends or loved ones, faster than those on earth can recall these same incidents from memory.

Freda will not accept a "maybe" or a half-way, uncertain reply to an impression, nor an attempted interpretation on the part of the phone caller. She will say:

"I am told such-and-such is the case. Let's find out why you can't remember or what you don't feel to be correct." In most instances, the information imparted by Freda is proved to be accurate.

As a convincing demonstration of her remarkable psychic ability, I am presenting an exact reproduction of a portion of this radio program wherein she is responding to a telephone voice.

> TERRY: Before opening up the phone to the party on Line 4, I'd like to explain because I really believe some people don't understand what is going on. When Freda gets an impression and asks you a question, don't restrict it to the four walls of your house or the immediate time you are in now ... it has to do with any experience of your entire life-time. So when you respond with a "yes" or a "no," please keep this in mind. Now, Freda, I'm giving you the Lady on Line 4 ...
>
> FREDA: All right—I'm ready.
>
> TELEPHONE VOICE: Good afternoon, Freda.
>
> FREDA (almost at once): The first thing I want to say to you ... I feel you have long fingers ... tapering fingers ... you possess unusual artistic creativity ...
>
> TELEPHONE VOICE: Yes, that is true.
>
> FREDA: This is shown in the way you select and buy things for your home. You are a person who would rather wait for the right things instead of going out and buying impulsively. Can you understand?
>
> TELEPHONE VOICE: Yes, I do.
>
> FREDA: With you, I get the color BLUE ...
>
> TELEPHONE VOICE: That's right.
>
> FREDA: Then I see you surrounded by colors green and brown.
>
> TELEPHONE VOICE: That's true.

194

FREDA: You are a very sensitive person—ex tremely so.

TELEPHONE VOICE: I am indeed.

FREDA: And have you got a BLUE ring, please?

TELEPHONE VOICE: Yes!

FREDA: Because I am fiddling with my own ring on my finger . . . and I hear a voice saying, "She has a BLUE ring."

TERRY (breaking in): Do you have a BLUE ring?

TELEPHONE VOICE: Yes, she's right . . . I have.

FREDA: I want FIVE in the family, please . . .

TELEPHONE VOICE: Yes, there are FIVE . . .

FREDA: I want the month of September . . . there are two important events in September . . . one in January, with you . . . I am going back to January of this year . . . when I feel that changes were taking place . . .

TELEPHONE VOICE: Yes, yes—that's true . . .

FREDA: And, please—who CRACKS their fingers . . . or CRACKS their knuckles?

TELEPHONE VOICE (laughing): My *daughter!*

FREDA: Thank you, because I feel I am CRACKING my knuckles.

TELEPHONE VOICE: She often does that . . .

FREDA: And she had a friend who loves horses . . .

TELEPHONE VOICE: She certainly does!

TERRY (breaking in): Let's go back a moment. That's incredible . . . Freda told you there were FIVE in your family . . . a daughter who CRACKS her knuckles . . . and that you have a BLUE ring!

TELEPHONE VOICE: Yes, yes . . . she's so right!

FREDA: You had a beloved dog . . . one no

longer here ... something was wrong with the under part of her ... the dog—was it a bitch?

TELEPHONE VOICE: Yes, she was a bitch ... you're right.

FREDA: I felt that strongly ... some internal trouble ... Now, please—have you recently been worried about finances, Madam ... going over financial things ... checking up ... adding up ... something you are trying to stretch ... as if you were trying to do without things, so you could use money for something you needed more—trying to squeeze ...?

TELEPHONE VOICE: Yes, we're building a home ...

FREDA: You, say—you are building a home ... I see you living in the house already ...

TELEPHONE VOICE: Yes, yes, we are ...

FREDA: You have "green fingers" ... I see you in your garden ... you love growing things ... plants ...

TELEPHONE VOICE: Yes, I do ... very much ...

FREDA: The spirits are telling me—you are concerned about an older woman friend who has memory lapses ... she is living by herself ...

TELEPHONE VOICE: Oh, that is true.

FREDA: Yes, I am being told that you can help this woman by stimulating her interest in outside things ... but, of course, she must be encouraged to help herself. She has been quite a trial for you ...

TELEPHONE VOICE: Very much ... oh, thank you for speaking of this ...

TERRY (breaking in): Freda—this is a most incredible thing ... you have hit almost everything. Madam, can you think of anything Freda has mentioned that you can't relate to?

TELEPHONE VOICE: No, I can't . . . it's quite remarkable.

TERRY: Would you like to reveal to us some of the things that Freda has just informed you about?

TELEPHONE VOICE: The ring is a blue one that I had given to me . . . There are FIVE in my family . . . My daughter does crack her knuckles . . . We have a dog that passed away . . .

TERRY: Freda said something was wrong with the under part of her . . .

TELEPHONE VOICE: Yes—her kidneys . . .

TERRY: And Freda sensed you were having financial problems . . . at present . . .

TELEPHONE VOICE: Yes, our home . . . trying to stretch our money, as she said . . .

TERRY: I think that's fantastic . . .

TELEPHONE VOICE: Right! Absolutely amazing. I agree.

TERRY: I want to tell you something, Freda, . . . I don't want to embarrass you . . . but I have worked, as you know, with spiritual mediums for the past few years . . . and I can say, without a question of doubt, that you are the best. There is nobody with whom I have worked who hits with the remarkable accuracy that you do . . . and you are much more sensitive than other people . . . Absolutely astounding!

FREDA: Thank you, Terry . . . Thank you very much.

TERRY: I'm going to give you a break for a couple of minutes because you have had a series of concentrated communications . . . and I would like to ask you a few questions.

FREDA: All right . . . I'll be glad to answer if I can.

TERRY: During the time that you talk to people over the telephone on radio and television

197

shows—how does this compare with the time
you give people in private readings or things
of this nature? How long do you generally
take with an individual when they are sitting
with you? I mean—once you get locked in on
something.

FREDA: Usually it takes three-quarters of an
hour . . . or an hour or so.

TERRY: Do you find that doing this on a private one-to-one basis—are you able to make
contact a lot deeper—and a lot quicker?

FREDA: Oh, yes . . . it helps a great deal.

TERRY: It's sort of a strain on radio or TV,
isn't it?

FREDA: It is, but one gets used to it. In a private sitting, one can get more specific help
from the Other Side. Also, people can ask
questions . . . and often have a two-way conversation with loved ones . . . but the greatest
thing about it is the comfort people can get
from it.

TERRY: Do you know . . . can you tell me the
kind of thing that happens in your mind when
you are talking to people? Is there anything
you can reveal? You tell me that you are link-
ing with people in the Spirit World. And I
don't disbelieve that because I don't understand the entire concept of it . . . but can you
tell me how this comes about—the kind of
feelings and the kind of things that you see
in the kind of "third eye" or the "inner sight"
that you have?

FREDA: Yes—I think so . . . I will try to make
it as simple as possible. When the contact
takes place, I have to heighten my own vibration. You see, we deal with vibration . . .
everything is vibration . . . and I have to lift
my vibrational rate to blend the two together
. . . When this takes place, the spirit forces,
using my mind and body as a channel, will

use different parts of my body to get impressions through ... like my fingers when I felt myself cracking my knuckles and knew these feelings were coming from some person on earth associated with this telephone caller.

TERRY: Amazing. If this impression of cracking knuckles had belonged to someone in the spirit world who was trying to identify himself, would you have known the difference?

FREDA: Oh, yes, I'm sure ...

TERRY: Do you see the spirit entities you contact?

FREDA: Sometimes I do, sometimes I don't ...

TERRY: But you FEEL something—there is a FEELING?

FREDA: Definitely I sense the feeling ... also they have to telepathically impress on me what they want to get through. If I hear clairaudiently, it is fine. I can repeat exactly what I am hearing.

TERRY: But you can hear voices?

FREDA: Yes, quite often I do hear. If a sitter challenges a statement and I have heard differently, I will stick to my impression and, in most instances, I am proved to have been right when they are able to recall or check up on the information.

TERRY: I've noticed that ... but I don't hear these voices ... yet you say that you can.

FREDA: Exactly ... Perhaps I can use this illustration to explain how I hear and you don't. It's all related to the higher frequency. You know there is a dog whistle that can be blown. The human ear cannot hear it—because it's too high—but the dog can hear it—and respond. So this is the kind of thing I am talking about. This is precisely what happens.

TERRY: I am wondering if it is not maybe something a bit more than that. I am talking generally to you and everybody who is listening in at present, and asking you—can you go back in your mind and remember things about a special occasion or about a special person in your life? . . . I personally can recall conversations or words that have been said. My mind is remembering it . . . but I am also hearing it in my mind . . . do you understand what I am saying?

FREDA: Oh, I do, too. Yes, that happens, too . . . yes, you can hear in your mind . . .

TERRY: Yes, you can hear it in your mind, as you say, because I can recall many things exactly that happened in my life. I can go back in my mind and reconstruct with my mind a motion picture, as it were, in color, of an event . . . remember the conversation . . . hear the sounds . . . see what is going on . . .

FREDA: Oh, this is what happens to us, too . . . You *see* in your mind and you *hear* in your mind—your inner ear . . . and when they flash a picture it is like a small TV screen in your consciousness . . .

TERRY: Almost like a Third Eye?

FREDA: Yes—it takes place between the eyebrows . . . it apparently has to do with the pituitary and pineal glands . . . these very sensitive areas both react . . . Some call them the "seat of the mind," where the Psyche or the Soul resides . . .

TERRY: Freda, I'm frank to admit that I can't explain some of the things you have done this afternoon . . . or other times in the past when I have worked with you. I cannot say it is "hocus pocus," or brush it aside, and close my mind and say "I don't believe it," as many people do. There are far too many things you are accurate on, and even taking it on the basis of chance—that you were able to take a telephone call and hit two or three things out of a person's life that anyone might be able to get, generally, but you don't do that. Take the case of the lady with the blue ring, for example. You were one hundred percent. You were more accurate than the listener who is calling because they, at some point or other, will recall what you have said. I think their lack of more complete recall is because their minds are not as open, at this particular moment due to their being under duress on the telephone, waiting, listening for what you have to tell them.

FREDA: Yes, that's probably true . . .

TERRY: And it's an emotional environment for them, while it is reasonably easy for you.

FREDA: Yes, but the point is . . . during demonstrations, many people say, "I hope she comes to me," but when I do, they often react just the opposite . . . they pull away, resist, act confused . . . reluctant to say even "yes" or "no." I've had many come to me afterward and apologize, saying they were so nervous and upset at the time, but wanted me to know now how sorry they were—but everything I had told them was correct.

TERRY: Freda, I wish there was some way of reaching and convincing people who really count. Let me ask you—if I would be able to arrange it, would you be prepared to sit down and talk to a group of psychologists, psychiatrists and possibly some scientists and physicists—and permit them to study you as an individual and have you give them some "readings," while they are recording "brain patterns" and things of that nature?

FREDA: I would be only too happy.

TERRY: Would you? I would really like to try that because I think it could not only be interesting but of great possible value.

201

FREDA: Well, I think that a lot more interest is being generated with regard to Psychic Phenomena in the scientific field today. I would be glad to do what I can to help.

Chapter 15

AN AMAZING DEMONSTRATION OF PSYCHIC MEDIUMSHIP

Pursuant to Freda Fell's expressed willingness to have her psychic powers tested, she accepted an invitation from Martha and me to be our house guest in our little home in north central Arkansas for a week, so that we could make appointments for some twenty of our friends from different walks of life, to whom she had consented to give "psychic readings."

For the past year, our ESP Research Associates Foundation has been engaged in Survival Research and Freda Fell came to us under our organization's auspices. We arranged for her to be with us in our home so we could get personally acquainted with her and observe her work at close range, checking every detail of the psychic impressions and spirit communications which came to her as she concentrated on the various men and women in an atmosphere of quiet, removed from big city vibrations.

Freda knew absolutely nothing about each sitter, not even their names, and we ourselves did not know too much about the backgrounds of these carefully chosen friends, most of whom had not known each other until they were introduced after the sittings were over, and the sessions were opened for discussion. The results were astounding in every case, described as "incredible ... amazing ... extremely accurate" by all concerned.

Freda sat quietly in an easy chair facing usually a small semi-circle of "sitters" and without going into any trance, started talking, selecting "sitters" at random as the "spirits" seemed to go to them, repeating to them what was said to her, as departed friends and loved ones identified themselves by relating past experiences or making comments about present situations concerning each "sitter," indicating a current knowledge of what had been happening to them.

The "sitters" came from as far away as Oklahoma and Missouri and other parts of Arkansas. It is now several months after the sessions and we are still getting appreciative "feedback" from the participants. One woman, a surgical nurse, remarked afterwards, "Does my face say all those things? How could Freda know so much about me and my loved ones?" Another "sitter" had his deceased father identify himself by showing a hand which had been crippled in later life, something he had never told his wife about, in their 17 years of marriage.

Because of the work we had been doing with A.J. and his telepathic communications with his wife, Wilma, we were anxious to arrange a sitting with Freda for him, and to see what would happen when these two sensitives were brought together.

A.J. hoped to tell Wilma telepathically what he would like to have her repeat to Freda from the Other Side, but this rather complicated experiment seemed to lead to confusion. However, Freda received many messages from Wilma which A.J. verified. You will see from this portion of the tape recording, how personal and detailed these impressions were. They started with Freda's sensing of A.J. himself, the nature of his character and personality, and that of his deceased parents.

FREDA (explained in the beginning): You have to understand that when impressions come to me, they may deal with your whole family at any time in their lives.

A.J.: Okay, I'll remember that.

FREDA: You've always been an independent individual, haven't you?

A.J.: Yes, I have . . .

FREDA: And if someone told you not to do it, you'd say, "I'll do it if I want to." And you have done it if you wanted to . . . and you have followed your own ideas . . . your own life . . . and if anybody tried to tell you anything different, you'd tell them to get lost.

A.J.: That's right!

FREDA: I feel strongly because of this, a lot of people would say, "You just can't talk to him" . . . and you'd say, "It's all right—I can do what I want."

A.J.: That's right.

FREDA: Your father is very similar . . . your mother tells me . . .

A.J.: That's right.

FREDA: . . . in his attitude . . . and a lot of things your father did have rubbed off on you, because your father was a very independent man . . . and a fighter, too—he'd fight . . .

A.J.: (laughing): Yes—that he would!

FREDA: And he didn't care who it was—or how big the person was . . . if he didn't like something, he'd tell you. Yes, your Dad was very similar. You could rub each other up the wrong way.

A.J.: That's right!

205

FREDA: That's the point ... you were both strong characters ... And your mother—she was a pretty busy, busy lady ... and she was mighty independent, too! My goodness me! You had a lot of independent people in your family around you. But she was not as difficult as your Dad to get along with. She was easier than your Dad.

A.J.: Oh, yes, a lot easier.

FREDA: But she still was stubborn.

A.J.: Yes, that's right.

FREDA: Still, she was the one who could handle your father better than anyone.

A.J.: She could, yes.

FREDA: She used to say to you, "I don't know why you let your father get you angry. He doesn't mean a lot of what he says." But she knew how to get around your Dad and she did it. With all that, your mother and father got along reasonably well.

A.J.: Yes, they did.

FREDA: No feelings of friction there ... You liked to work for yourself even when you were younger ... you didn't like anyone bossing you around.

A.J.: I sure didn't!

FREDA: You were bound and declared you were going to be your own boss ... and you could turn your hand at almost anything at one time ... and you *did* ... you could take on this and that job ... and as long as it was bringing in money, that's what made you happy ... and at the same time, you had quite a lot of ... I'm going to use the word "ingenuity."

A.J.: I suppose you'd call it that ...

FREDA: You didn't mind as long as you were working for yourself ... you'd tackle anything that appealed to you ... You've got the kind of mind that will grapple with getting

things together—putting things together ...
you've always had that sort of mind. You've
done many things in your life and many people wouldn't dream you've done what you
have done ... "But that's all right," I can
hear you saying. "I don't care what they
think—I know what I've done and can do."
For that reason, you've been very much a
loner ...

A.J.: You're exactly right!

FREDA: Your mother, from whom I am getting many of these impressions, tells me you
were always a "loner." Were you the only
son?

A.J.: No—I've got two brothers.

FREDA: Well, why do I feel you were more or
less separated from them? I don't feel you
close to them ... as though you did your own
thing in life apart from your brothers.

A.J.: We all lived in different parts of the country ... out of contact with each other.

FREDA: That explains why I am getting such
a distant feeling. I know you had another wife
before Wilma. Your mother tells me you did
not get on very well ... It was a life of frustration.

A.J.: Yes, it wasn't smooth.

FREDA: As I say—frustrating. It was very difficult for you ... your wife got bored ... she
didn't have enough to do ... she was left too
much on her own resources ...

A.J.: We had retired ... built a big country
home ... she painted all the time.

FREDA: But she didn't have enough to do outside the home ... You might almost be able
to say she had become a "recluse." She lived
too much within herself.

A.J.: That's the way she got started drinking.

FREDA: And at the same time, she didn't mix
enough with people.

A.J.: That's right.

FREDA: Your mother is telling me your first wife developed quite a temper ... she'd as soon throw something at you as hand it to you ...

A.J.: That's right!

FREDA: Didn't you have long absences from home?

A.J.: When we were drilling oil wells ... I would be away ten days or more at a time ...

FREDA: That's what your mother tells me ... and these absences didn't help, resulting in quite a bit of friction ...

A.J.: It certainly did ...

FREDA: I now seem to be in touch with your *second* wife ... I'm getting impressions ... Did your wife go into a coma before she died?

A.J.: What do you mean?

FREDA: Was she unconscious?

A.J.: Yes, she had a stroke that day. I had a feeling ... I stayed home from work. I told Wilma, "I'm not going to work today." She said, "Well, I'll be perfectly all right." But I told her, "I'm not going, anyway."

FREDA: Yes, but did she ... ?

A.J.: She had arthritis very bad. She had pneumonia a couple of months before that ...

FREDA (putting hand to her head): I'm going to my head ... I'm getting confused thoughts and feelings ... Did she ... ?

A.J.: Yes—before she died ... a couple of weeks ... she'd get crazy ideas in her head ...

FREDA: That's what I mean—I'm getting feelings in my head ... your wife is pointing to her head and nodding ... she is indicating a lapse of memory ...

A.J.: Yes, she was confused ...

FREDA: Loss of memory.

A.J: It would last for thirty minutes or so ... then she would say, "I feel funny ... what

208

have I been doing ... what have I been saying?" Then I would tell her.

FREDA: That's exactly what your wife is telling me now ... I feel strongly that because her head had been affected in this way ... your second wife, Wilma, didn't like to be alone too much. She had not been feeling well for some time. She didn't know when these spells would come on her ... and the idea of being alone in the house when that happened, really worried her.

A.J.: Yes, I'm sure that is true.

FREDA: Also, she is showing me—her hands were badly affected, crippled, because they were just like this ... (Here Freda made claw-like fists of her hands and twisted her arms in imitation of what she psychically saw Wilma to be doing.)

A.J.: Oh, yes,—that's just the way she was ...

FREDA: Yes, she's looking at me now ... as I am demonstrating ... and nodding her head ... and telling me how painful it was ... her hands ... and she seemed to go into a severe decline eighteen months before her death ... her health deteriorated from that time on ...

A.J.: LET ME INTERRUPT FOR A MOMENT. I JUST ASKED WILMA MENTALLY IF SHE WAS TELLING YOU THIS—AND SHE SAYS "YES," SHE IS TALKING TO YOU!

FREDA: I KNOW SHE IS.

A.J.: THAT'S WHAT SHE IS TELLING ME.

SHERMAN: That's great—that's definite CONFIRMATION!

FREDA: Yes, I have a fine contact with her now. She is saying to me, as she is showing me, that she couldn't straighten her hands ... and, at times, when she needed to get up, it was just like this ... (Freda demonstrates physically, what she sees Wilma to be doing.)

A.J.: Yes, yes—that's right.

FREDA: Try as she might ... she couldn't straighten up ... her elbows ... such pain ... she had great difficulty in getting around. I feel she hated putting her hands in cold water ... because it just made her jump ... and she couldn't even put her hands up ...

A.J.: Oh, no—she couldn't!

FREDA: She couldn't even wash her neck ... she couldn't do anything like that! ... and even touch her face, she couldn't ... and this distressed her because she couldn't ... she was a very clean lady.

A.J.: In other words, she'd get mad at times because she couldn't ...

FREDA: Yes, but as I said, she was a very clean lady.

A.J.: Oh, yes—she certainly was!

FREDA: And she's telling me she had to have help to get to the bathtub ...

A.J.: That's right ... she couldn't get up—no way. But she would insist that I take her to the bathtub every day ...

FREDA: Yes, she is recalling how it was .. she was so worried about keeping herself clean ... and getting to the tub ... trying to pull herself up on the rail ... and also, she tells me, her knees would swell up like balloons ...

A.J.: Like what?

FREDA: Her knees—so painful—they'd swell like balloons.

A.J.: Oh, yes—they sure did!

FREDA: Your wife is telling me—there was fluid on her knees ... would ache so ... as though they were on fire ... and then they would get cold as though she needed to keep them warm.

A.J.: Yes, that's right.

FREDA: Like I'd want to wrap something around to keep my knees warm . . .

A.J.: More or less—a cloth that stretched.

FREDA: Elastic, yes . . . knees warm . . . She is saying, "Oh, that was awful!" And now she is saying she is happier where she is.

A.J.: That's what she's told me.

FREDA: She tells me, too, they put her on cortisone.

A.J.: Yes, they had to take her off.

FREDA: Yes, because it made the fluid worse . . . Suddenly I feel sick like I couldn't keep food down.

A.J.: Yeah, for the last three or four months, she couldn't . . .

FREDA: She was so sick . . . couldn't keep the food down . . . trouble with pancreas . . . liver . . .

A.J.: They gave her so much medicine . . . I don't see how she stayed alive . . .

FREDA: Anyway, that's what she is showing me . . . and I believe she had a sister or two. She wasn't the only girl in the family.

A.J.: No, she wasn't.

FREDA: One sister—they weren't such good friends. Am I right?

A.J.: No, they didn't get along.

FREDA: Your wife tells me when she died, her sisters all attended her funeral.

A.J.: That's true.

FREDA: Your wife, before she married you had a lot of frustration and unhappiness in her first marriage.

A.J.: That's right.

FREDA: In fact, I get the feeling, she was worried about getting married because she didn't quite know how it was going to turn out.

A.J.: That is correct. Her folks tried to keep her from marrying him . . . told her she'd never be happy with him . . .

FREDA: Anyway, your wife is saying—"All right—it happened." My impression is that she was pretty willful when she was younger.

A.J.: Yeah, I guess she was.

FREDA: Pretty strong-minded ... rather independent but, at the same time, whether she married beneath her the first time or not, or what it was—even her sisters did not like the idea of her marrying that man.

A.J.: No, they didn't.

FREDA: It wasn't just her parents ... but she wouldn't listen to them or her sisters ... She was defiant because I am being given to understand that her family was a little on the narrow side.

A.J.: They are *still* on the narrow side.

FREDA: And she did not like the restriction that was placed on her ... on account of this narrowness.

A.J.: That's what did it.

FREDA: Now I'm being shown the home where you and your wife lived ...

A.J.: In Oklahoma?

FREDA: Yes, I am in your living room ... and I see colors green and yellow ... around the windows.

A.J.: There was some brown too ... on the window curtains ...

FREDA: Yes, I see them now ... The telephone—it has numbers 9 and 8 in it.

A.J.: That's part of our Oklahoma Area Code number—which is 9-1-8 ...

FREDA: Well, I wouldn't have known that ... Let me ask—did you live in a place near a bridge ... Wilma is telling me about a bridge.

A.J.: A *highway* bridge.

FREDA: But she's talking about *running water*.

A.J.: There's a creek running right by the house.

212

FREDA: Then that's what she's talking about—*running water* . . . it's not wide—but I heard the word "bridge" so now I know it's a big concrete bridge . . . the creek beside it . . .

A.J.: That's right.

FREDA: Your wife tells me that she is much happier . . . better off where she is.

A.J.: That's what she tells *me*.

FREDA: She is much happier because she is not crippled in body . . . not disfigured in any way . . . She is in a new state of being . . . She can go around when she wants to . . . she has no pain . . . she repeats, "I'm much happier."

A.J.: She's told me that a lot of times.

FREDA: She's telling me now about her life over there . . . One of the things they've taught her is to "bury the hatchet" . . . In other words, to not bear grudges . . . They are learning lessons on love and on understanding . . . how to communicate . . . how to grow, soul-wise . . . because the soul has to progress . . . this is the important thing . . . and it's through forgiving and going forward that the soul advances . . . and you can reach higher planes of being.

A.J.: I know . . . Wilma and my nephew . . . and others . . . tell me the same thing.

FREDA: She's telling me—have you got a watch belonging to her . . . a wristlet watch that was hers? That didn't go . . . that she didn't wear very often. A timepiece . . . a watch . . .

A.J.: Yes—she had three watches . . .

FREDA: But one didn't go very well.

A.J.: Yes—the last one her sister sent her for her birthday . . . didn't operate—it kept stopping.

FREDA: That's the one—she is repeating, "It didn't go very well."

A.J. (laughing): Yes, I heard her mention that.

213

FREDA: And one of the watches was a *silver* . . .

A.J.: That was the last one, she's talking about.

FREDA: Right—because I asked her the color . . . and she said it was a *silver* color.

A.J.: How's that?

FREDA: Are you wearing a ring—Have you worn a ring that belonged to her—because she keeps repeating—you've got her ring . . .

A.J.: Yes—it was her graduation ring she got from high school . . . (He holds up his hand.) I've got it on.

SHERMAN: Do I understand—you're wearing that ring now?

A.J.: Yes—I wear it *all* the time . . .

SHERMAN: It's worth emphasizing—you're wearing Wilma's ring.

A.J.: This is her ring. I said she got it when she graduated from high school.

SHERMAN: It's interesting and significant that A.J. has telepathic communication . . . and *you* have it, Freda, in your way . . . and what you have been doing now is to provide cross-checking. Very unique.

FREDA: Yes . . . yes . . .

A.J.: I don't know . . . when she's talking now . . . she says she's been thinking to tell me something for the last fifteen minutes . . . and she's not hearing you say that . . . ?

FREDA: No, when I am saying other things, she's telling me other things . . . She can only talk to me in one way and that's what she's doing . . . telling me about the watch that was silver . . . it didn't go very well . . . you were wearing her ring . . . she can't be talking one thing and then trying to tell me something else.

A.J.: Well, all the things she has been telling you—to which I agree—she hasn't talked to *me* about . . .

214

FREDA: Look, sir—I don't know you . . .

A.J.: HUH? . . . What?

FREDA: I have never met you before.

A.J.: Well, I meant—she doesn't mention the things that you are mentioning. Maybe it's because I already know . . .

FREDA: Maybe so—but I don't know . . . I have to hear her talk before I can repeat what she says . . . and you've been telling me right along, they are true.

A.J.: Yeah . . . I realize you couldn't have any way of knowing.

FREDA: Right!

A.J.: Nobody else has tried to talk to you?

FREDA: Your wife has been doing the talking!

A.J.: She is the only one who has been talking?

FREDA: Yes—apart from your folks—your father, in the beginning—and your mother.

A.J.: Yes?

FREDA: And after them—your wife took over.

SHERMAN: It was very natural for Wilma to take over since she has been connected with you right along.

A.J.: I see.

FREDA: Your wife is talking again . . . she is telling me about your equipment that you use in tape recording. Are you thinking of using some new kind of tape?

A.J.: New kind of tape?

FREDA: Yes—some new kind of technique?

A.J.: Well, I've thought about it . . . but I've told Wilma I can't use it . . . because you have to have a new special type of tape recorder . . . it's a steel tape, I think it is . . .

FREDA: Well, she's telling me that you have been thinking of making and using some new kind of tape.

A.J.: I have been thinking about that but I said to Wilma, I've got to go out and pay a thousand dollars for a tape recorder if I'm going to use that—and I still don't think it will be any good.

FREDA: No—it's no good—*leave it alone.*

A.J.: Yeah—that's what Wilma said ... I shouldn't spend that money for ...

FREDA: No—*leave it alone!*

A.J. (laughs): She keeps after me to spend some money for something ... *I've been waiting for her to tell you about that.*

FREDA: No—but she's just talking about the new kind of tape that you are thinking of using—and she just says "leave it alone." I am only repeating what she says.

A.J.: I know—I hear you.

FREDA: Sometimes your equipment gets interference on it ... although you say it's good—it's refined—it's still not refined enough. There seems to be some discord.

A.J.: It's "white sound." You know what "white sound" is?

FREDA: No, I don't.

A.J.: You get that on tape recorders all the time.

FREDA: It's like distortion.

A.J.: No, the voices are not distorted.

SHERMAN: It's an extra-terrestrial interference that every ...

FREDA: Well, that's distortion ... interference is distortion ...

SHERMAN: It picks it up all the time ...

FREDA: No, no—you've misunderstood what I'm saying ... What Wilma's telling me is that there are certain distortions on the tape ... in other words, if you're getting extra sounds ...

A.J.: The extra sound is called "white sound."

SHERMAN: That's right ... that's what it is called.

FREDA: It's the "white sound"?

SHERMAN: Yes—"white sound."

FREDA (laughing): Interference—distortion . . .

A.J.: Yes—I see what you mean.

FREDA: Anyway, the equipment that you are using now is adequate for now . . . but I *do* feel that later on you are going to make some changes with it . . . It's like you're trying to add something to it . . . or refine it in some way.

A.J.: Yes—I'm considering some changes.

SHERMAN: Sounds like Freda's right on the beam.

A.J.: That's right—we've found some more sophisticated equipment . . . but we can't find the engineer . . .

FREDA: Wilma just said you will be doing that.

A.J.: Yeah . . . she did.

FREDA: Sometime within the next 18 months . . . in fact, in six month's time . . . you'll be having a different approach.

A.J.: How? . . . You mean new tape?

FREDA: More sophisticated . . . more sensitive equipment.

A.J.: I wish I knew what that was . . .

SHERMAN: You've worked so hard . . . so many months on that.

FREDA: It has to do with the electrical equipment which will be more sensitive. You'll be led to it . . . you'll be talking to someone about your need for improvement . . . and you'll be led to it . . . Wilma says, "Don't worry about it."

Because of the remarkable accuracy of Freda Fell's impressions, some of which might be attributed to telepathy, I have felt that you, the reader, might wish to study the transcript and decide for yourself how much of this unusual "sitting" could be credited to actual spirit communications.

The consistence of accuracy and the personal nature of the impressions is certainly indicative of extraordinary sensitivity. A.J. himself, who feels he has become accustomed to telepathic two-way conversations with his deceased wife, Wilma, was increasingly amazed as Freda continued to receive impressions on subjects which Wilma had previously spoken of to him, or topics that were related to the present moment.

At one time, as you have noted, A.J. reported Wilma as telling him that she was indeed talking directly to Freda! This was a type of development that I had hoped could or would happen—for spontaneous testimony to be offered by A.J. that Wilma had informed him she was really in communication with Freda. That this testimony did take place contributed a great deal to what I consider the marked success of the test.

But all "sittings" as I have said, turned out to be as accurate and impressive in their way. Freda told me that she has had years of experience in working with her "spirit helpers" who aid in lining up the "spirit communicants" and she can seldom remember a time, no matter what the conditions, the degree of doubt or belief of the "sitters," when she has not been able to function reasonably well.

This is most unusual because there have been many times, working with psychics who were trying to demonstrate, when the sensitive would say: "Sorry—the power is not there at present ... I can't seem to get anything ... I'll have to wait until another time." More often if psychics wished to impress me or the "sitters," they started guessing—putting out feelers—first names of purported spirit entities, hoping someone would recognize a name they could build a message on. It has been most disappointing, even suggestive that the psychic did not possess the claimed communicative ability. There is such a narrow line of demarcation between imagination and genuine impressions that if a psychic medium seeks to get informative help from the "sitter," he might be judged to be "suspect."

Documented Record of
Amazing Spirit Communication

One of the couples Martha and I invited to have a "test sitting" with Freda Fell during her week's stay in our home, was a distinguished attorney, who must be known by the initial T and his talented wife, L. This couple, so prominent and favorably known in the Arkansas city where they lived, felt it better not to disclose their identities, more so because some of their departed spirit friends were equally well known, and the messages which came through were of such a personal nature.

You need to know just a bit about the unusual Mr. T before you get into his wife's documented report of the extraordinary "sitting" which their presence occasioned. T, several years before, had been given an award as the "Outstanding Disabled Veteran of the Year" by the Disabled Veterans Association of Arkansas, as the "disabled veteran who had accomplished the most in spite of severe difficulties."

On October 23, 1963, Pilot T's Skyraider 8D-5, suffered an engine failure after being launched from the carrier by a steam-powered catapult which accelerates the plane from 0 to 100 miles per hour in a distance of less than 250 feet. The plane crashed into the ocean. Pilot T and a radio technician were picked up by a rescue helicopter. The radio officer whose first name was "John," was lost.

For the next two years, T, who was paralyzed below the waist, was confined to hospitals where he recovered from a back injury and underwent rehabilitation to learn how to maneuver without the use of his legs. In 1966, he returned to his home town in Arkansas and entered law school. After graduation in 1969 he joined a local firm and eventually resigned to practice law on his own. His advancement since that time in civic, political, church, public service and business affairs has been spectacular.

Two weeks prior to the visit of T and L to our home, a very dear and close friend of theirs, a prominent surgeon, had committed suicide. They wondered, even hoped, that this friend would try to communicate with them through the psychic powers of Freda Fell, as well as the radio officer, John, who had lost his life in the plane crash.

T's wife, L, took shorthand notes of the "sitting" which she checked against the tape recording in writing her report of what took place. It is so well and accurately done that I am presenting it exactly as she prepared it. You will see that she addressed her personal transcript to me and with this lightly sketched background you will be easily able to identify with all particulars.

Upon arrival, we were very careful not to give away information that might give clues to our background or to those who have passed on. This I felt was only fair in a real test of the psychic's ability.

I did have a few questions that I asked which helped me decide the nature of the thing. One question I asked Freda Fell was how did these sessions affect her physically. Evidently, she receives energy from it and is not depleted by it.

Also, Harold, we did not contact you in an effort to hear about this friend who had passed over, but were very interested when you called us to come and see Freda Fell.

220

We were interested in learning if our friend, a doctor by profession, had made the transition and was at peace. We were so close to him that we never felt the separation of death. There was a great deal of personal remorse in our lack of ability to talk him out of this suicide, and I deeply regretted this for his wife and children.

T is in a wheelchair. He was involved in an airplane accident nearly 17 years ago. T was a pilot in the Navy, and he had total engine failure on takeoff from the aircraft carrier. They were on the edge of a typhoon and the waves were 20 feet high. The plane pancaked on the water. T was knocked out on impact and there were two others in the plane. S got out before the plane went under, but a very close friend, J, did not get out. When T regained consciousness, the water was black and cold; his seat belts had jammed and he couldn't get free. Finally, he tore the belts loose. He could faintly see J's legs moving, but he never knew whether it was the water moving them or whether he was struggling to get out. Because of the construction of the plane, T couldn't help his friend, and because he was the pilot of the plane, he has felt personal responsibility for the death of his friend. We wondered whether or not J would come through, but here again, we were very careful not to mention any details.

FELL: I noticed you came the way you did (referring to the chair) but I have to congratulate you, because I feel that after the first couple of years you adapted and horizons opened up that you never thought possible. And I want to say to you because of the mishap that would have devastated most anyone else, and because of the life you led before, you were able to rise above it. You were very sports-minded. The very fact that you could not participate or do was really very agonizing, and they understand this and appreciate this. But you see, you were destined for things you never even thought would be possible. Horizons opened up for you that you never dreamed about, and one can honestly say that you may have been deprived of the use of your legs, but you have been more than rewarded in other ways.

I feel I must say yes. You never really became bitter, but many times you came very close to it, and it was "why?" always, "why?" But now, you say, "Well, if this hadn't happened, so much that I have come to appreciate might not ever have entered my life." Because of it your whole evaluation has completely changed. You've prospered a lot more in the material than ever before. And people who know you now think, "Well, he seems to have gotten a midas touch. It's like, well, I'll cast my bread upon the water, but it doesn't come back as bread, but two and three fold." Your whole life has become richer spiritually, mentally, and financially.

You've got terrific insight—I don't know if you're aware of it or not, but you have. I believe your faith in God has increased—more than it ever had been in your life, and people who know you would say, "But how come?" and you say, "Because of the peace and quiet, because of all I've gone through, I've gotten nearer to God than I ever had been before." And you have—you really have—and you feel strongly that God is in the lead, guiding your life. That God is with you every day. You never cease to thank Him for so much—both of you—because you've both gotten a bond that has gotten stronger every day. And I tell you, nothing will ever break it, and it will go on right through the end of time. Well, I don't know, Harold has heard me talk and has never heard me talk like this. You two have got something that all the money in Christendom couldn't buy. You have an understanding, a love that's deeper than the ocean.

EXPLANATION: This we feel is all very true. Before the accident we were basically self-centered parties, but not at peace within. But since we have made God the center of our lives, it has not been without trials, but we are able to face them with strength and together.

FELL: You've had your tests—oh, boy, you've had your tests, I'm not denying that, but by and large, you've stood the test of time. I feel rather wonderful about this relationship, I really do, because at one time, you could hardly stand it. It was, "I'm going. That's it." But all of that is long since gone, and that's the beautiful part. You've not only achieved a lot mentally and in your own expansion, but I feel there have been surprises with people at the progress you've made ... that they were not expecting you even to sit up.

EXPLANATION: This is not entirely true. Because of the level of the spinal cord injury, it was expected that he would sit up, but he has made remarkable recovery, and most of it has been since the six month period; but even though he cannot walk, he is a very active attorney and we had a little girl, our second, six years ago, which we were told not to even hope for.

FELL: The fighting spirit started to manifest and worked on positive thinking.

I don't know if Harold helped in the initial stages, but they are pointing to him that he was the trigger that started you off to imagery—that you lost hope, got it back again—

EXPLANATION: Harold, you have been a tremendous help to us with various problems.

223

There was a particular case that comes to mind. Soon after T passed the bar, a coed at our school was brutally stabbed to death, and a young man was picked up not far from where the body was found who had blood on his clothing and had apparently been on drugs. This young man hired a friend of my husband to represent him. If an attorney knows a man is guilty, you take one approach, but if you are convinced that he didn't do it you take another. Even though T didn't think he did it, no one knew. To make things more complicated, the victim and the client had the same blood type. So since you, Harold, had been successful in other cases of this type, we were most anxious to have your impressions. We called and simply stated that there had been a murder in our town, and you said, "Just a minute," and you described how the murder had taken place—where the knife would be found—that the man being held was not guilty—and that the man who actually committed the murder had a lot of pornographic literature in his apartment. The client was released, but the man who they think committed the murder had the pornographic literature in his apartment all sliced with a knife and had left the country.

But I do hope we weren't a nuisance.

FELL: But look at you now—I feel strongly that it's all stations "go," and you are more active now even in your business life than you ever were before, and what's more, you *do* know where you are going now, where before, there were so many ifs and buts that you couldn't make up your mind. You've done remarkably well, and you never would have knuckled under to anybody in any profession or in any job situation, because you had a temper you wouldn't believe—you were a rebel and very outspoken and almost chauvinistic. You've always been ambitious—to get ahead, nobody was going to tell you what to do; you hadn't worked this hard for nothing, and you were darn well sure that you were going to be recognized, and if anybody was going to take the ground from under you, then they had better think again, because it just wouldn't happen.

EXPLANATION: This was all very true of his preflight class, always a favorite of everyone. Even as an ensign, he was asked to dine with the admiral. His future looked very promising with the Navy.

FELL: However, what happened, happened—and yet I feel at the time it happened you had gotten yourself in a way—you were tense, you were mentally pressurizing yourself beyond your own endurance power. I'm having to look at my watch and say, there's not enough time. It was just one round of a highly pressurized movement. You didn't even give yourself enough time to eat properly.

EXPLANATION: Just before the accident, T was worried because he couldn't pass a physical that his blood pressure was too high. That after a shore leave, it was taken and had returned to normal and that he was reinstated to flying status—that was related in a letter I received after the accident but written before.

FELL: Then just when everything was running smoothly, when you were beginning to win, when you were beginning to get on top, bang. Because you had quite a future, and it was, "Oh, God, I've gotten so far and just when I'm in sight of it." That was the biggest blow that you could take, and yet, sir, if you had gone that way, you would have been totally destroyed. You would have destroyed yourself. If anybody would have told you you could settle for the quiet life, you would have never believed them. The one thing you had to guard against was boredom.

EXPLANATION: We truly do have a quiet, peaceful life. We live on a farm.

FELL: I don't know who Mary is, but I am hearing Mary calling—(Affirmed). I don't know, but Mary has been a little bit off key or off color. I do not feel a 100% power with Mary. Somehow there is either a mental worry or anxiety. Things are not all that they could be. Emotionally, I am feeling that it is not all that it should be. I get a worrying kind of nature. That type of worry is minor to you.

EXPLANATION: We do have a lovely sister-in-law named Mary, and they were awaiting the results of her husband's bar exam.

FELL: So that's how it is being explained to me regarding dear Mary.

And Harris and Hot Springs.

Have you been to Vancouver? Have you been to B.C.? (Answer L: "I have.")

Now, I'm coughing. Someone has a cough and it's from smoking too much (looking at L). Did you used to smoke too much?

ANSWER: I do still smoke too much and I have a cough.

FELL: Because it's you they are looking at and talking about. When you were in Vancouver, please, was it B.C.?

ANSWER: Yes.

FELL: I heard Harris and Hot Springs.

ANSWER L: I have an Uncle Harris who took treatments at Hot Springs.

FELL: And also, to a name Vickey and I want the month of August. It is a birthday and it is on your husband's side of the family. It is also an anniversary.

ANSWER: T has a niece Vickey who may have a birthday in August.

226

FELL: I'm hearing the name of Nelson—wait a minute, did you know someone who visited London? I'm visiting London and I'm not too far away from Trafalgar Square—Nelson's column—China crossroad.

ANSWER: We brought a horse from Vancouver and he is insured with Lloyds of London.

FELL: I keep on being shown a draftsman's plans—has there been talk of expansion?

ANSWER: In one of the businesses that T has an interest in. Ground was broken the preceeding day for a new building and T was going over plans.

FELL: It's about time you got this thing off the ground, because it is going to go great guns. There has often been laughter about who wants to be a millionaire. You're not doing too badly, because I feel that the energy and the effort that is being put into this project is going to be well worth the while. And you have more than realized your investments anyway.

ANSWER: The three owners of these stores began with an investment of $100.00 each and in five years, it has grown to be a rather nice income for all.

FELL: And what's more, the sky is the limit. I'm asking where I'm getting my information from, but so far my informant is rather a strong minded man, a man who—would no—yes, personalities when they come close to you can judge, and a personality to me speaks volumes, and yet, he is saying, "I'm doing this because they wouldn't have known me any other way." And the man in his way was dictatorial and I get an arrogance with him, and yet—well, he was rather dictatorial and demanding sort of man but deep inside him, he was a pussycat once you got to know him. But outwardly, if people saw this man outwardly working and doing, they think, "Who is he? He is so arrogant. He is so egotistical," and mind you, the name really fitted, because he was all these things. But he would say, "If I roar, they'll run."

EXPLANATION: We know that this is a very dear friend, F, the physician, who had committed suicide ten days ago. And I knew it was him when he was talking about my coughing and smoking too much. He was reportedly a terror around the hospital. The nurses had many occasions to run when he roared. It is told that late at night he would walk up to the nurse's station, look mean, and growl, "Don't you have any patients to take care of?" This would be if they were talking or reading a book. Or in the operating room, he would throw a look or say, "Where did you get your nurse's training?" Then at home, he would crack up about how mean he was.

FELL: But it was a joke. It was quite often a face that he put on. People do not look beyond their noses. This was the kind of man he was. This is how he is putting it across. I just said to him, "Come on, hurry up," and he just said, "I'll take my time," and then I felt him crumbling up with a grin to give me the complete picture of how he was.

EXPLANATION: This is a true picture as we knew him and he wouldn't be hurried but was good natured about it.

FELL: But certainly this man wasn't family.

ANSWER L: Just a very close friend.

FELL: But he must have been a very close friend—extremely close—like he was one of the family. I'll tell you one thing about this man. He was a very clever man. He had a mind razor sharp.

ANSWER: He was well known as one of the finest surgeons in the state.

FELL: This man in essence is certainly helping you, and he is very fond of you, because it is as though I want to put my hand on your shoulder, and when he did that it is as though there was a lump in his throat. But he wouldn't let anybody see that emotion because he was too supposedly tough, and yet he wasn't tough. And he thinks a great deal of you and he has been with you for some time. I don't know why he is saying "Buddy, Buddy." I don't know what he means by that.

ANSWER: Buddy is part of his name—part of his son's name, and also call words on a C.B. that he and I used to use.

FELL: He very much believed in individuality. No one would get the better of him. I tell you about this man—he was a businessman right down to his fingertips. And he said there's no sentiment in business. He worked extremely hard and studied extremely hard, and was to be reckoned with, and very well respected in his profession. He had a good mind. It is like a legal mind, it is as though he would assess everything, he would leave nothing unturned.

ANSWER: All is a very accurate account. He was consulting with lawyers on medical cases—very brilliant.

FELL: I do feel when he passed over it was like a quick (snap) passing. The passing was so quick that shock waves were generated by this. Because to all he seemed fit, but he knew he wasn't well. He says, "I was stubborn and would not admit to not feeling well," and this was part of his masculine pride. He wouldn't allow the thought of illness to enter into him. And he had been working very hard the last five years building up to something, and particularly the last year and a half, because it seems he put every ounce of energy and effort into it either promoting or building something, because he felt the culmination of things almost within his grasp. Before he fully realized the totality of what and how his efforts have been rewarded, then—snap—

But he said, "I have walked with you ever since"—and he wants you to know that. And he says that he will always walk with you because he says you couldn't have loved each other more if you had been brothers.

He was a bit of a terror though, a raker we call them—he was, you know . . .

ANSWER: We know.

FELL: But he's just laughing and saying, "Well, you work hard, you play hard—otherwise you get bogged down."

I think he was dark haired, this man.

ANSWER: Yes.

FELL: He's not showing me his face, but his hair was dark. Although he wasn't a bad looking man, and he had a sort of charisma—very much so far as the ladies were concerned.

ANSWER: True.

FELL: A red car—a ruddy colored car. It was not a fireman's red, it was more a dull red—he says, "Come on, you had a red car—not my car, you had the red car."

ANSWER: Yes. This is true. I had a red car, but we did not drive over in that one that night.

FELL: Bill (possibly a close friend here). Do you remember Mike he says? Correction, "Mack." Do you remember Mack and the three of us getting together and there seemed to be a good natured tug of war because it seems they were always trying to outdo each other with their repartee backwards and forwards.

ANSWER: "Mack the Knife" was his call name on the CB radio, and we would talk going the same direction on trips. When we passed his final resting place, T turned the squelch all the way up on the CB and asked, "Calling Mack the Knife, do you have a copy on this Iron Side?" more as a salute—however, something did try to break in as answer.

FELL: He is showing me a car wheel bouncing along on its own.

ANSWER: He had a very beautiful car and had lost the hubcap on one wheel and he was most upset over this.

FELL: He just said F, so he's given you his name. This man was a real live wire. He's laughing and saying, "Friend of hundreds."

ANSWER: He was a marvelous physician who deeply and personally cared about his patients. Each one was a personal challenge to do all he could for them.

FELL: Was he known by a lot of people? It's as though his name could have been a household name, as though he was known by a lot of people.

ANSWER: In the area he was.

FELL: He's laughing and speaking as though a fishbone was stuck in his throat. Someone has choked on something in the throat.

ANSWER: L has an esophageal hernia and frequently does choke. It isn't serious, but inconvenient.

FELL: Really you should not eat food that needs a lot of chewing, and he's laughing and saying, "Why don't you get a mincer like a baby, and all you have to do is swallow it. No problem there at all."

ANSWER: Well, he knows that isn't going to happen, and here he is giving me a barb—there was a lot of joking between us.

FELL: He tells me you've never felt healthier in your life (referring to T). You've never felt

231

so fit and healthier in your life.

    Affirmed.

FELL: I get the initial "R," as in Rod—Run.

ANSWER: This is possibly the initial of Red, a horse that we are boarding for his widow. He also had a special affection for this animal.

FELL: He is saying Leonard Nimoy. Are either of you interested in science fiction?

ANSWER: L is.

FELL: I was wondering why I was being shown this picture of Leonard Nimoy with this Star Trek and stuff like that.

ANSWER: Laughingly T answered, because F thought L might be one.

FELL: Is there some relationship there?

ANSWER: No, I was always interested in things of that nature, and he thought I might be a little weird. He's giving another shaft from the other side.

FELL: Well, if you understand it that's all right, because it isn't up to us to understand, just transmit what is given to us.

ANSWER L: It is certain his humor stayed intact.

FELL: Project #3.

ANSWER T: 3 was a definite number in my life at one time. Explanation: Everything connected with the plane crash was repetitive of the number 3. It happened on October 23, 1963, the number of the carrier was 33, the number of the plane was 73. The sister squadron was flying in from the Philippines that day, Squadron number 33, there were 3 men in the aircraft, it was the 3rd launch of the day, the injury stopped at the 3rd lumbar vertebrae. T even wrote an article after the accident entitled, "My lucky number is not 3."

    We knew with this that F was no longer

speaking, but J. the dear friend who was killed in the accident.

FELL: Well, that's how he put it—number 3. He speaks to you as the month of February as a special month. Birthday—wedding—passing . . .

EXPLANATION: His only son, T, was born February 14, 1963.

FELL: Yeah—he just said, "Surprise—surprise he still gets around," a good sense of humor this man, I like him very much. There is a . . . do you know an Uncle J?

ANSWER: Yes, not a real uncle.

FELL: There's a J here and he just says, "Hi." I don't think J and this man knew each other, because it's as though your friends stepped back and this J stepped in. I didn't get the feeling of "hello," it was just as though they didn't know each other. He's giving me the feeling that on earth they didn't know each other. (T interjected that he hoped they would know each other.) I get a young man who died quite quickly as a result of an accident. I asked J about it, and he said he died quite quickly and it was the result of an accident, but he was reasonably young. So he said, "I'm fine and happy, having a ball." He didn't know what hit him—he didn't suffer—had no pain. He wants you to know that as well.

EXPLANATION: This was very important for us to know, because T was the pilot (even though the accident was rated 100% engine failure) and the burden of J's death has always weighed heavily. But this was the first notice that he had died without pain. T was under the water when he woke up and was unable to help J because of the design of the plane. He did see J's leg move, but never knew whether the movement was from the water or from J's own struggle.

FELL: He didn't suffer at all.

ANSWER: I have always wanted to know that.

FELL: And it's in a boat, because he's talking about the boat—it happened on the boat. He could swim quite well too—he was a very good swimmer. A lot of people might say, "Well, he was a good swimmer. Why, why?" He says, "Well, you can't swim when you're knocked out." Some sort of an explosion . . . I'm feeling a bang and my head—so that's why he didn't get out of it. I like him, I like the feel of him, very lively, happy, friendly, physical, nice person.

He is speaking of a Susan (his brother's daughter).

Something Ann (no explanation).

John was not the only child, I don't think, because I asked him if there were any others. He said, "No, I wasn't the only child." Thank God, because his parents took it hard.

EXPLANATION: Upon later checking, we found he had a brother and a sister.

FELL: A tomboyish sister. I'm hearing the name of Queen—something . . . Queen or Quin—Anything (possibly Anthony Quinn who played Zorba the Greek)—Greek, Zoro . . . something to do with Zoro—

ANSWER: J's nickname was Zeek.

FELL: All right, I'll buy that. Oh, and someone has suffered from hay fever badly—allergies—I feel that I ought to sneeze. Hay fever is an allergy.

The name of Guin or Quinta (J's wife's niece). Gentleman, getting on in years, coming toward me. I feel this man was ill, he was in the hospital. I feel he lost quite a bit of weight. I gradually feel the weight falling away from myself. I am certainly getting the feeling of a mustache at one time. I'm get-

234

ting the initial "W," and the man was in the hospital. I get the feeling of a sudden collapse. They had a medical—artificially fed—and passed over in the hospital—75 or 76. And who is Peter—Pete was his name.

EXPLANATION: This would be L's grandfather.

FELL: I see 2 dogs here. They're not living now, they've passed over. One seemed to be long eared type dog. I don't feel these 2 dogs you had at the same time. Different times for these dogs. One seemed to be the ears darker than the rest of the body. The body itself seemed to be mottled. As I'm seeing this dog come up and lick you in the face, and she used to roll over so you could scratch her tummy.

Maybe this friend of yours that came in the beginning is having a joke—I want this explained, because he is talking about a monkey—who had a monkey? I don't know who Tammy is, but I'm hearing Tammy and again I'm seeing this monkey now—

Did you know someone who has a game reserve or is attached to something like that? I am seeing different animals.

EXPLANATION: F did compare our house to a zoo because we always had many and various types of animals.

FELL: There was someone who did have a parrot or a bird that talked.

ANSWER: Parakeet, T's parents.

FELL: They have it and the name of Rodger or Rodgers.

ANSWER: F bought his horse from a man named Rodgers.

FELL: Did you also know a gentleman connected with the family that had bad problems in the digestive tract and liver problems?

ANSWER: L's uncle.

FELL to T: You're still doing your exercises

235

aren't you? Well, you should still do them because he has suddenly come right down to you about your exercises. Keep at it because it will pay off—will you make sure he does that please—keep those exercises moving. Have you been getting tingling or pins and needles in one of your legs?

Affirmed.

FELL: Because that's good—he says—and he must keep on with his exercises—no getting out of it—no saying "I'm too busy, I've got this to do." No one should be too busy to give themselves a little extra time in the day.

Speaking of New York—Washington, D.C. Also speaking of Chicago.

ANSWER: Possible friends there.

FELL: Did you know someone named Ed out East?

ANSWER: Yes.

FELL: Going toward that New York area with this man Ed.

ANSWER: Not sure.

FELL: Regarding yourself, it would seem you have been making changes in your business structure. It seemed you have cut away certain things, but you have added others. One avenue of resources dried up, so don't waste any more time on them.

ANSWER: This has been exactly what has happened with the stores; some have been sold, others added to.

FELL: The first man is a beautiful feeling of influence to you.

ANSWER: We felt F's presence several times. T has seen him on two occasions.

FELL: Was there a blonde lady associated with him?

ANSWER: His second wife was blonde.

FELL: We've mentioned his third wife, D, and he said, "She dyed her hair."

236

ANSWER: Even though D was in her early 20's, she did color her hair because she was prematurely gray.

FELL: He speaks of something blue with a plush blue pile to it.

ANSWER: In their home was a blue velvet painting. He spoke of the gun.

FELL: There were two guns.

ANSWER: Indeed, there were two guns. On Monday, he gave one to a relative and came up and talked with us, but then on Friday, he was determined to go through with this, and there was another gun.

Our last communication from him was, "I have a daughter." While he had four boys, he had a very special relationship with his daughter.

This was a truly remarkable evening. I felt Freda Fell was a sincerely gifted person, and there was no way anyone could know this much about the different events in our lives. While I weigh the advice given here I do accept this as advice and reserve the right to decide all things for myself—one must be very careful of that to which you give up your will—it should be to God alone.

Chapter 16

THE REMARKABLE MECEVITCH CASE

This case I am about to report is taken from my book: YOU CAN COMMUNICATE WITH THE UNSEEN WORLD, now no longer in print, but it is of such an exceptional and evidential nature that it must be kept in circulation.

There are countless current cases of automatic writing. Many books have been written by variations of this method, most of them subconsciously conceived; but there are others in which contact has apparently been made with higher intelligences or discarnate entities, and information seemingly beyond the possibility of ordinary sensory awareness has been produced.

I have generally warned against the indiscriminate use of Ouija Boards and the experimentation with automatic writing because both mediums of attempted communication with those in higher dimensions open the mind to possible influence by what I term "earth-bound entities," men and women who are close to our plane of existence and who might seek to possess a living mortal.

There is increasing sober evidence that "spirit possession" is more prevalent than has yet been recognized by the psychiatric and medical professions, and it is due, in my opinion, to mankind's widespread use of drugs of one kind and other, excessive drinking coupled with the high-tension living. Such practices so upset the mental and emotional and sexual stability of people that their normal resistance to any external influences has been lowered, and other minds, of a designing and covetous nature, can move in and take over partial or complete control.

You have probably heard disturbed friends and loved ones say: 'I don't know why I did it ... Something made me do it ... I was not myself ... I wanted to kill myself (or my husband or wife or children) ... I can't understand where these filthy, obscene thoughts and feelings are coming from ... I am hearing voices which seem to be coming from people who say they are dead ... They are keeping me awake nights, talking all the time, mostly about sex ..."

These are obviously experiences to avoid, or not to invite, or from which to escape if some of the unsavory and evil influences have been encountered. It is for this reason that I have cautioned against permitting one's self to get psychically involved, even though there are occasions when use of the Ouija and automatic writing may prove highly inspiring and evidential.

AN ASTOUNDING CASE WORTHY OF STUDY

As if to bear out the statements I have just made, and also to indicate that "an exception proves a rule," I received a remarkable letter a few years ago, as well as an automatically written transcript from Vitold Mecevitch, New York City, whose permission I obtained to share with my readers. First, the letter:

Dear Mr. Sherman:

Tonight, I have concluded reading your interesting book, YOUR MYSTERIOUS POWERS OF ESP. It is most gratifying that, throughout your book, you have repeatedly warned against invasion of the living by discarnate spirits, and of the dangerous ill effects upon those who, without proper understanding, indulge in spiritual communication via automatic writing. My wife and I have had many unpleasant and horrifying experiences in the past, and this is the reason why I deeply appreciate your warning.

And yet, when we have communicated with my deceased father-in-law, we felt his loving presence, his anxiety in explaining to us his present state of existence and his strong desire that we believe him—that there is life after bodily death and that the soul of man never dies, but lives on and on.

On March 10, 1964, he communicated with us for the last time, and at this last seance, certain phenomena occurred which have been on my mind ever since.

One of his last written words were: "This is the Truth that I was and am with you."

At this instant, the pencil stopped moving, and my wife and I heard the loud bang of some object striking the paper on which the above-mentioned words were written. We put full lights on and looked about us. The fallen object was in the shape of a small potato, brownish-gray in color, very hard (like stone) at first initial touch. A few seconds later, however, it became very soft, and we were able to extricate from it a small, metallic statuette of a man. Upon further examination, we found the solid mass in which this statuette was originally encased to be in reality just plain earth

There was NO earth (soil) in our apartment, neither did we ever possess a statuette of this sort. We still have the statuette and the papers used in our seance in our possession.

I am sending you a translated Russian transcript of all the seances conducted with our father via automatic writing, from February 13, 1964 (nine days after his bodily death) to and including his last seance with us, March 10, 1964.

Vitold Mecevitch

It is doubtful if you will ever read in any literature a more touching and convincing series of communications. To preserve the genuineness and feeling of the communications which took place in the Russian language, I have not sought to alter the translation in any way. The form in which this report has been made to me has also been reproduced so that you can get the full impact and can evaluate for yourself:

1st Seance   *Feb. 13, 1964—2:30* A.M.

MYSELF (Vitold Mecevitch): Is it possible that we will meet in the world beyond with those whom we loved?

FATHER: They went forward (further). There are many trains, destination unknown. Some will leave earlier, others will remain.

MYSELF: Is our future life there dependent on our lives here?

FATHER: The truth is in your heart and if I did not steal, I look bravely into anyone's eyes, and I am not afraid. This is why I will take a seat on the train without fear. This is my right.

MYSELF: It is better for you to leave us. Peace be with you.

FATHER: And with you also.

241

4th Seance   *Feb. 22, After Midnight*

MYSELF: Once more we would like to speak to a kind spirit we were talking to the last time. Just where are you, Father?

FATHER: As yet, I am here. Not far ...

5th Seance   *Feb. 23, 1:30* A.M.

FATHER: There was the creation of the visible and invisible worlds. Visible, it is firmament of earth and planets, world of reality, heavy road. Visible would be seen by human eyes because it is a physical reality as is everything else that man goes through in this life. Also, there is invisible world and it is likewise real, but incomprehensible to human consciousness and unseen by physical sight. The difference is this: that earthly man does not know anything of this world and, on the contrary, the invisible world knows everything of earthly life and sees it, but differently than Man. He knows physical acts but there are not many here who can read human thoughts. First step from physical state of existence will inevitably bring us into this world ... I'm looking for clear words for ... it is like on earth ... different development—civilization and cannibalism is divided here.

MYSELF: If it is hard for you to control, you should not, we understand and we will wait until tomorrow. (No answer, pencil moved straight ahead. It is now 3 A.M.)

6th Seance   *Feb. 24, 1964—2:15* A.M.

FATHER: The invisible world is combined with the visible and is in a state of gravitation, one to the other. The more strong attachment, passions, love, animosity (malice) unfulfilled desire on their part to come back. We can divide the inhabitants of the invisible world into several categories.

(1) There are those who by any means possible, wish to come back to earth. About that possibility (feasibility) I do not know as yet.

(2) Such beings who did not leave anything on earth, except affliction (sorrow). They are inert.

(3) Those that are satisfied and who have made surroundings to their own tastes, want to remain.

(4) Those who are conscious of inevitability to go forward and who are without fear, are ready for it.

MYSELF: If you think it is becoming more and more difficult for you, we will wait until tomorrow. (Father did not answer and left us in the same manner as yesterday.)

7th Seance   *Feb. 25, 1:30 A.M.*

FATHER: Correction about Group #2. They are not inert, but they are forgotten. They are enjoying everything here and are afraid of the change. Strangely enough, all categories know about this division but cannot change places by themselves and they are bound together and are attached (gravitated) to earth, except those in Group #2. There are no seeming boundaries as on earth, but it is an impossibility to cross from one group to the other. There is a law here: No punishment but impossibility. Each group in its own surroundings is free. Group #3 cannot penetrate to Group #2, but between themselves they have their own will (point of pencil broke) in natural reciprocity and concern to go as far ... enlarging by their own ... (pencil was pulled out from our fingers, and the thought left unfinished)

MYSELF: Father, if you have difficulty to con-

243

tinue ... (I did not say any more as pencil began to move again)

FATHER: I want to help you ... to open first secret because I love you. If I will be given opportunity to give you a proof of reality of that which I am writing ... people without evidence would not believe you.

MYSELF: We were reading today an article by Mr. Krymoff. What do you think of him?

FATHER: With sadness, he is looking to find justification and the cause of life and his realistic mind would not believe anything without proof, that is without a miracle, which could astonish him. (our conversation was momentarily interrupted by some spirit)

MYSELF: I love you, father ...

FATHER: We should not cry. Love lives on. You are also dear to me, my boy. (It was now 3:50 A.M.)

8th Seance   *Feb. 26, 1:30 A.M.*
(Started seance at 12:30 A.M. There were other spirits, and father came finally at 1:30 A.M.)

FATHER: Dear Children (not word "children," here he again uses old Russian letters) Could not unite with you sooner. Was trying to comprehend new sensations and discovery. I am afraid that by my quick judgment I will lead you astray, and instead of helping you, I may harm you. It seems to me that Group #1 is divided into two parts and could mean danger. (Pencil was pulled out from our fingers, and unfinished word "Danger" was crossed out.)

MYSELF: If it's too hard to speak—do not speak. For us it is more important not to cause you any harm, (or displeasure).

FATHER: No, my children should be guarded.

MYSELF: Father, please be careful. In our previous experiences, many times the pencil was pulled out from our fingers and spirits were not permitted to continue with us. In such cases, they just left us. We do not wish this to happen to you, because we want you to remain with us as long as possible.

FATHER: No, in past times we took towns. We will see yet. (at this point seance was temporarily interrupted and during this interruption, my wife was telling me about bombardment of train near Paris during the last war, and on which my wife and father-in-law were riding. I asked my father-in-law if he remembered a certain episode)

FATHER: Of course, I remember—the nice cutlet was lost. Brave Manusha. Well—ask questions. What is bothering you?

MYSELF: Nothing bothers me. Only, Father, please be careful. We know a lot from you and other spirits. We are afraid for you and ourselves, because we wish that you could remain with us for a long time.

FATHER: I will try but I am not sure for how long.

MYSELF: Did you wish that we publish your labor?

FATHER: Only in such case—if you could get positive proof.

MYSELF: Would you change anything in your book, MAN IN THE CREATION if you could ever return to earth? (Father had been a well-known Russian author)

FATHER: I would change many things because, knowing a new world ... the only question is—would I remember anything of my being here?

MYSELF: If you feel tired and wish to leave us, it is all right with us. We will understand.

FATHER: Light and Love be with you.

MYSELF: Could our loving thoughts help you?

FATHER: Love is prayer (Russian word "molitva"—prayer was written with capital "M." Seance ended at 2:44 A.M.)

9th Seance   *Feb. 27, 1964—1:30* A.M.

FATHER: Very important. From Group #1, there is a possibility of possession. (Here a Russian word was used which meant, according to Dr. Nandor Fodor, "an invasion of the living by a discarnate spirit, tending to a complete displacement of normal personality for the purpose of selfish gratification") . . . also from . . . (next word was crossed out) temporarily which is da . . . (word was unfinished and we believe that this word was meant to read "dangerous") Understand?

MYSELF: We understand everything. If it is getting to be difficult for you to continue, please don't, and we will ask only simple questions.

FATHER: Ask questions until it is not too late. I am looking for means to help you, and if I will find out, I will let you know.

MYSELF: Father, what do you think about telepathy, Dr. Rhine, and also about possibilities of man to influence inanimate things, like dice?

FATHER: Rhine is very gifted man. Yes, it is absolutely possible, but one has to be used to a particular dice and must teach dice to obey. This I can see clearly. But in Casino, one cannot teach dice to obey, because they are already taken by others, and each dice could "not be benevolent." (We are omitting quite a few personal and many other unimportant questions that were asked by us and were answered by my father-in-law.)

MYSELF: How can you know this now?

FATHER: Past can be seen by us.

MYSELF: In the past, we used saucer in our

246

communications with spirits, and we have
had very dreadful, horrifying experience.

FATHER: Those creatures are half alive
corpses. Be saved. In the future, be careful
because . . . (Pencil was pulled out)

MYSELF: Father, you have heard my
thoughts.

FATHER: We need to speak and I also feel your
love.

MYSELF: Do you wish to say "goodbye" to us
until tomorrow?

(No answer—as always—straight lines.)

Open Date   *Feb. 28, 1964—2:15* A.M.
(Father did not come. Some friendly spirits told
us that "he is busy and he is temporarily absent." We asked spirits to tell our father that
we wish him to make further progress and
that we will patiently await his return.)

10th Seance   *Feb. 29, 1964—1:30* A.M.
FATHER: Dear Children: I am sorry that you
have waited for me in vain, but I could not be
without being active. It was necessary to find
out more and to understand. Can I explain?
This is not the end. At some distance, which
cannot be humanly measured, there is something like—I am looking for words—a MEM-
BRANE through which it is impossible to
pass (to penetrate). If one goes near it, unseen
forces jostle one away (pushed off). At the
same time, there is a solution, and under certain circumstances, creatures of this world
pass through it, when they begin to feel some
sort of call (invitation) which is getting more
and more persistent and stronger. When it
happens, they cannot resist this call, but out
of their free will, they cannot go through.

MYSELF: Some spirit who called himself "passerby," told us about it, and a few days before

247

he felt this call (invitation) his manner of speaking changed; he became very serious and sad. He did not joke with us anymore.

FATHER: Yes, it is so. This is like a magnet. Many do not wish to go, and this is why the change of character as you have noticed.

MYSELF: Do you keep contact with those who are on the other side of this so-called MEMBRANE?

FATHER: I suppose you can, but man on earth cannot. Some of us see this—no, that is not the right word—rather we FEEL, that those who have already passed through will never return to earth. From Group #1 there are many possessions.

MYSELF: Are you having some sort of radiation?

FATHER: Of course we have but only spiritual. Even so, earthly man is surrounded by individual auras.

MYSELF: Why should people have their seances at night and why is it necessary to conduct it in semi-darkness? (We have a 7½ watt red bulb burning before the Icon.)

FATHER: Firstly, because of its quietness. Also, elements of light are disturbing (hinder) as for instance, in the Cinema. This is fine that you have light burning before "Love." It drives away (repulses) evil.

MYSELF: How about knocks and noises? Is it because spirits want to make contact with us?

FATHER: I did not touch yet upon *temptation*. (seduction) . . .

MYSELF: Would it be different if one commits suicide or dies a natural death? Would he go to the same place in any case?

FATHER: It is important that he should not have any hatred in a moment of transition.

MYSELF: At times, before, during and after a seance, we experience many happenings; saucers being broken, chain on the door shaken, different objects being displaced, and so on.

FATHER: It is to be understood. It all happens. It was a time of temptation. I am not strong, but there are those to whom all this is possible. Before my departure I will ask that I be given the possibility (opportunity) to do so. Would you believe then?

WIFE: If you would ask—I do not wish that anything could be taken away from you because it may hinder you to go further.

FATHER: Love be with you.

11th Seance   *March 1, 1964—1:30* A.M.
(Before the start of this seance, we were discussing the possibility that, perhaps, in reality, we are not speaking with our father—but that it is our subconscious minds that are responsible for all this writing.)

FATHER: All your feelings are understandable. I went through all this myself when I was on earth, and it was never in my mind that I, once more, will be able to exchange thoughts with you.

MYSELF: What is faith?

FATHER: Faith could be of several kinds. Self-suggestion. Suggestion of people around you. Faith, as inside consciousness; it is like the music of the composer, who is taking it from there (from inside consciousness). But faith is also a search for the sense of life and if there is a search, there is a sense (meaning).

MYSELF: Are you speaking of the Sense and Cause of life?

FATHER: Justification. You, my little girl, believe, (have faith) although you do not think so. Earthly death is not the end. There is no end of human life. I cannot be with you too long. Ask questions, if you wish.

MYSELF: Do spirits take "Warmth"?

249

FATHER: Yes, without a doubt. Every contact
with the living gives out "warmth" or the er-
zatz of it.

MYSELF: Is there a difference in duration of
time (passing of time) between your and our
earth?

FATHER: Yes, on earth—time is slower.

MYSELF: Is it possible for the spirits who have
gone over to the other side of the MEM-
BRANE to communicate with us?

FATHER: Yes, for those who dearly love you
and are not afraid.

MYSELF: Father, you have said that you cannot stay with us for long.

FATHER: There is something that you should
try to understand between the lines. What I
want to tell you is this—there are two forces
(powers) of creation. In Music—MINOR and
MAJOR . . . stay with the joyfulness, children
of mind.

12th Seance   *March 2, 1964—1:30* A.M.

FATHER: With much sorrow I am telling you,
my dear children, that I begin to feel a call
(invitation) but only a faint one (weak). Do
not worry. There is time yet. We should not
lose time. If you have any questions, ask me.
I will answer, if I will have a chance. I want
most important for you, and I know that it is
material. Did you understand about MINOR
and MAJOR?

MYSELF: Why is it that the most powerful
force cannot be victorious and destroy the
weaker one?

FATHER: Sometimes those who are straight-
out and strong cannot conquer weak ones because they are deceitful, not straight-out and
strong—worthy and false. This is only my
thoughts (opinions).

250

MYSELF: I believe we should not deepen our search in order to understand more.

FATHER: Yes, yes—It is impossible to know everything, not only for you, but for us also.

MYSELF: Father, you are leaving us soon. We are very sorrowful.

FATHER: Maybe not so soon. Do not be grieved. (Following this there were some questions and answers of mostly a personal nature.) This is what is most important for you to know. THERE IS NO DEATH—It is only a transition to a different sphere of consciousness. In the beginning, I wanted to tell you about everything that encompasses us, but I see this is difficult for human comprehension. Earthly life is not the end. Again I warn you about uninvited guests and enticing propositions. This is very important.

MYSELF: We promise to be careful in the future and will take your advice. You have been speaking to us at length. Do you wish to say "goodbye"?

FATHER: Let love save you . . . I am counting on you. You are good son and husband, and, besides, she has nobody. I am leaving her in your name and I trust you.

MYSELF: On my part, I will tell you, Father, we will be together always . . . and I will never leave her.

FATHER: I trust your word. Let Love and Light guard you, and you also, *Detotchka* (*Detotchka* is a sentimental Russian word meaning "a girl") should never part.

WIFE: We will be together always.

MYSELF: Shall we continue with the seances after you are gone? I think we should not be interested anymore. What you have told us is most valuable and important.

FATHER: Do not deepen yourselves with it

when I am gone. Remember about "Wolf in sheepskin clothing."

MYSELF: We are not going to have seances often, only when we want to find something important for us.

FATHER: I will tell you something strange—it is them that are using you, and you are caught in the mirror (fall into).

MYSELF: Do you wish that we discontinue seances altogether?

FATHER: Don't say so. There will be temptations yet. You do not understand that by being together you are strength and their first problem is to divide you. This is why I took word from you both, and you are accountable for it. It is like an OATH.

13th Seance   *March 3, 1964—1:30* A.M.

MYSELF: Father, you came earlier than expected.

FATHER: I am very pleased by your desire to speak with me.

WIFE: Would some of the spirits like to return to earth, if possession is possible?

FATHER: I imagine that those very happy on earth would like to repeat their life again.

MYSELF: Father, we were in contact in the past with a kind lady spirit and her friend "passerby." Please give them our love. Also give my love to my departed sisters and all those we loved so dearly.

FATHER: It is a noble wish and I may do so earlier than you think. For clearness sake let us say that there is a strong apparatus of telepathy, as I have already experienced, and your wish will be fulfilled.

MYSELF: Thank you very much, Father.

FATHER: I am able to feel everything. Your love will be united with your dear ones, no matter where they are. There are some forces

252

(powers) white, black and red. I am afraid that I have confused you but it is like, in ancient religions, and also some following religions—the triangle was saved but in latest ... was not properly understood. Do you understand? ... And so, children of mine ... I have seen plenty and I am convinced ... Love be with you.

14th Seance   *March 4, 1964—12:25* A.M.
(We were told by some friendly spirit that Father would not come today and that he is busy examining (looking over) the "ribbon" of his earthly life. We waited for an hour. He did not come.)

15th Seance   *March 5, 1964—2:00* A.M.
FATHER: KEEP STRONG. (These two words only were written with great difficulty. Pencil was shaking on all sides and at the conclusion of word "strong," the pencil broke. We waited for another hour—Father did not come anymore.)

16th Seance   *March 6, 1964—1:15* A.M.
FATHER: Dear Children: I am still with you. For how long, I do not know. Do not be grieved. Ask what is on your heart and mind, but above all—do not be sad.
MYSELF: Father, were you looking over your "ribbon" of your past life?
FATHER: Sad picture of IMPERFECTABIL-ITY ...
MYSELF: We were happy that you are still with us. Hope you will stay for a while longer. You wrote yesterday "keep strong." We understand everything and we shall keep strong.
FATHER: Do not worry, my boy. Even if I will leave you—I will keep watch over you and you would not be left alone.

MYSELF: We are very happy about it.

FATHER: And besides all, I think that ...
PROOF that I was with you ... someone will
give me ... not from our world, but your
earthly world ... something that you have not
in your house ... something that you even
cannot guess or think of ... but money I am
not permitted (to give).

MYSELF: Don't Father, if you may have some
difficulty. We believe you.

FATHER: It is because you will forget.

MYSELF: You have spoken about two forces
in the creation.

FATHER: Creation and forces—differentiable
(differential).

MYSELF: But you spoke about three forces—
white, black and red.

FATHER: One senseless—and two with sense—
but hostile to each other. (Father started to
write some word but did not finish and left us
without saying goodbye, which was unusual
for him.)

17th Seance   March 7, 1964—1:20 A.M.
(Father did not come for a long time. We were
communicating with other spirits. Finally he
came at 2:15 A.M.)

MYSELF: We wanted so much to speak to you
once more. We love you.

FATHER: I love you also. It is beginning more
and more difficult to resist ... but I will come
to you ... Soul and heart do not lose. Stay
with Love and Light.

18th Seance   March 10, 1964—1:30 A.M.
FATHER: Dearly beloved children. Perhaps
this is my last appointment with you. Do not
grieve, *Detotchka*. Love connection stays (remains) forever. My last covenant to you. BE
ONE WHOLE—ONE BODY, HEART AND

SOUL ... AND IN ETERNITY BE INSEP-
ARABLE. I unseemingly will guard and love
you. Let LIGHT and LOVE be your GUARD-
IANS. Your Father always loving you. And
THIS IS THE WHOLE TRUTH THAT I WAS
AND I AM WITH YOU. Do not be afraid. Be
of good cheer—OPEN EGG—in it—there is a
MAN IN A SHELL!
WIFE: Forgive me, Father.
FATHER: Forgive me, too, my *Detotchka*.
LOVE and LIGHT be with you!

A PHENOMENAL HAPPENING!

"At the conclusion of the words "THIS IS
THE WHOLE TRUTH THAT I WAS AND
AM WITH YOU" we heard a LOUD BANG
of some OBJECT striking the page on which
those words were written.

"We put full lights on and started to examine
this object. At first, we thought it was a stone
and I tried to cut it open with a knife. I could
not. After a few seconds, perhaps forty to sixty,
this object became, in our hands, softer and softer, and we were able to extricate a little ME-
TALLIC STATUETTE OF A MAN.

"The MASS in which this STATUETTE was
originally surrounded was, in reality—just
PLAIN EARTH, which finally completely dis-
persed (crumbled).

"We give you now a FULL DESCRIPTION
of the STATUETTE. It weighs about one and
one-half ounces, and measures about three-
fourths of an inch in length (from head to end
of legs) a little more than one-half inch in
width, at the shoulders. It is heavy for its size,
so I believe it is made of silver.

"It is a figure of a man, dressed in ceremonial
costume (perhaps of Middle Age period). In his
left hand he is holding a drinking cup, and
the key is hanging from a shoulder belt,

255

touching his left leg. The legs are short and evidently were broken off or were corroded and eaten up by the elements of nature. Eyes, mouth and nose were plainly visible through magnifying glass.

(NOTE: I went to New York City and met Mr. Vitold Mecevitch and held in my own hands this extraordinary apport. I also had Mr. Mecevitch take the statuette to a photographer and had greatly enlarged pictures made of it, which I have in my files.) Harold Sherman

Of all the thousands of communications to which I have been directly exposed during my life, or which have been reported to me, these transcripts of the Mecevitches' communications with their Russian father have to be among the most convincing and meaningful. They have the ring of truth in them, dramatically punctuated by the materialized apport, significantly the STATUETTE OF A MAN, embraced in earth, "the dust of the ground" out of which man was created.

The expressed desire of the Russian father (whose name must remain unknown for respected personal reasons) that he be permitted to leave some material evidence of his actual presence, was fulfilled in this startling but most impressive manner.

The contents of the transcripts themselves deserve careful and thoughtful study, both for what is indicated between the lines as well as the specific statements made. The significance of these messages cannot and should not be underestimated. Not only can they be an inspiration but they can also serve as a protection to those of us seeking greater knowledge of the Beyond, and who might otherwise involve ourselves innocently but dangerously with harmful rather than helpful psychic forces.

Years ago, one of the most spiritually endowed men we will ever know on this planet, Harry J. Loose, who is mentioned in my books HOW TO MAKE ESP WORK FOR YOU, YOU LIVE AFTER DEATH, and HOW TO KNOW WHAT TO BELIEVE, warned Martha and me that, as we delved deeper and deeper into these psychic mysteries, we must see to it that we maintained unfailing love and harmony between us as an "insulating shield" against possible attempted invasion by evil spirits.

Since that time, we have had ample reason for blessing Harry, on many occasions, for his wise importuning. This is not the book or the place for the recitation of experiences we have had, wherein other individuals and even groups sought to put a "hex" on us, to call down the wrath of their concept of God and higher beings upon us because we had become aware of their fraudulent and wrongly motivated practices. It has not been our mission to seek exposure of such persons but we have had a need to know the truth about their activities so as not to be drawn into them or brought under their influence. Martha and I strongly feel that there is no area of investigation that requires more honesty of approach, nor is there an area in which it is more difficult to separate the illusory from the genuine in all phases of psychic phenomena.

This is largely because the whole field has been honeycombed with psychic imposters, religious fanatics, voodoo, witches, Satanic worshippers, magicians posing as psychic sensitives, phony mediums and well-meaning but self-deluded men and women.

On what is often referred to as "the other side of life" or "the life after" the researcher encounters all manner of spirit entities, from the low and degraded, seeking a parasitical attachment through possession of the minds and bodies of living mortals, to the much more rare but highly developed spiritual beings, or friends, or loved ones like this Russian father-in-law of Vitold Mecevitch.

His admonition to his daughter and son-in-law for them to "BE ONE WHOLE—ONE BODY, HEART AND SOUL," and to LET LIGHT AND LOVE be their GUARDIANS, was strikingly similar to the counsel given us so many years ago by our friend and mentor, Harry J. Loose.

If all the discordant tensions that might exist between any husband and wife could be eliminated through new understandings, then new tolerance toward the faults and weaknesses of each, new and deeper love and harmony and a hitherto unrealized happiness and health of mind and soul would come to pass.

No outside destructive influence, either in this life or the next, could then break through the magnetic barrier set up by the shield of LIGHT and LOVE. Any husband and wife, or two or three or more people who venture to make contact with the "spirit world" without such an established aura of LIGHT and LOVE, are doing so at their own peril. They are too apt to become involved with "earthbound spirits" who may masquerade as friends or loved ones, claiming and promising everything until they can gain control, and then the party or parties possessed can no longer detect the real from the unreal. They are psychically and emotionally "hooked," to use an expression, and it is often most difficult to get free of the incessant voices and unbidden physical urges they are experiencing.

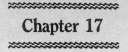
THE RAYMOND CASS REPORT

One of the most authoritative and articulate Electronic Voice Phenomena researchers in England is my friend, Raymond Cass, who heads his own Hearing Aid Company and who, as an Audiologist, with vast experience in sound projection and detection, has recorded and analyzed thousands of what he considers to be paranormal voices, and has prepared this extraordinary report.

It has to be the most definitive account of what had been taking place in Europe, especially in Sweden, Germany and England with respect to this significant as well as exciting and controversial phenomenon.

When you couple this report with the information furnished by Sarah Estep in Chapter 4, of research being done on the American scene, and especially A.J. Plimpton's remarkable experiences, you will realize that the EVP project is an expanding one and may well play an evidential part in the scientific investigation of Survival after death. I am presenting Raymond

Cass's report exactly as written, starting with his description of what he calls:

The Experiment

The 23rd of August 1976 was a routine day in the life of a Hearing Aid Consultant. Unlimited reserves of tact and patience are necessary in this difficult but rewarding occupation. I was at that time heavily involved in research into the Electronic Voice Phenomenon (EVP) but as our business grew I found less time and spare energy to apply myself to the tiring process of recording playback and interpretation of the fleeting paranormal voices.

On this late Summer evening, however, when the last patient had departed, I sat quietly for awhile, had some refreshments, and feeling a little revived, resolved to try for two-way dialogue with the mysterious voices. As the exact parameters governing successful contact are still virtually unknown, each experiment remains very much a hit and miss affair. I had never been able to emulate Jurgenson's lengthier contacts lasting 10 minutes or more, but considered that any clear and unambiguous contact at all, especially an instant response over the radio to my voice, was in itself a staggering achievement. For years I had hesitated to attempt the direct response method and felt slightly foolish addressing thin air.

I am located in downtown Hull, an industrial city on the North Eastern seaboard of England. After 6 P.M. the bustle of the inner city subsides and the swirl of traffic ceases. My EVP results had always been better in this location, possibly aided by stray EM fields which created a lively flux around my office as against my home further North overlooking the North Sea. In the United Kingdom I seemed to be well ahead of the field in the matter of clarity and sound volume of voices but still lagged far behind the Swede who was able to devote all his time to this often gruelling and time consuming research project.

It is important to realize that the EVP is sporadic and unpredictable ... dependent on a rare combination of factors ... geophysical, meteorological, and Solar. If a favorable flux exists at the moment of recording and if the experimenter is able to hold his concentration and ignore the sensory data of the world of "ordinary reality," a moment may arise when disembodied minds are able to ... for a mere instant in time ... bridge the gulf between their world of pure energy and our dense world of matter! No techniques exist at present, whereby these parameters may be defined or quantified. An extraordinary mental "set," plus undeviating mental intent, probably accounts for some of Jurgenson's success, but I have no doubt at all that he is a favorite target for transmissions from disembodied minds who find in him the optimum experimental subject. Under these circumstances some of the Geophysical factors may be less important.

One thing is certain ... the experimenter cannot stand apart from the experiment ... even if he starts his recording apparatus, then leaves the scene as I have done, invisible threads connect him with the room and the apparatus. Nevertheless a British Government scientist, working on reports of "voice intrusions" at a radio monitoring station near Darmstadt, West Germany, told me that in his view, abnormal meteorological conditions facilitated EVP production. *Examples from my archives together with samples obtained by the Government from other sources had been digitally processed and computer analyzed for purposes of comparison with thousands of known radio signals from normal sources.*

261

At 6:30 P.M. on 23rd August, 1976, accompanied by my assistant Ingrid Feuchte, registered audiological consultant, and a successful voice experimenter in her own right, I retired to a small room at the top of the building reserved for EVP activities. On this occasion we used the radio/mike method where a battery powered miniature recorder stood on a table near a multiband receiver tuned to the Airband at around 127mhz. There is little air activity over this part of England and no Airport within 50 miles so the band was quiet and unfrequented. The Juliette radio is sensitive to high frequency interference, such as car ignition sparking in the street below, but not subject, as some have thought, to breakthrough from local taxi, police and other PSB transmissions. Under good conditions voices broke in with sudden attack and decay, and experts who had evaluated my set-up theorized that *an emanation from an unknown source was "beating" with the selected airband frequency* and producing a transient condition which enabled the voices to manifest. Emanations from a Mass X-Ray Unit only 30 yards from my location have been suspected and it is curious that the decline in my experimental results coincides with a rundown of this Unit's activities.

After years of scepticism concerning the possibility of two-way communication with the voices, we swung into action this Summer evening and addressed the invisible source. The band was quiet with occasional interference from a faulty flourescent light in the corridor outside, or the passage of an automobile in the street below. The tiny Sony TC 150 cassette recorder stood ready to record this, also my words of greeting to invisible entities plus any response over the loudspeaker of the radio. As always I felt slightly foolish addressing thin air, but warmed to the task of establishing a bridgehead between the Two Worlds and achieved in a few minutes that peculiar one-pointed, expectant mental "set" thought by many to be a vital component in a successful EVP experiment. Writing this now in 1980 the exercise of addressing a machine does not seem so outrageous as I am actually contemplating upgrading my existing telephone answering service with a machine programmed to spill its messages on recognition of my voice from a call box anywhere in the United Kingdom!!

The specific object of this experiment was to contact, if possible, the surviving personalities of K. Raudive and/or his Latvian Parapsychologist friend, Sonje Liepene, who had already burst into our tapes with crucial and evidential material. Within seconds and immediately following a specific request for such a contact a hoarse voice intervened but failed to achieve full breakthrough . . . seconds later and riding on a piercing pilot tone of approximately 12KHZ, the voice called dramatically and as if over vast distances and in slightly bowdlerized German . . . *"Here's Raudive . . . waiting at the bridge."* A mathematician has calculated that the chances of this very rare name being called on a radio tuned to the Airband in the North East of England at the precise instant of my request are so infinitesimal as to be almost nonexistent.

Some years later in a lecture hall at Karlsruhe University, West Germany, this voice example produced a stunned silence and a few cries of protest from the body of the hall as sceptics wrestled with the concept of *two-way EVP communication.* Together with many other samples this voice example has been examined on both sides of the Iron Curtain. The *shock of an answering voice out of nowhere trapped on magnetic tape* . . . with accents and intonation of a deceased person's voice is difficult to convey . . . one has the sensation of something which if eventually stabilized and enhanced, will bring about deep changes in consciousness . . . an information revolution as the futurologists term it, will

263

occur. A vast and strange hinterland of communication and intelligence may one day be tapped as discarnate minds bridge the gulf between two dimensions.

That the major contribution to this coming revolution is being made at this moment in West Germany, where about 1000 experimenters, scientists and members of the German Voice Phenomenon Association are actively engaged in pushing forward the frontiers of the unknown, may be partly due to historical accident ... partly to the peculiar Germanic capacity for close concentration and attention to detail allied to technical expertise. One factor arising out of the successful experience of hundreds of investigators has been the *decline in importance of the results of any single individual. The one to one confrontation between psychic and sceptic no longer applies.* The EVP rests on a broader base and may exponentially expand to a universal experience when common consensus stabilizes its terrestrial manifestation.

A POTENT CATALYST

Jurgenson received a stream of communications from the hidden source. Reception implies transmission which implies intelligent direction. The Voice Source revealed an overall strategy and the Swede quickly realized that he was a focal point or even a target. In RADIO LINK WITH THE DEAD, unfortunately untranslated into English, Jurgenson revealed the blueprint for the next couple of decades. His personal communications, from deceased friends, relatives and old colleagues were to him totally convincing and decisive. The broader strategy as revealed by the Voice Source for graduated intervention in terrestrial affairs via a form of radio propagation powerful enough to override many earthly transmissions, aroused scepticism and even hostility in some quarters. The Swede himself, realizing that he had perhaps revealed too much too soon, let it be known that any further editions of the book would be subject to revision with certain deletions.

I found the book dramatic and compelling reading, confirming and underlining many of my own experiences in the realm of the EVP. Indeed I found it a catalyst ... my tapes became alive ... the voices assumed new authority. Lena, Jurgenson's scintillating female "guide" and Boris Sacharow, his mentor in the field of Yoga and Theosophy, cropped up on my tapes announcing themselves by name. I could not emulate the Swede in terms of time available for experimentation nor in funds available for elaborate equipment, nor had I the contacts in the media which enable Jurgenson to reach a wide audience in a comparatively short period of time ... *but in encapsulated form and within the time available to me I experienced most of the dramatic audio effects described by the Swede.*

Dr. Ralph Determeyer, who was able to use a sealed studio at Munster Radio Station for his experiments, also confirms the following brief summary of the wide range of audio acrobatics performed by the "Voice Entities." Firstly, the Voices used a polyglot mode of speech using the elements of two or more languages in fast, terse, highly compressed "blips." Unusual neologisms, idiosyncratic grammar and syntax, try the patience of linguistic purists.

The Voices, however, are not robotic ... they are, on the contrary, lyrical, musical, entrancing and sometimes siren like. Jurgenson differentiated between two types of entities ... 1) Copyists who, using unimaginable skills and technology, are capable of instantly metamorphosing a standard broadcast ... spoken or sung ... and emerging at the precise termination of the passage with a coherent message, usually addressed to the experimenter himself. 2) Popsers ... (an unfortunate term) who are able to insert in between the spoken words of, say a Newscaster, in the precise interval, words and names, again with relevance to the experimenter and his immediate circle. Furthermore, a voice appearing at one speed on a reel recorder is found to say something quite different at a higher or lower speed.

Even more startling, a tape reversed, which normally produces an incoherent babble, may be found to have intelligible voices imprinted on it by some unknown process. Voices range from hoarse whispers to loud exclamations. Passages are sung with great passion and emotion . . . many of the female singing voices tug at the emotions and display an astonishing range. The Voice Source shows a close monitoring of the experimenter's thoughts and actions and makes appropriate comments or predictions.

In my work as a Hearing Consultant, I use audiometric pure tones for measurement of hearing loss. Once during an EVP experiment, accurate facsimiles of tones from 250 to 6000 HZ appeared on the Band. Again whilst reading Richard Sudhalter's stunning biography of Bix Beiderbecke, the brilliant cornetist who died tragically at 28 in New York, my tapes were invaded by cryptic references to obscure passages in the book which assiduous search later brought to light! All this recorded, and preserved on tape for as long as magnetic tape retains its impressions!

Once after a conversation with an Aunt who recalled with amusement my father's liking for a certain lady during his lifetime, an angry voice interrupted an experiment . . . "You shouldn't talk like that about Bobby Cass and me." Again, a member of a local sub-aqua club described to me the discovery of a World War II German bomber on the seabed off Scarborough, skeletons of the crew were seen in the fuselage. Later that day during a routine experiment a guttural voice broke in "Would you please get these fishes off my face?"

The Voices display humour, anger, sadness and the gamut of emotions . . . all this rapidly, musically, and in the strange rhythm characteristic of the EVP. Once trapped on tape the samples may be examined at leisure . . . studied for clues about ethnic origins, computer enhanced, digitally processed to remove unwanted static and compared with normal transmissions to establish possible paranormality.

Content of personal significance to the experimenter, response to his most intimate thoughts, mention of his name and his locality, preclude confusing the Voices with normal transmissions or the mechanical utterances of police, taxi, and other stereotyped PSB transmissions. But this is only the beginning . . . using the radio microphone method, the experimenter may experience the staggering instant response voices who answer him back and in Jurgenson's case argue with him for several minutes. He has published a tape where an angry male voice castigates the human race for its cruelty to the animal creation. All this not the sole prerogative of a restricted elite but eventually intended to be a universal facility made possible by the intensive research of spirit scientists of a parallel dimension.

In the two decades since Jurgenson's initial contacts, the number of active and successful experimenters has grown steadily. What was thought to be a fad based on wishful thinking and self deception and doomed to early extinction, is alive and kicking with no signs of abatement. But the pace of discovery varies, for reasons not clear, from country to country with the Germans well in the lead with over 1000 regular experimenters after wide TV and media coverage. The game is well and truly afoot!

HISTORICAL ASPECTS

After the onset of wireless telegraphy and before the turn of the Century, the Austrian psychic researcher Baron Hellenbach predicted in his book BIRTH AND DEATH the evolution of electromechanical means of communication. He foresaw that the content of the earliest contacts might suffer from the inherent difficulties of bridging a gulf between two dimensions and warned against undue optimism. Nevertheless he was one of the first to discern the coming possibilities in wireless propagation. He was followed soon after by Nikola Tesla, Marconi and Edison, who attempted to translate theory into practice and, according to some accounts, succeeded in making mysterious but transient contacts. The reader is referred to standard works and biographies for more details.

In the twenties the English writer Thorpe, who had developed what he called "Etheric Vision" whilst a prisoner in Germany, promised his readers details of mechanical means of detecting what he called "The Voice Phenomenon" in a further book ... this unfortunately never appeared, but his original work ETHERIC VISION, now a collector's item, displays acute awareness of events due to materialize twenty or thirty years later. Alice A. Bailey, following in the Theosophical tradition, stated categorically that radio confrontation with discarnate beings would become reality before the close of the 20th Century.

Whilst Spiritualists experimented with various pieces of apparatus designed to augment the energies of Mediums, radio hams around the world reported transient, sporadic signals from unknown sources. *These two developments ran parallel courses, but never connected.* In Italy the late twenties gramophone recordings were made of the Direct Voice through the mediumship of an Italian aristocrat, Count Centurione

268

Scotto at Millesimo Castle. The Count had contracted the gift, seemingly by "psychic contagion," from the controversial Valiantine. After World War II an Electronic Communication Society was formed in Manchester, England, where serious attempts were made to amplify by electronic means the pervading energies of the seance room.

By 1950 the stage was set for the final countdown leading up to Jurgenson's decisive discoveries, but first we should mention the pioneer work of two lesser known experimenters. Although a chapter on the EVP is nowadays almost obligatory in popular surveys of Parapsychology, the name Atilla von Szalay is frequently omitted. Already in 1947 von Szalay was experimenting with phonograph discs and wire recorders and had succeeded in capturing faint whispers ... Raymond Bayless had repeatedly tried to set the record straight and obtain recognition for the pioneering work of this New Yorker.

In Chicago in 1950, one John Otto, patent engineer and radio ham, together with a group of local radio amateurs, had detected unusual signals of unknown origin on undisclosed frequencies. Lyrical voices using what we now know as the polyglot mode, sang and spoke in rapid bursts which the group recognized were unlike anything transmitted by regular sources. These transient signals were sporadic and hard to pinpoint ... regretfully they were not recorded.

In 1950 distribution and use of tape recorders was not so universal as today. In my own work I have found that very few of the transient "blips" can be deciphered on first hearing. Recording and subsequent playback transforms the situation, however. Eventually the Otto group abandoned the time-consuming search; boredom and the "decline effect" set in, followed by rapid demotivation ... I mentioned this early group on several of my tapes circulating in the USA in the hope that indigenous researchers would unearth further information on these Chicago experiments. Nothing has so far materialized.

Around this time, George Hunt Williamson, author of OTHER TONGUES—OTHER FLESH, published by the Amherst Press, was logging reports of intrusive voices of unknown origin on tape whilst another American, John Keel, investigating UFO reports world wide, came up with dozens of reports of voice intrusion culled from military and civilian sources. In OUR HAUNTED PLANET, Keel devotes an entire chapter to these rogue transmissions and in OPERATION TROJAN HORSE, he exhumes press reports from the thirties when unidentified voices plagued the military in Scandinavia along with early UFO sightings. Eventually the Nazis were blamed, but examination of German archives after the War revealed no evidence of German involvement.

There are some conflicting accounts concerning the exact date of Jurgenson's original discoveries. One widespread report has it that his original voices were discovered on tape whilst recording birdsong at his country residence near Molnbo, Sweden. According to Jurgenson himself and more recently, intrusive voices appeared on studio tapes whilst making a documentary film. The time was 1958-59.

It is a part of EVP mythology that the Swede stumbled on the Voices as a totally new and unexpected happening, but in fact Jurgenson was well versed in occult and psychic matters and had *already had a premonitory feeling of impending invasion from a transcendental source* although he was not aware of the exact form this would assume. He was probably unaware of the imminent persistence and scope of the psychic invasion when it suddenly materialized, and he relates in RADIO LINK how, fed up, and satiated with the Voice infestation, and exhausted by prolonged listening sessions, he packed away his entire recording gear and attempted to concentrate on his normal professional activities. Before long an upsurge in *clairaudient sensitivity with voices modulating environmental sounds* such as running water and the like, forced him to dig out his apparatus and record the voices objectively on tape. Later a similar experience was reported by the American experimenter, A.J. Plimpton.

The millions of words which have since issued from the pens of dozens of writers worldwide flow directly from Jurgenson's discoveries and researches which still continue at the time of writing. Only sketchy reports of his activities reached the Anglo-Saxon readership during the sixties through magazine articles in FATE and lesser known Occult journals. RADIO LINK WITH THE DEAD somehow escaped the translator's pen. Able to read German, I found it fascinating reading.

The entry of Konstantine Raudive onto the scene has been amply documented . . . the voices quickly became known as the Raudive Voices, a term now defunct. After visiting Jurgenson in Sweden, the Latvian Psychologist returned to the Black Forest to pursue his own researches. Subsidized by his wife, a famous European novelist and translator of Russian classics and by royalties from his own weighty and rather pedantic philosophical works, Raudive was able to devote all his waking hours to the long and tiring process of sifting through the thousands of tapes accumulated in hundreds of hours of EVP recording.

The result was a book which enjoyed a small circulation in Germany but which translated into English, revised and expanded to contain sections by experts in Electronics, Linguistics, Psychology and Theology, catapulted Raudive into the eye of the storm in England and the USA. The publishers of the book BREAKTHROUGH, Peter Bander and Colin Smythe, were directly instrumental in bringing the EVP to a much wider public, contributing in one stroke, in a skillful public relations exercise, to the rapid dissemination of the fact of the existence of paranormal voices on tape.

Raudive irritated the parapsychologists by his claim that the Survival problem could be solved in one stroke where generations of philosophers, psychic researchers and scientists had failed to arrive at any consensus despite 100 years of psychic study. He insisted on listening to and deciphering faint "C" quality recordings which I for one would have erased and discarded. His multi-lingual comprehension enabled him to fit an interpretation onto passages meaningless to his contemporaries, and it was at this point that charges of subjectivism and delusion were leveled at him, principally from sources within the British parapsychological establishment. Subjectivism and self-delusion is the central plank in the opposition to the EVP as a viable contribution to parapsychology. I have repeatedly asked listeners to my published tapes to point out misinterpretations or faulty translations. My interpretations must be near the mark as I have had no response . . . no complaints. I will immediately withdraw any sample shown to be from a normal broadcast source. I accept and endorse the rigorous weeding out of ambiguous and subjectively colored interpretations. Raudive was not so forthcoming and defended every last voice. His dogmatism aroused opposition and resentment. I have listened to his voice samples, the audible ones, and found many of them to bear all the known characteristics of the EVP; I do not know what percentage could be attributed to pure subjectivity . . . *I do know that he did, in fact, record many hundreds of genuinely paranormal samples.*

In Europe a more balanced view of his contribution to the subject predominates but amongst British and American parapsychologists his credibility suffered after an adverse report in 1974 by young Cambridge scholar, David Ellis, who was awarded the Perrot Warwick studentship in Psychical Research, 1970-72. Young and inexperienced, his footsteps were guided by SPR veterans John Cutten and Manfred Cassierer whose hostility to Raudive was well known and has never abated. David Ellis collated a vast amount of published material on the Voices for his projected book THE MEDIUMSHIP OF THE TAPE RECORDER (privately published), which is a useful reference work on the activities of early voice experimenters in the seventies of which I was one selected for investigation.

I was, however, disappointed with the scope of the inquiry. This consisted of a hurried visit to my home in Bridlington, an exchange of anecdotes and mutual EVP experiences, a short 10 minute listening session to my latest voices and a lengthy meal when David entertained with comic impressions of some of Raudive's voices. No experiments ... no serious work! In Ellis's subsequent book I emerged in a more favorable light than most, but concluded that his final verdict of thumbs down to the Voices, quoted later all over the world, was based on a hurried, under-financed and incomplete investigation.

Ellis's survey of the historical aspects of the EVP up to 1973 and his collation of the available literature on the subject was invaluable to the researcher but his conclusions published in 1974 to the effect that the so-called EVP was merely projection of the minds of the experimenters onto random noise or even mechanical noise of the tape recorder with a generous measure of self delusion, was a hasty and unfortunate generalization. It cut no ice in German research circles, and instantly cut David off from further continental contacts. To Anglo-Saxon parapsychologists, however, the Ellis report was manna from heaven. They were able to go back to sleep or return to statistical studies ... or continue to research into the raw and undifferentiated forces of the Poltergeist! The consensus was that the young Briton had exorcised the ghost of EVP. Having solved the mystery and defused the time bomb in 1974, David Ellis is in 1980 . . . *still investigating the Voices!!*

Meanwhile in Europe the work has continued without loss of momentum. The names will be familiar to readers: Prof. Alex Schneider of St. Gallen (Physicist); Franz Seidl of Vienna (Engineer and Audio Technician); Prof. Hans Bender (Scientist); Fidelio Koberle (Industrial Psychologist); Dr. Ralph Determeyer (Electronics Specialist); Theodor Rudolph (Electronics Engineer) and many others . . . most of them after 20 years have elapsed maintaining a lively interest in the EVP. Their ranks have since been augmented by newcomers to the field, especially in West Germany. The majority opinion is that there is some outside influence at work.

The Psychokinetic Theory, ie. that the Voices arise from the subconscious of the experimenter runs into grave difficulties. Electrical output from the brain is extremely weak . . . too weak to influence magnetic tape at any distance. Little of a factual nature is known about the subconscious mind *except by inference* and the bewildering variety of the Voices, their linguistic virtuosity, their animated forceful expression, and above all, their ability to instantly respond via the radio/mike method, imposes great strain on the overworked Unconscious Mind Theory.

There has been little interest in the ranks of the British SPR in this new phenomenon; only two members undertook extensive experiments to test the theories. One was Richard Sheargold, veteran member and radio ham. Sheargold, with an acute ear for radio transmissions, postulated a theory akin to the old theosophical "thought form" concept. According to Sheargold the voices are encapsulated fragments within the psyche of an individual, the residue of all the experiences and contacts of a lifetime galvanized temporarily into life, like the spooks and astral shells beloved of the Theosophists! In EVP the entities discharge their energies and are dissipated, thus accounting for the "decline effect" experienced by experimenters. One point emphasized by Sheargold, whose hearing faculty was trained in a lifetime of audio work, was that the voices were absolutely objective on magnetic tape. Victor Spencer Wilson, a languages teacher with an acute hearing capacity, was a successful experimenter in his own right, leaning to the spiritistic theory.

Another member of the British Parapsychological Establishment, Stan Gooch, dipped one toe into EVP waters coming up with the statement that everyone had been listening to taxi, police and other PSB transmissions . . . in other words, RF breakthrough. No one with normal hearing could possibly mistake the stereotyped utterances of the Police and Fire Brigade for the lyrical, soft, rhythmic paranormal voices. Nevertheless, Stan Gooch's lapse will no doubt be quoted in parapsychological journals as a new discovery!

Meanwhile in Germany a new generation of experimenters . . . among them scientists, technicians, electronic experts, are probing the secrets of the Voices. Hans Otto Konig of Ratigen has announced the discovery of a high frequency pilot tone on voice examples. This is paralleled by my own experience. I judge the tone to be in the region of 12KHZ. Konig is working on an automatic detector system, which, scanning the wavebands, will instantly recognize the tone and go over into the recording mode. The voice transmission will then be hopefully captured.

Fortunately, in Germany, the accent is no longer on whether this or that individual claims to get voices . . . personal attacks fall short of their target simply because there is a large collective operation going on which yields sufficient evidence to confound the para-psychologists.

Here are a few of my voice examples:

SIGNIFICANT VOICE EXAMPLES

"Raymond ... look ... we use recordings" ... an attractive female voice tells me that the entities use a technical process.

"December starts an evil struggle" ... an urgent female voice recorded at the time of the Middle East crisis in December, 1973, warns of an impending struggle!

"Carefully with nerve gas," ... a guttural male voice warns against chemical weapons or perhaps the accidental spillage of chemicals.

"Cass's Centre for hope and joy." ... a tinkling female voice pays a flattering compliment!

"You ... the present sleepers" in an accusatory tone, an older female criticizes our "head in the sand" attitude.

"Lilo Shipley ... she doesn't bother" ... a very young female voice breaks in, mentioning an acquaintance by full name. The girl proved right ... Lilo Shipley, recently widowed ... ignored my wife's attempts to inform about the Voices.

"Take a walk and ventilate your feelings" ... We had been discussing our sedentary life and lack of outdoor activities ... a guttural male voice. *"Breathe through the nose ... and no troubles follow"* ... a curious sing-song voice followed a discussion about summer colds and hay fever.

"The cold soldat" (the cool customer) a polyglot voice breaks in as I questioned Jurgenson's superior results. Apparently I am too calculating or cool and should meet them emotionally, half-way.

"I say this . . . taking all the troubles . . . these are yours" . . . a beautiful female singer laments. Clearly we are the architects of our own troubles.

"From the mystic worlds . . . you close us out" . . . a soaring female singing voice regrets our preoccupation with material things.

"Bardon" . . . A powerful singer gives his name. Franz Barden was a well known German occultist whose book I had read about this time.

"He's my true Freddy" . . . and, *"I've just been speaking to the Freddy,"* in her enchanting voice, Lena, Jurgensen's guide, breaks in onto my tapes. (1972)

"Kersten . . . Germans visit Frederick" . . . a male voice, that of Felix Kersten, Himmler's masseur and an old friend of Jurgensen, who had often manifested on his tapes, tells us that Germans had visited the Swede. This was later found to be correct . . . a German TV team with Prof. Bender, had filmed at Jurgensen's location near Stockholm.

"This is Raudive—waiting at the Bridge" . . . a stunning instant response voice caught by the radio/mike method.

"Raudive . . . strong as oak . . . towards the grave!" . . . a sombre prophecy of Raudive's eventual demise. Recorded in May, 1972. This voice couched in Archaic German.

"Focus scores again" . . . a delighted voice comments on the fact that, on one afternoon, I fitted three identical "Focus" hearing aids. This would seldom happen as we have many brands of deaf aids available.

"Smith seems to be responsible for the tape" . . . a thoughtful female at a deliberate pace, answers my unspoken inquiry in my mind, "Who is in charge of our experiments on the Other Side?" Smith was a deaf client, occultist and philosopher, who had died shortly before I started the experiments. He was the first to give us a clear Christian and surname on tape—*Mir-*

iam Smith—the name of his wife. We checked out the "*Miriam*" and it was correct.

"*The only theft which is justifiable*" . . . a male voice speaking perfect German. Only minutes earlier I had remarked to my secretary that time and money spent on the EVP would detract from our professional work and was perhaps a theft from the business.

The EVP will persist and expand . . . at what speed, it is at present impossible to judge. Eventually it will contribute to a shift in human consciousness. It is part of a process which started around 1848 and will be completed within the lifetimes of some of us. It will be a part of the total revision of human attitudes which Alvin Toffler has called the "Third Wave." For the present it is doled out to us in small doses. This appears to be deliberate. Sudden forays into our airwaves are just as suddenly withdrawn, as the Lamoreaux brothers have confirmed, and as predicted by Jurgenson.

Finally the projections of Marconi, Edison, Hellenbach, Tesla and Sir Oliver Lodge will assume reality and as Alice A. Bailey predicted we shall come face to face with discarnate humanity via radio propagation. Let us hope that this influence will divert us from our headlong dash to nuclear holocaust!

≈≈≈≈≈≈≈≈≈≈≈≈≈

Chapter 18

≈≈≈≈≈≈≈≈≈≈≈≈≈

DIMENSIONS OF LIFE
BEYOND LIFE

In deference to the many millions of religious believers in a life after death, assured by faith and not by evidence which the scientific world can accept, my dear friend, John Hefferlin, retired Religious Science minister, has granted me permission to publish his inspired essay, "Dimensions of Life Beyond Life."

From a spiritual point of view, I doubt if you will find anything more beautiful in the current literature, and I feel it deserves a place in the consideration you may be giving to the question of Survival.

In all thinking people there comes a time of deep questioning, when they ask themselves, "What is life?" and "What is death?" Before these questions can be answered satisfactorily, however, the most basic question of all arises, "What is God?" To this, no man can possibly give a complete answer.

We have progressed so far beyond the old anthropomorphic concept of a God with human attributes and characteristics, that many people who formerly considered themselves to be atheists or agnostics are now accepting the more modern and scientific approach to God as Infinite Mind, Infinite Intelligence, Infinite Energy and Substance, Infinite Wisdom and Love. The magnitude of God is so tremendous as to be beyond the scope of man's imagination! God is so vast, so enormous. Everything which exists or ever did exist or ever will exist is within God—from the most inconceivable tiny particle to and beyond the outermost galaxies within the infinity of space.

I cannot possibly tell you what God is, but if you will allow me, I can share with you what God means to me. Try, if you will, to imagine the most beautiful and perfect tiny baby you have ever seen . . . a few days before birth, still in the womb. Imagine that you can communicate with this little one and ask the question: "What is your world like?" Listen carefully and you hear, "My world is a wonderful world. Here I am snug, cozy and warm. I'm surrounded with love and my every need is provided for even before the need exists. I hope I can stay here forever."

Now you ask another question: "Where is your mother? What does she look like?" You can almost imagine the little facial expression changing to one of quandary. Listen again and you hear: "My mother? I don't know what you're talking about! What is mother? Do I have one?" You smile to yourself as you realize this little one cannot possibly know anything about her mother until long after she's born and she learns of the parent-child relationship. And yet, she will never be any closer to her mother than she is right now, since she lives, moves and has her being within her own mother.

Then, though living in a world of comparative

darkness, where the horizon is limited to smooth moist walls and surfaces within the womb, the unborn baby is suddenly filled with but one extremely urgent and miraculous desire, to reaching out for broader horizons. Thus the time for birth arrives and the child is born.

Where does the baby go when it is born? It doesn't go anywhere, since it is already here. And yet a whole new universe has come into being, where the horizon is ever expanding. What is birth? Beyond the biological and physical experience of being ejected from the womb, birth is actually the transition of consciousness as the baby passes from its seemingly one dimensional world in the womb, out into the world of three dimensions.

Following birth, the little one grows through infancy, childhood, adolescence, and finally reaches maturity, taking its place in the world of adults. Then, eventually death occurs. It may be the result of an accident, illness, or old age, but death does come.

It is now that we face two of the most significant questions in our entire existence.

"What is life?" Life is the manifestation of the vital forces of God, individualized in man as an individual entity. Because God is All-in-all, we live, move and have our being in God. That which we are is some part of God, individualized in us as us. We live, therefore, that God may be more adequately and abundantly expressed.

"What is death?" Death is the passing beyond this three-dimensional world into other worlds of varying dimensions—into an ever-expanding universe with ever-broadening horizons. We die, but we live! Life, as we know it in this three-dimensional world, will continue just so long as the body retains sufficient channels through which the vital energy of God can flow. When enough of these channels cease to function, the body dies.

281

It is like discarding old clothes. In Corinthians, 15-40, the Bible says: "There are celestial bodies and bodies terrestrial, but the glory of the celestial is one, and the glory of the terrestrial is another."

What happens when the individual passes through death? Where does one go? Just as the unborn baby must pass through the process of birth so that life shall continue, the individual passes through death for exactly the same reason—to experience greater life!

Where do we go when we die? We don't go anywhere, since we're already there. Like the process of birth, when the baby passes from its world of "one dimension" within the womb and moves out into the world of three dimensions, death is the passing from the three-dimensional world into that world of many more dimensions. Our consciousness continues to expand in direct relation to the ever-expanding Universe, with its ever-broadening horizons, as it unfolds before us.

Just as the unborn baby cannot possibly perceive that its world is part of and within the three-dimensional world, we apparently cannot and do not perceive that our world is part of, and also is within other worlds of innumerable dimensions beyond this one.

Jesus said: "Let not your heart be troubled. In my Father's House are many mansions. If it were not so, I would have told you." The mansions to which Jesus referred equate to what we might call "dimensions."

Death is not the lonely thing it appears to be. Remember the experience of birth when the newborn babe is greeted by a "Welcoming Committee" of friends and loved ones.

Since Consciousness is the only Reality, our Conscious being which is the Spirit of God in us as us, will always clothe us in such form as may be appropriate so that we shall conform to the needs of whatever Dimensional World we may be living within.

In God, we live, move and have our being, for Life is Eternal!

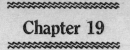

Chapter 19

THE CONTINUITY OF LIFE

Foreword: Walter and Mary Jo Uphoff of Oregon, Wisconsin, are perhaps the best known husband and wife Psychic Research Team in the world today. They have, for years, been affiliated with our ESP Research Associates Foundation in Little Rock, Arkansas, and have traveled extensively in many foreign countries, visiting outstanding mediums and other psychically endowed men and women as well as scientific investigators.

This has resulted in their authoring of two comprehensive books, NEW PSYCHIC FRONTIERS—YOUR KEY TO NEW WORLDS (Third Edition) and MIND OVER MATTER, containing the latest developments in the field of psychic phenomena. Both books are obtainable through the New Frontiers Center, Oregon, Wisconsin, 53575, and Colin Smythe, Ltd., Gerrards Cross, England.

As the Uphoffs' contribution to the evidence presented in this book, I have asked them to summarize

284

their findings and convictions having to do with personal survival after death.

You will first hear from Walter Uphoff:

Mankind, at least as long as history records, has yearned for, or believed in life after death. Of course believing something does not necessarily make it so, nor does disbelieving it necessarily make it untrue. With the advance of knowledge about the physical and biological sciences there has come a materialistic and mechanistic view of life which has tended to raise doubts about survival of the personality and has produced a polarization between religion and science that has tended to keep both from looking at the entire range of evidence. The concept of survival was either accepted or rejected on "faith."

We were reared with the traditional religious view and then exposed to the college laboratories and an intellectual environment which was bound to raise doubts and questions. When this occurs many tend to gravitate to one extreme or the other. Either they embrace the concepts of science as providing the most rational answers, or they retreat to the "faith of their fathers" and hesitate to question or explore. From what we have read and observed about the universe, it seems to function in an orderly fashion, adhering to the laws of cause and effect; it presents mysteries only insofar as our experiences and intellect limit our capacity to comprehend. There is no room for contradiction in an orderly universe. What is true must fit the same paradigm. Wherever apparent conflict or contradiction appears, either science or religion is in error.

Making progress toward understanding calls for a high degree of "ambiguity tolerance." The minute one becomes a true believer or disbeliever, he or she has "turned off his/her hearing aid" and is unlikely to learn much more about the subject under consideration. If one can learn to defer making final judgements, letting the evidence accumulate and putting it into some rank order from the most likely to the least likely, and remain flexible enough to modify that order as the evidence warrants, one can make progress toward greater understanding and toward approaching certainty based on experience.

Through years of exploring we have come across so much evidence that there is something that survives bodily death that we now put it as the most probable reality—a reality we cannot deny and yet be honest about what we have seen and experienced. If it can be conclusively demonstrated that the phenomena we have witnessed and experienced are all part of a worldwide conspiracy or mass self-delusion, we will be glad to modify our rank order. At this point we do not expect this to happen.

Here is a summary of some of the evidence that to us very strongly suggests survival, not in terms of conventional theologies, their concepts of rewards and punishments, and for some a purgatory added as an intermediate stage, but based on evidence of psychic experiences. One thing that emerges is that our beliefs create our own "reality" for us, that we create our own "heaven and hell" by the lives we live and the beliefs we nurture—not a location but a state of being. No one is there to judge us. We become our own judge. "Karma," that term accepted by some and rejected by others, is most likely nothing more than a recognition that laws of cause and effect are a part of the way the universe functions.

The books written by Harold Sherman translated into other languages have provided insights for many. Our travels and explorations at home and abroad have also given us insights to be added to the pattern which portrays life as it is, or seems to be. Psychic experiences are so extensive that coincidence, chance, delusion and deception are inadequate to explain the range of phenomena reported by people in all cultures. Virtually all of these experiences are suggestive of survival. Here are some types of experiences we consider most evidential:

CLAIRVOYANCE AND MEDIUMSHIP

Some persons are able to pass on precise information about deceased relatives and friends that would indeed be difficult or impossible to obtain even if there were a worldwide computer information bank, secretly financed and secretly kept. One experience will illustrate what we mean.

My mother-in-law had died in 1975 and my mother passed on in September 1978. In the spring of 1979 we made a round-the-world trip to investigate psychic phenomena, via Hawaii, Japan, the Philippines, Sri Lanka, Switzerland, Germany, Holland, and England. In London we stopped by to visit Ena Twigg, one of the world's best known and impressive mediums. After talking about developments in parapsychology, she abruptly said to me, "I see your mother standing behind you," and proceeded to give details of what my mother was communicating through her. I asked permission to use my tape recorder and almost an hour of meaningful messages were recorded. More than ninety percent of the statements which could be verified were accurate. There were comments about her physical condition and illness before she passed on, her funeral, her family and her beliefs. What Ena Twigg said was so much in character, both for my mother and for my mother-in-law whom she said she had met, that survival is by all odds the most likely explanation. Mother had been in a nursing home, had broken her hip twice, had great difficulty walking and was on heavy medication. Toward the end she had great difficulty eating and drinking, suffered attacks of coughing and had great discomfort in breathing. She was propped up on pillows in bed and the day before she passed over, could no longer talk. Ena Twigg described these circumstances accurately and in great detail, saying that Mother knew we were with her before she "died," that she had a feeling of being both in and out of the body, and that she was glad finally to be free. She had been tired of medication, "tired of being tired" and was no longer afraid to die.

Reared in a fundamental religious environment which viewed psychic phenomena as "the work of the devil," she did not approve of our interest in parapsychology and was distressed that we were involved in it. She could not comprehend why we did not accept the attitudes toward life and death and life *after* death as taught in Sunday school.

She was showing herself in bed with a lot of pillows behind her, Ena said, saying, "I can't breathe. I can't breathe."

"She wants you to know that she has met the rest of the family," Ena said, "and is 'so much easier in my mind and body,' " which caused Ena to chuckle and remark, "She hasn't got a body!"

"She's saying, 'It's so marvellous to be free! I am more than glad to be able to say, I'm sorry! You two were right and I limited what could have been something beautiful. It caused some distance between us.' She says, 'Do you forgive me?'

"She hasn't seen Jesus and she did think he would have sent one of His disciples ... 'I've had lovely golden lighted figures round me who said, "Don't feel sick! Don't feel sad! Be whole again!" '

" ... She's showing me a little, old-fashioned organ. (We still have the roller organ with the rolls of hymnal music.) She was very orthodox in her beliefs, you know, and a great lover of hymns. 'When I was ill and couldn't get to church, I would follow the hymns in the service and feel much happier. I felt near to God, but lost ... I know you couldn't get there much towards the end.' "

Then Ena said, "I see a big capital 'E' flashing in front of me. Do you know what that means? (My father's name was Emil.) Your father had a naughty sense of humor at times ... Your father's chemistry and your mother's chemistry didn't always match, you know. They got on together but they weren't really a pair."

The messages continued with Ena relaying to us what she was hearing, "I am sorry that I let my rigidity inhibit a very good relationship ... You made a good wife for him, you know." (Turning to Mary Jo, Ena explained. "She gave you her boy but it was on a string at first.") I had great difficulty in letting go."

" ... You've got a mass of tape recordings that will be the part of another step forward. You've got my blessing on it. You wouldn't have believed that possible, would you? ... I've got a lot to learn ..."

"Her new world was a very good school to learn in, she said," Ena continued. "She is asking me to tell you that everything is looked at, nobody's blamed, everybody's understood where she is." Ena broke into a gale of laughter, "She says 'There's no scandal here!' How funny! I've never heard that before! What does that mean?" We took this to mean that she was referring to the small talk and gossip that was so much a part of the community life where she lived. "She was a very fastidious person. Everything had to be just so. Her handkerchiefs had to be ironed just so. She did not like the younger generation wearing too casual clothes ... She's been around your house and you've had a room redecorated, she says. 'It looks good and I like it because you didn't change it too much. It's restful.' (Mother had visited our home once more than five years before. At that time the living-dining area had but one coat of an off-white paint, but about six weeks *after* her death, we had covered the walls with a light vinyl so similar in color that most people have not noticed the change.)

"She says, 'It's such an adventure. I haven't broken through before.' (To Mary Jo) She's seen your mother and says, 'We've both got a lot to learn.' Toward the end she couldn't drink. She was very thirsty. Her throat hurt ... She says, 'My love will burn even brighter now that I've put my conscience at rest by saying you were right and I was wrong ... '

"She had an old Bible that was a great friend of hers and she used to mark it. (Correct) She was very fond of 'The Lord is My Shepherd.' She would like that to have been sung at the funeral you know, but it wasn't. 'I was there,' she says. 'It was a lovely funeral, though. It was quiet and dignified.' "

These thoughts were interrupted by cautions to me about the car and the farm tractor which we used, followed by a short message from my mother-in-law saying that she was looking after my mother and remarking that, "I feel as if I've got the layout of where I am now," definitely an expression she would use. Ena continued, "She's quite content. She says, 'You do realize mine (her death) was purely old age,' but she suffered. 'I deserved that beautiful death ... I just slipped out when I died.' " Ena mentioned that my wife had not put her mother's rosary into the casket. (Correct) "They were my friends, my companions." (This was not given in disapproval, however, but apparently merely as "evidence.")

The messages from my mother resumed. "You went to some place where there was a pagoda or temple and you went up a lot of steps." (When we were in Baguio City in the Philippines, we visited the Bell Church, a Chinese Temple, where there are long flights of steps leading to an inner temple where incense is offered before four large figures of gods and goddesses. Joss-sticks were lighted and placed in large pots of sand and we joined in that ceremony with others who were present.) "You caught a feeling of great reverence and great joy and peace in that place. We all came along but we didn't understand it." Here Ena observed, " . . . I can smell the incense."

We could give other excerpts equally evidential but these should suffice.

THE HEALING HELPERS

Virtually every phenomenon in the area of the paranormal has a component which implies the continuity of personality. All the well-known healers whom we have known, with one exception, have carried on their work with the full conviction that they are helped from "The Other Side" or that they are merely channels or instruments through which others carry out their healing mission. Harry Edwards, George Chapman, John Cain, Rose Gladden, Olga Worrall, Ethel De Loach, The Philippine healers, Gerard Croiset, etc. all believe they are (or were) intermediaries in the healing process. In the case of George Chapman, it was established that Dr. William Lang, an ophthalmologist who practiced in Middlesex hospital, London, died in 1937 and continues to work through Chapman at his healing center in Aylesbury.

When a group of Dr. Lang's collegues were assembled with Chapman in trance, he gave them information about themselves and their families and used medical terminology which Chapman, who had no medical training, could not have known by "normal" means. These medical men were convinced that they were in fact in contact with the surviving personality of Dr. Lang.

An investigation of hauntings and poltergeist activities has produced evidence that when people commit suicide, or are murdered, or meet a sudden death, what survives often does not realize that it is "dead" and therefore hangs around, earthbound, to haunt the premises. New owners of haunted houses are sometimes given a difficult time until the entity somehow learns or is shown that it can move on to a better, happier place in another dimension.

Dr. Carl Wickland's book, THIRTY YEARS AMONG THE DEAD, an account of his experiences with the treatment of the mentally ill, makes a compelling case for possession as an explanation or cause for some cases of mental illness.

The extent to which one's belief system shapes one's reality is demonstrated in numerous ways. In a fascinating book, THE AWAKENING LETTERS* by Cynthia Sandys and Rosamond Lehman, each of whom had a daughter who died as a young adult, numerous short scripts of messages via automatic writing give vivid and evidential items supporting the survival of bodily death. One of these comes from Lady Cynthia Sandys's brother who had been in the British diplomatic service in Moscow before he died. He tells how he went to the aid of the Russian cosmonauts whose craft had crashed and found that they had been so firmly indoctrinated in their materialistic view of life that they did not realize they had left their physical bodies and assumed that the speed at which they had been traveling in space had put them into another dimension.

"... So, once they'd left their bodies and found that they were alive outside the capsule, and able to pass through, into and out of the capsule without friction, they were astounded and ready with pencils and paper to work out the pressure of air gravitation, etc. They got the idea that owing to having been in space for so long they had, as it were, passed through another sound barrier; only in this case, it was a barrier that brought freedom from gravitation down to earth. All this time they completely ignored their own physical bodies and I wondered if they actually saw them—they were so much absorbed by this new power to pass through solid matter and still remain above the earth's surface . . ."*

THE DIRECT VOICE TAPES
OF LESLIE FLINT

Of all the evidence I have come across, nothing has been quite as impressive and evidential as the material contained on the hundreds of tapes recorded by S.G. Woods and Betty Green during sittings with Leslie Flint, a British direct voice medium, over several decades. According to an article by Peter Andreas in ESOTERA (September 1978), a German publication, Mr. Woods accumulated about 800 such tapes. He reports that a researcher, using voice print equipment, ran 500 of the tapes through the machine and found no two alike, effectively ruling out ventriloquism. Flint has also been tested with a microphone taped to his larynx, his mouth taped, and colored liquid held in his mouth. Yet voices, both male and female, manifested. We have about fifty of these tapes and find them enlightening, stimulating and provocative. No two personalities are alike. Some are sophisticated. Others simple or earthy, as they were in their physical bodies.

On one of these tapes, Bessie Smith who identifies herself as a Negro slave who worked in the

---

* THE AWAKENING LETTERS, Sandys and Lehman, Neville Spearman, Ltd. Jersey, England (1978)

cotton fields of Alabama for 45 years, tells how surprised she was that "she didn't have no wings" when she arrived on The Other Side. She had always been taught that when you went to heaven, you had wings, and "the better you was, the bigger your wings was." For a time she was worried that she "might have been sent to the bad place."

Oscar Wilde manifested on August 20, 1962, with the same wit and humor that characterized his writings during his lifetime on earth. Dr. Anna Gasto, who said she died in the concentration camp at Dachau, told about the difficulties of those killed in the camps who remain earthbound to the place. The conversion of the concentration camps to memorials, she maintained, tends to keep the souls of many who died there from moving on to other dimensions.

Direct quotations from entities who passed on ten, thirty or fifty years ago illustrate how reality is created by one's belief. Alf Pritchett, killed in battle during World War I didn't realize he was dead, so he kept on running wondering why the Germans didn't capture him. Later when he met a comrade who had been killed several months before, he realized that it was not a dream and that he had to join others in the Great Beyond. There was no pain, he felt light as a feather as he glided along, eventually meeting his sister Lilly who had died as an infant but was now grown up.

If you have need for tea or something to eat, you will be able to have it for a time, but eventually you will discover you do not need such sustenance any longer. Mary Ann Ross, a Scottish spinster, met her beloved who had passed over before her and was thrilled to find him waiting to teach her to play the piano. Flowers grew as tall as houses and the colors were so magnificent and intense that words were inadequate to describe them. Lionel Barrymore says he has met Shakespeare and that they were still producing plays in the modern idiom with a moral and a purpose. Ted Butler tells of seeing his body lying on the street after a lorry went out of control and crushed him against a wall on a London street. After all the commotion of getting an ambulance, he rode to the hospital with his weeping wife and the nurse, but left in a hurry when the body was transferred to the mortuary. After attending his funeral, he rode the trams for something to do until another "dead" person on a rescue mission persuaded him to come along to another plane of existence.

PERSONAL SURVIVAL TESTIMONY

By Mary Jo Uphoff

Attitudes toward life and dying and death are built up over a lifetime, an ever-changing view altered by the experiences one has had, the books read, and the people one has known. Obviously this is the only way one can acquire a knowledge and a belief about death. For most of us the death experience which closes this lifetime, will come but once and will be final. Those who have read the well known books by Dr. Elisabeth Kubler-Ross, Dr. Raymond Moody, Karlis Osis and others know about the experiences of persons who experienced "clinical death" but were revived and lived to tell about it. The euphoria of release from pain, the brilliant light, beautiful surroundings, and the meeting with family and friends who have preceded them in death are reported so frequently that a pattern emerges which points to the survival of bodily death in surroundings which are suggestive of an idyllic life on Earth, but of a finer, etheric dimension. Less well known are reports that those who have led lives of degradation and evil have experienced darkness and terror.

One of the most moving of the personal accounts is RETURN FROM TOMORROW, a book written by Dr. George Ritchie, a psychiatrist who has spoken and written about his personal encounter with dying in an army hospital during World War II.*

It is highly evidential to me that there is such an overlay of experience on the part of those who have been "revived" from apparent death in hospitals, after accidents, in surgery, heart attacks, etc. Many of these recall viewing the "death" scene from a point outside their bodies, hearing what is said, observing the efforts of the medical personnel, the grieving responses of relatives, yet experiencing euphoria, the complete absence of pain, the intense all-pervading light, and often the presence of others, some of them sometimes recognized as dead relatives or friends. When this occurs within one's own circle of relatives and friends whose integrity one does not question, the report of the experience is not easily dismissed.

There are many published works which have purportedly been dictated or impressed telepathically by the dead on the living. These accounts have an authentic "ring" of true experience, and although they vary in details, the survival of con-

* RETURN FROM TOMORROW by George Ritchie, M.D. with Elizabeth Sherrill, Chosen Books Publishing Co., Ltd. (1978)

sciousness seems clear and unmistakable and not unlike the accounts of out-of-body experiences which are not at all uncommon.

Accounts of past lives which emerge from age-regression under hypnosis raise some profound questions about birth and death experiences more or less vividly recalled or called up. Certainly, these are not to be passed over lightly, regardless of the theories one holds about hypnosis and the role of the subconscious. Nor can the cases suggesting reincarnation which have been studied and investigated by Dr. Ian Stevenson and others be easily dismissed.

The paranormal voices on magnetic tape provide some of the strongest evidence for survival. Voices which should not be there, voices saying something of important personal relevance to the person doing the recording have been found or deliberately captured on tape by tape recorders. The patient research and hours of recording such voices by Friedrich Juergenson, Dr. Konstantin Raudive, the Lamoreauxs, Veilleuxs, William Welch, Raymond Cass and many others have amassed tapes bearing so many references, names and personal comments that the explanation that these are "stray radio signals" borders on the ludicrous.

In the summer of 1975 at the request of Harold Sherman, we visited the L family in Michigan. Both their daughters had died unexpectedly some months before, the elder in childbirth, the younger at age 14 in an auto accident. The deaths occurring so close together, the bereavement of the parents was acute. Following the loss of their daughters, the L's took a foster daughter, Lynn, into their home and it is to be assumed that this could not have been communicated to their deceased daughters by what are accepted "normal" means. In a sitting with a medium after the daughters' deaths, the younger daughter's voice appears on the tape just after the medium had said, "I believe she was Daddy's girl," saying brightly, "Daddy's girl! That's me!" Later on another tape, her voice is heard saying, "Hello, Mommy! Hello, Daddy! Hello, Lynn!" In view of the time sequence, how could Lynn's presence in the family have been known to the L's younger daughter unless she had survived bodily death?

The S family, whose two-and-a-half-year-old son was run over by a car out of control as he played on the walk in front of their home, heard his little voice say in the presence of both parents, "I'm not dead, right, Mom?"

There is the voice of Dr. Raudive's deceased secretary, who had not believed in life after death, exclaiming joyfully on one of his tapes, "Bedenke! Ich bin!"—"Just think! I exist!"

Poltergeist activity is conceded to have at least two possible sources: the application of mental energy to physical objects by either living or deceased persons. Two experiences come to mind which could well be manifestations of presence of those we call "dead."

Two years ago this summer we visited my sister in North Dakota. On our arrival on a Friday evening, she told us that several times in the preceding days, she had found our family picture, unbroken, on the floor below where it had hung.

Each time she had put it back on the wall, puzzled as to how it had fallen. Since the ring on the back was still firmly attached, the picture would have had to be lifted off the hook fastened in the wall. "I think it's Mom letting us know that she knows we will all be here together," my sister said. My skeptical brother-in-law looked amused and said nothing. "Mom and I used to joke and say that whichever of us went first would come back to let the other know."

Next morning, my sister and I drove some distance to visit an elderly relative, leaving our husbands at home. My brother-in-law was reading the morning paper in the kitchen; Walter was reading a book in the adjoining room, when both were startled by the sound of the picture falling to the floor in the bedroom. Both rushed to the scene, and examined the picture which was unbroken; the hook in the wall was intact. By this time all of us were in agreement that this poltergeist activity was our mother's way (she had died the year before) of letting us know that she was very much aware of our presence and that indeed she did, like Dr. Raudive's secretary, *exist*.

Another event which seemed to be directly related to survival occurred in Switzerland while we were visiting the Affolters. Just a week before Paul's father had died and Paul told us that there had been unexplained noises on the ceiling in the living room since his father's death. He hoped, he said, that we would not be disturbed by them. We assured him we would not.

Our host and hostess had errands, so we were left for a time in the house by ourselves. We had just arrived in Europe and I was still very tired from "jet lag," so I decided to take a nap. When I woke the house was extremely quiet; outside a gentle rain was falling in the fading afternoon light and I could think of no reason why I should not enjoy a little longer the delicious half-awake relaxed state I was in. I heard the click of the bedroom door latch and immediately thought Walter must be calling me to come to dinner, but the door did not open. In that moment I was aware of an intense localized cold in the area of my solar plexus and the thought entered my mind that this was the poltergeist. Another click. Again the door did not open and I *knew* with the strange "knowing" which often accompanies a paranormal experience that this was the Affolter's poltergeist.

When the door latch clicked again I was ready for "flight." This time, however it *was* my husband who put his head in the door to announce that dinner was ready. "Were you here before?" I had to know. "No," he said, "I just came down."

Lyall Watson presents the thought that there is no *death*—that even the physical body, in so-called death, becomes part of the living, pulsing Earth or of its creatures. This transmutation to another form of life is discussed in his book, THE ROMEO ERROR,* for which he proposed the word "goth" and says that without death—or GOTH—there would be no life.

We, however, think of the on-going of life in terms of the spiritual or conscious part of ourselves—the expression of consciousness in our personality—our "person-ness." So far we have been able to experience only glimpses of what on-going life might be. Some of us delve in the Scriptures for our understanding, or gain insight from

* Watson, Lyall, THE ROMEO ERROR, Doubleday & Co., New York (1974)

our own mystical experiences, or those of others. Now, having paid homage to science for most of our lifetime, some of us are hoping and expecting that scientific proof of survival may be forthcoming.

May I be so bold as to ask whether scientists are more to be relied upon than others in such matters? All depends on certain assumptions of reality; even in accepting the verdicts of science, those of us who are laymen rely heavily on our "faith" in the bottom line of the laboratory report. May I further suggest that the answer to this all-important question may lie *within* each of us whereby we ourselves, by our lives, our experiences, our thinking, and our expectations, are creating the reality which is our heaven, hell, eternity. Here we are, creatures five or six feet tall, trying to comprehend a cosmos extending infinite light years on the one hand, and the infinitesimal universes of atoms on the other. Those who have delved deeper than we into these mysteries do indeed maintain that the cutting of one blade of grass disturbs the universe. Does this not imply that we have a role in the Great Scheme which encompasses all this in some intelligent form—that we too are a surviving, ongoing, spiritual part of this life?

I doubt that all the evidence which can be compiled—outside personal experience—will convince any doubter who is not willing to accept the possibility, probability or certainty of life after bodily death. Discovering the purpose of our lives is a personal quest, to which our own experiencing, thinking, evaluating, weighing and seeking will provide an answer for each of us. It is, to be sure, the most important quest of our lives—a search which each of us undertakes with whatever help and experience we are fortunate enough to get from others. Debate and laboratory research may supplement or reinforce, but it cannot take the place of the individual adventures of the spirit and the mind.

Chapter 20

YOUR PREPARATION FOR
THE LIFE TO COME

If you were to go on a trip abroad to visit a country in which you had never been, you would probably seek to know all you could about it before making the journey.

And yet, you are destined, one of these days, sooner or later, to leave your present place of residence—your physical body—and to depart on a one-way trip to an uncharted place to which many friends and loved ones have already gone, and of which you know next to nothing.

There are no guide-books to this land from which there is no return, and no dependable directions as to the safest and best way to get there; no absolute guarantee of the conditions you will find on arrival, or who may be waiting to greet you.

Up to now you may not have given the matter of your departure from this earth much thought. It has not been too pleasant or happy a subject to reflect upon—and there may have seemed little you could do about it, anyway. Better just put off facing it as long as possible.

In this book which you hold in your hands, you have read the individual testimony of many sensible, sensitive men and women who profoundly believe—who not only believe but feel that they KNOW—that there is personal survival after physical death.

Such people have one thing in common—they are free of fear—they say, as a result of psychic or spiritual experiences they have had; that they are sure they can face the time for their departure from earth without apprehension, with, instead, a feeling of anticipation, that they are not nearing an end of life but a new beginning.

The dictionary, in giving a definition of fear, lists "awe and fear of God" as one of man's strongest emotions. This fear, approaching panic and terror in the lives of many, has plagued humanity for centuries, and because it has been difficult to visualize life without a physical body, many have been led to a belief in Reincarnation, wherein the soul returns to live again in a physical form through the agency of a new set of earth parents.

My research has convinced me that there are other possible explanations for what seem to have been past life experiences—among them possession by earth bound spirit entities who infuse the minds of living mortals with vivid feelings and images of their own past lives; or, genetic recall—the genes containing the records of past life experiences, not of their own, but of their direct line ancestors; and, through dreams or visions or hypnotic suggestion, they may get partial playbacks in mind of these experiences.

A writer of Science Fiction can produce an endless variety of imaginatively fabricated accounts of past civilizations, realistic life forms and every manner of personal experience. The power of suggestion is so great that, given an impetus through hypnotic direction or one's own imaginative compulsion, the mind of the average individual can conjure up fantastic seeming past life experiences which he relates to himself.

Today, with all the research that has been done and all the impressive-sounding philosophies that have been built around the idea of Reincarnation, and the often realistic hypnotic regressive recollections of past lives, there is still no scientific proof that Reincarnation is a fact.

One of the top scientists who has devoted years to a study of Reincarnation, who has traveled to distant foreign countries to personally examine young children who seem to have had a recall of past lives, said to me recently: "Many of these cases are strongly suggestive of Reincarnation but, in my opinion, they have not been proved." He expressed himself as strongly opposed to hypnotic regressive therapy and hypnotically induced readings on past lives.

A simple method of demonstrating the fallacy of past life readings is to do what I did some years ago. I answered the advertisements of three "past life readers," who promised readings taken from the "akashic records." In placing my order, I told each psychic that I was especially interested in knowing about my *immediate* past life and would they please include this report in whatever past life readings they sent me.

You guessed it! I received three DIFFERENT immediate past life readings, each having to do with a different time and place in history. I had been a female once and a male twice. *Totally fictitious!* Doesn't it stand to reason that, if "akashic records do not lie," the *same information* of immediate past lives, should be determined from each past life reader?

And yet, countless believers in Reincarnation are placing reliance on the truth and accuracy of these "revelations" and making life-changing decisions based on them!

There are studies being conducted today by past life therapists, who claim that they are relieving patients of physical and mental illnesses which had their origin in past life experiences, and that once these experiences have been recalled and the causes of the present life sickness have been revealed, spectacular healings have often resulted and great improvements in health have taken place.

However, it is a psychological fact that a patient can be confronted with a fictitiously conceived account of a past life experience as an explanation of a patient's illness and if the patient accepts the accounts as true, the hypnotic power of belief and suggestion alone, is so strong that, like a placebo effect, the patient is often enabled to relieve body and mind of the ailment.

One individual reveals that his wife's first baby was born dead and explains the death of this apparently perfectly formed baby body by saying that no reincarnating spirit was present at the moment to occupy it!

Are we then to assume that all fathers and mothers, either in or out of wedlock, are simply creating bodies to serve the karmic needs of those desirous of re-entering this life? That these bodies possess no souls of their own? That they have not been newly created? And that no *new* souls are coming into being? That all are limited to the reincarnative process?

Among those who believe in Reincarnation, few claim they have any clear-cut, evidential knowledge or memory of a past existence. All the friends and loved ones they may have known and with whom they may have had developing experiences, are gone. Their relationship would no longer be recognized in subsequent lives since they might appear as father, mother or brother instead of husband, wife or daughter or whatever.

A basic point that is seemingly overlooked is that when an individual is deprived of his identity and memory, he becomes a non-entity and has to start over again as an entirely new personality, possessing no awareness of any mistakes he may have made in any past lives for which he is supposed to make atonement in order to expiate karma.

A wise earthly father would not punish his child until he had first let him know what he was being punished for. If we fail in school a grade, we must take this grade over again but we know what we are doing it for—and WHY. There is something very wrong about the concept of Reincarnation as it is commonly accepted.

Certainly, as we observe the present status of the human race—man's savage inhumanity to man—we are willing to agree that the "spiritual gravity" of many is so low that they cannot hope to gravitate to higher states of being until they have been rehabilitated. But this does not mean that souls must return to earth for that purpose.

What we are beginning to learn about the earthbound areas and the millions of low grade spirit entities that are confined there until they can be helped out of their confused state, indicates that some provision has been made by Higher Intelligences for their care and guidance on a colossal scale. It explains also why those who have left this earth existence, finding it is impossible to re-enter this life through another physical birth, often seek to possess living mortals so they can experience again through them, the feelings of the flesh.

The question of Reincarnation is a big and provocative one and probably can never be settled because it has been ingrained in human consciousness for so long.

* * *

In preparation for the life to come, what can a person do to be as ready as possible for a sudden or a lingering passing into the Next Dimension?

The loss of a young child to death always seems to be most regretted since he or she has been deprived of many maturing experiences which a longer life could have brought. When these early departures happen, we are getting frequent reports obtained through spirit communications, that these infants and younger children are lovingly cared for in what are described as Nursing Homes or Development Centers, and that grandparents and other relatives are often in attendance or keep them in their spirit homes. Here in these higher dimensions or so-called "heaven worlds," these young people grow to maturity, much as they would have on earth, and can be reunited with their fathers and mothers as they arrive, if desired. The Bible makes the statement, "as above, so below" and it appears that surviving spirits have found it possible to create homes resembling in many ways the ones they had on earth.

Perhaps your religious convictions are such that you have left the thoughts of death to the church and have given little conscious thought to it yourself.

In fact, you may have been willing to accept Survival on faith alone, and have put off thinking about it, until the actual time comes.

Or you may have felt like a prominent businessman friend of mine who, when facing the possibility of death, lost no time in joining the church of his choice. "I don't know whether this faith is right or not," he said to me, "But if it is, then I'm saved, and if it isn't and there is no life after death, it doesn't matter!"

There is, however, a strong probability that you, like many people, have an inquiring type of mind, regardless of your religious teachings, and have had, as a consequence, your doubts and wonderments.

"Can personal survival really be true? How can I be sure—or can I, or anybody, ever be sure?"

Quite possibly, if this has been your attitude, what is presented in this book may be reassuring. From a study of this evidence, you may have decided that the grounds for life after death have been pretty well established. If you accept them as such, then is there any way you can prepare yourself to meet death when it comes, as calmly and fearlessly as possible?

Well, for one thing, if you have a brief prayer or meditation period each day or night, you can address your concept of the Higher Power, Your Inner Self or the God Presence, and let yourself develop a *knowing* feeling that this Intelligence within can and will care for and protect you in time of need, either Here or Hereafter.

As we grow older, and I, myself, am now past the age of 84, infirmities and illnesses often appear and test your courage and your faith. There are so many inequities in life, so many undeserved tragic happenings; little or no evidence of a benevolent Father-God— a God, instead, who seemingly permits widespread wars, wanton criminal acts, abject poverty, great pain and misery; together with Nature's punishments of storms and earthquakes and floods. Are prayers to such a God of any avail?

Scores of letters have come to me from critically and terminally ill men and women, seeking relief and healing or asking that they be permitted to die if there is no hope. My own dear mother, partially paralyzed by a stroke at age 89, was kept alive by intravenous feedings for weeks, while she pleaded for the doctors to let her leave her worn-out body, saying that most of her friends and relatives had preceded her and there was no sense in her remaining. Mother's case can be multiplied by millions. Thankfully, Dr. Elisabeth Kubler-Ross's contributions to the problems of "death and dying" have brought about more humane attitudes and practices on the part of doctors and nurses. Underlying all these human sufferings is the fear of death, where many cling desperately to the only life they know, uncertain that there is any other.

Of course it is our concept of God that has to be wrong. Our unthinkably great Creator has provided us, as creatures of free will and free choice, with universal laws of Cause and Effect which function in every aspect of life, and when we misuse these laws, by polluting all the elements as well as man's mind, we must and are suffering the consequences.

It is my feeling, based upon a life-time of study, that what I call "God, the Great Intelligence," indwells each human consciousness and that this God Power is actually Cosmic Energy in action, which responds to our needs as we clear our minds of destructive thoughts and harmonize with the God-given Creative Forces, which can and do magnetize conditions around us, attracting what we desire to do or be or have.

The functioning of this God Consciousness is always impersonal, playing no favorites with any part of Creation, helping materialize whatever we visualize, whether it is good or bad for us.

Therefore, when you, through meditation, place images in your mind of what you want or need, you can be certain that you have personalized a sensing of the God Presence within which is the one dependable source of supply and protection.

It is well, if you have not developed this *knowing* contact with this possibly new concept of God, that you take a few moments each day to experience the deeper feeling of inner security which comes through your union with the eternal part of you.

Here in essence are some of the conclusions we have arrived at as a result of our Survival Research:

1. THAT—we possess a higher vibrating, ordinarily invisible, spirit form which indwells our physical body and corresponds to it in Imagery, except that it does not reflect any deformities or infirmities that our Outer Shell may have acquired at birth or in life through injury or illness.

2. THAT—this spirit or astral entity can leave our physical body, either consciously or unconsciously through the sleep state, to travel varying distances in the physical universe, or occasionally on short visits to the Next Dimension.

3. THAT—our spirit form is attached to the physical house it lives in by what is often called a "silver cord" of unusual magnetic elasticity, which is severed only when death occurs, at which time our spirit entity is liberated for existence in the "life after life" state of being.

4. THAT—there are thousands of people who have testified to having had out-of-body experiences wherein they have described an awareness of separation from the physical as well as visits to places and people, either known or unknown to them.

5. THAT—the most prevalent of out-of-body occurrences have been reported as having taken place in and around the moment of "clinical death" when dying persons have seemingly been transported into realms or states of being wherein they found themselves being greeted by friends and loved ones or spiritual beings.

6. THAT—most individuals who have had realistic near death experiences, when they felt themselves to have been in touch with loved ones who had gone on, declare that they have lost all fear of death and, on many occasions have protested against the efforts of doctors to bring them back.

7. THAT—the Next Existence appears to be only a dimensional step away from the physical

because there are countless records of people who have communicated through psychic mediums, reporting having met with instant death through accident and found themselves almost immediately aware of their existence outside the physical body; observing the accident scene; accompanying their lifeless physical form to the morgue; staying close to earth and loved ones; witnessing their own funeral; still not willing to let go of their past earth life; temporarily resisting the efforts of departed loved ones to help them adjust to the fact of transition.

8. THAT—the reaction of different individuals to the death experience greatly varies since those who have been long ill and suffering before passing, seem to have found themselves in what might be termed "hospital-like Rest Homes" where they are permitted to sleep for a period in the care of spirit doctors and nurses and in the presence of friends and loved ones waiting to greet and take them to their homes that seemingly have been prepared for them.

9. THAT—these "Rest Homes" appear to extend over the surface of the earth, at intervals, designed for the accomodation and care of thousands of human creatures who are constantly making the transition.

10. THAT—newly conceived spirits, denied a physical life experience by abortion, or who pass on at birth, or shortly thereafter, or die in infancy, are entrusted to the special care of doctors and nurses, or departed friends and would-be relatives, and brought to maturity in the "heaven world."

11. THAT—each individual of whatever age, possesses a body form that seems every bit as substantial as the one he had on earth but whose vibration is such that he finds he can pass through objects such as doors and walls and

buildings, or even living mortals whom he passes on the street.

12. THAT—when a spirit entity leaves the earth scene and enters one of the so-called higher planes of existence, he finds himself surrounded by objects he feels to be as solid as any he has experienced while on earth.

13. THAT—the mode of travel of a spirit entity is not by car or plane or train, but in response to a wish to be at a certain place and he is immediately there, limited only by his degree of "spirit gravity."

14. THAT—those who have long gone before us, and have been joined more recently by our departed friends and loved ones, have prepared a place for us through the exercise of visualization and creative powers which have taken the form of great communities in all the different dimensions, containing educational centers with vast libraries and auditoriums and outdoor amphitheatres; special types of industries and research laboratories; recreational areas and gardens; mountains, woods and lakes beyond description.

15. THAT, however—when we arrive in the Next Dimension, we cannot expect to find ourselves in a "perfect world" because death of the physical does not confer "perfection"—it only affords us an opportunity to review and evaluate our past earth life and to correct, insofar as is possible, the mistakes we have made and the harm we may have done others.

16. THAT—there appear to be vast Lower Regions close to the earth where millions of discarnates are temporarily held, awaiting rehabilitation, since their vibratory rate in consciousness is so low that they are not ready nor qualified for any higher realms of existence, because, it is profoundly true—each soul takes over into the Next Existence only what he has developed here.

313

17. THAT—as one views our world today, one sees that mass humanity is pretty low in the scale of spiritual growth—that on every side, in every country—in every class of citizenry—we are confronted by lawless, criminal, murderous—even bestial conduct, which has opened the door to possible possession—like attracting like—by low grade, earthbound spirit entities.

18. THAT—many earthbound spirits, bereft of their physical bodies and obsessed with the desire to return to earth, roam about seeking opportunities to attach themselves to the consciousness of living mortals who may have left themselves open to possession through use of the Ouija board, automatic writing, excessive indulgence in alcohol or drugs, or as the result of nervous breakdowns or sordid misuse of sex.

19. THAT—there are others whose lives on earth have largely been spent in criminal and unspeakably vicious pursuits, and who are required to suffer the self-punishing experience of dwelling in what has been described as "dark, dismal areas," where they seem to be fixated on acts of their unsavory past—a state which might be likened to the Catholic concept of "Purgatory" or the Christian idea of "Hell."

20. THAT—there are those who have attained by their earth thoughts and acts a high enough "spirit gravity" to by-pass completely the lower earthbound regions, to reach directly what might be called the "first heaven world" where friends and relatives and possibly "spirit guides" are waiting to greet and care for and help them get acquainted with their new existence.

21. THAT—there are many people in many countries who die indoctrinated with different religious faiths, whose first thought is to seek a replica of their churches, and the company of like believers, as well as the presence of the Spiritual

314

Leader they consider their "Savior," and with whom they hope to dwell throughout Eternity.

22. THAT—many who follow their faith in death create the illusion of whatever they desire which, for a time, is very satisfying to them but which they gradually outgrow as friends and loved ones and spirit guides acquaint them with the New Reality which enlarges their concept of whatever has been their religious faith.

23. THAT—since every human creature appears destined to survive death, regardless of his faith, and shares a portion of the unthinkably great Creator in his consciousness, he carries this awareness with him and, as he evolves through the experiences yet to come in the timeless era ahead of each soul, he expands his understanding of the God Presence within.

24. THAT—we may expect to learn one day in the Life Hereafter, how and when we originated as a self-conscious human creature; from what forms of life we may have evolved; who our actual antecedents were—but it seems enough for us to know now that "we live and move and have our being" and exist as an imperishable part in the plan of Creation.

The Urge to Return to the "Home of the Spirit"

The sensation of "going somewhere" rather than dying, when death of the physical body is near, is caused by a subconscious memory dating back to the moment of conception, when a minute segment of the "Mighty I Am" split off from the Creative Source of All Things in the invisible realm beyond materiality and started another soul on its journey through Time and Space in search of the Source of its origin—the Source beyond earth parentage that brought it into original being.

This is not an illusion. The feeling is inborn and manifests itself in many ways during earth life; the vague awareness that the soul came from somewhere beyond earth life and that it had a previous existence— not necessarily through other earth lives but in, perhaps an unseparated state of being, in the mind of the unthinkably Great God, awaiting its time of individual manifestation to become a conscious part of the Eternal Now.

Among the effects of my dear mother, Alcinda E. Sherman, who had been widowed for over forty-three years and who left this life at the age of eighty-nine, I found a little verse, author unknown, which she had copied in her own hand. My father, Thomas H. Sherman, had been the one love of her life, and she had looked forward, all these years, to a reunion with him when her time came to go.

I hold the little scrap of paper in my hand as I transcribe the verse and feel Mother's vibration as I seem to hear her say . . .

Goin' home, goin' home
I'm goin' home.
Quiet-like, some still day,
I'm just goin' home.
It's not far, just close by,
Through an open door,
Work all done, care laid by,
Goin' to fear no more.
Mother's there, expecting me,
Father waiting, too,
Lots of folks gather there,
All the friends I knew,
All the friends I knew.

316

Morning star lights the way,
Restless dream all done,
Shadows gone, break of day,
Real life just begun.
There's no break, there's no end,
Just a goin' on.
Wide awake, with a smile,
Goin' on and on,
Goin' home, goin' home.
It's not far, just close by,
Through an open door.
I'm just goin' home.

About the Author

Harold Sherman, founder of the world renowned ESP Research Associates Foundation, devoted nearly 70 years of an active and versatile life to extensive research and experimentation pertaining to various phases of Psychic Phenomena, now popularly referred to as Extra Sensory Perception.

Mr. Sherman's unusual psychic abilities first came to world attention as the result of his experiments in Long Distance Telepathy, conducted with the famed Arctic Explorer Sir Hubert Wilkins, in the year 1937–38. At this time Sherman, acting as Receiver from his apartment house home in New York City, received impressions transmitted from the mind of Wilkins on a regularly appointed basis, during the five months that Wilkins was in the Far North searching for a crew of Russian fliers, who had been forced down on an attempted non-stop flight to the United States some 200 miles from the Pole, and never heard from again.

The experiments were witnessed by pre-arrangement, with Dr. Gardner Murphy, then head of the Psychology Department of Columbia University. At their conclusion, it was found that Sherman's several hundred recordings checked against Wilkins' diary and log, had an accuracy of some 70%. The complete account of this adventure in mind-to-mind communication is contained in the book *Thoughts Through Space,* written by Wilkins and Sherman—a mental feat since acclaimed as a classic of its kind.

Since that time, Harold Sherman has participated in many tests and experiments, and has been called upon to use his developed sensitivities to help locate missing planes and people, to provide psychically determined clues in murder mysteries and other crimes, and to offer intuitive solutions for countless personal problems.

He is the author of more than twenty books on Self-Help and ESP, many of which have been translated into foreign languages. Today Sherman is regarded throughout the world as the Elder Statesman and outstanding Lay Authority on ESP.

Through it all, Harold Sherman has been motivated by the desire to obtain, through Survival Research, positive proof of Life After Death. He wrote his first book on this subject, *You Live After Death* in 1945, which has remained a best seller ever since, and has brought comfort to thousands who have lost loved ones.

Rev. Norman Vincent Peale said of it: "Inspiring, convincing ... of immense importance to every one of us."

Now, Harold Sherman has written what might be called a sequel, under title of *The Dead Are Alive,* containing evidence of the reality of Survival. It seems destined to take its place alongside of *You Live After Death* as an authoritative companion.